Women of Bible and Culture

Published by
Kachere Series
P.O. Box 1037, Zomba, Malawi
ISBN 99908-76-02-9 (Kachere Theses no. 3)

The Kachere Series is represented outside Africa by
African Books Collective Oxford (orders@africanbookscollective.com)
Michigan State University Press East Lansing (msupress@msu.edu)

Layout: Mercy Chilunga and Klaus Fiedler
Cover design: Mercy Chilunga

Printed by Lightning Source

Women of Bible and Culture

Baptist Convention Women in Southern Malawi

Rachel Nyagondwe Banda

Kachere Theses no. 3
Kachere Series
Zomba
2005

Kachere Series
P.O.Box 1037, Zomba, Malawi
kachere@globemw.net
www.sdnp.org.mw/kachereseries/

This book is part of the Kachere Series, a range of books on religion, culture and society from Malawi. Other Kachere Theses printed and forthcoming and further related Kachere titles are:

Yonah Matemba, Matandani. The Second Adventist Mission in Malawi (Kachere Theses no. 1)

Hany Longwe, Identity by Separation. The History of the Achewa Providence Industrial Mission (Kachere Theses no. 2)

Jonathan Nkhoma, The Use of Fulfilment Quotations in the Gospel according to Matthew, (Kachere Theses no. 4)

Patrick Makondesa, The Church History of Providence Industrial Mission, (Kachere Theses no. 5)

John Lwanda, Politics, Culture and Medicine in Malawi: Historical Continuities and Ruptures, (Kachere Theses no. 6)

Jurgens Johannes van Wyk, The Historical Development of the Offices according to the Presbyterian Tradition of Scotland, (Kachere Theses no. 7)

Patrick Makondesa, Moyo ndi Utumiki wa Mbusa ndi Mai Muocha wa Providence Industrial Mission, (Buku la Mvunguti no. 3)

Harry Langworthy, "Africa for the African". The Life of Joseph Booth, (Kachere Monograph no. 2)

Joseph Booth, Africa for the African (1897), edited by Laura Perry, (Kachere Text no. 6)

The Kachere Series is the publications arm of the Department of Theology and Religious Studies of the University of Malawi.

Series Editors: J.C. Chakanza, Fulata L. Moyo, F.L. Chingota. Klaus Fiedler, P.A. Kalilombe, Martin Ott, Shareef Mohammad

Women of Bible and Culture

Baptist Convention Women in Southern Malawi

Rachel Nyagondwe Banda

Kachere Theses no. 3
Kachere Series
Zomba
2005

Kachere Series
P.O.Box 1037, Zomba, Malawi
kachere@globemw.net
www.sdnp.org.mw/kachereseries/

This book is part of the Kachere Series, a range of books on religion, culture and society from Malawi. Other Kachere Theses printed and forthcoming and further related Kachere titles are:

Yonah Matemba, Matandani. The Second Adventist Mission in Malawi (Kachere Theses no. 1)

Hany Longwe, Identity by Separation. The History of the Achewa Providence Industrial Mission (Kachere Theses no. 2)

Jonathan Nkhoma, The Use of Fulfilment Quotations in the Gospel according to Matthew, (Kachere Theses no. 4)

Patrick Makondesa, The Church History of Providence Industrial Mission, (Kachere Theses no. 5)

John Lwanda, Politics, Culture and Medicine in Malawi: Historical Continuities and Ruptures, (Kachere Theses no. 6)

Jurgens Johannes van Wyk, The Historical Development of the Offices according to the Presbyterian Tradition of Scotland, (Kachere Theses no. 7)

Patrick Makondesa, Moyo ndi Utumiki wa Mbusa ndi Mai Muocha wa Providence Industrial Mission, (Buku la Mvunguti no. 3)

Harry Langworthy, "Africa for the African". The Life of Joseph Booth, (Kachere Monograph no. 2)

Joseph Booth, Africa for the African (1897), edited by Laura Perry, (Kachere Text no. 6)

The Kachere Series is the publications arm of the Department of Theology and Religious Studies of the University of Malawi.

Series Editors: J.C. Chakanza, Fulata L. Moyo, F.L. Chingota. Klaus Fiedler, P.A. Kalilombe, Martin Ott, Shareef Mohammad

DEDICATION

This book is dedicated to my first husband Jande Macson Paul Banda. His liberation spirit as regards women was the first condition that allowed me to embark on the challenging study. He was able to stay on for six months with me in Australia when he had already completed his masters degree with Australian National University (ANU). It was this period of waiting that enabled me to finish my first degree in Theology that was necessary for entry into the Masters Programme. During this period, I went through a difficult time of loosing my only brother, Andrew Medson Gwang'wang'wa Gondwe, in his early twenties. As if this was not enough, I also lost my niece Mwawi Kanyerere Gondwe, also in her early twenties. Through all this, am very much grateful to Jande, my family and Hughes Baptist Church in Australia for providing me with the necessary spiritual and emotional support.

When Jande went to be with the Lord on the 25th of November 1999, I was already a year old into the programme. During these initial stages, Jande became my main encouragement. He provided moral support as well as a study area for me to study from 1998-1999. This work would not have been possible without my two sisters and their husbands: Alice Judith Mkandawire and Col. Macbeth M. B. Mkandawire, Mercy Grace Gwang'wang'wa Gondwe and Maxwell Kanyerere Gondwe. They were very key sources of inspiration for me to complete this study. I am very much indebted to them and all my nieces and my nephew: Noela Pamela, Marion Jane, Christian Lilian, Tawonga Sharon and Lusungu Cassandra Mkandawire and Donaless, Bettie and Spencer Kanyerere Gondwe.

I am also grateful to my children, Moriah Jacob Zion Banda, Joseph Esau Banda and Mordecai Isreal Jande Banda, for their support especially during my research and writing period of this work. Many thanks to Lotia Chithabwa my niece, and Elizabeth Kayira my cousin for the tremendous support during this time.

This book is an extract from an academic study which would not have been possible without my patient supervisors; Dr Klaus Fiedler and Dr

Felix Chingota of the Department of Theology and Religious Studies (TRS) of the University of Malawi. To them, I am truly grateful.

For the production of the book my thanks go to Mercy Chilunga and Olive Goba of the Kachere Series and with much gratitude I want to acknowledge all the information and help the Baptist women (and some men, too) here in the South gave me, So that I could do the research.

Finaly I want to thank God for providing me with God loving parents who have cared for me since I was born. Their Godly attitude concerning the worthness of girl children is what brought me to this level of writing the book

Rachel Nyagondwe Banda
2005

CONTENTS

Abbreviations

APIM	Achewa Providence Industrial Mission
BACOMA	Baptist Convention of Malawi
BWUA	Baptist Women's Union of Africa
CCAP	Church of Central Africa Presbyterian
CLAIM	Christian Literature Association in Malawi
EC	Executive Committee
MCP	Malawi Congress Party
NIV	New International Version
PIM	Providence Industrial Mission
SBM	Southern Baptist Mission
SDA	Seventh-day Adventist
T/A	Traditional Authority
Umodzi	*Umodzi wa Amayi a Baptist*
WMU	Women's Missionary Union

INTRODUCTION

B APTIST CONVENTION WOMEN ARE ALL WOMEN THAT ARE MEMBERS IN THE Baptist Convention and not only women belonging to the women organisation *(Umodzi).*[1] In this church Baptist polity does not force women to be part of this organisation. As such this reflection on the lives of women in the Baptist Convention is broad, and not restricted to *Umodzi* women. A reflection on women in Baptist Convention needs to start in the Southern Malawi because the history of the Baptist Convention in Southern Malawi is an important segment of the history of the Baptist Convention in Malawi. The Southern Region is where the work of the Baptist Convention started, and from here it spread to other regions in Malawi and to Mozambique. As such it is important to begin reflecting on the experiences of women in this region.

The scope of this study is the Southern Region of Malawi and in this, Baptist Convention of Malawi is divided into two sub regions: South South and South East. The South South sub region consists of the Lower Shire (Chikwawa and Nsanje districts), Thyolo, Mulanje, Phalombe, Chiradzulu, Mwanza, and Blantyre districts. The South East sub region consists of Zomba, Machinga, Mangochi and Balaka districts. Baptist Convention women are found in all the districts of the Southern region, but some districts such as Zomba and Chikwawa have more than others.

Women in Southern Malawi come from mainly matrilineal ethnic groups such as Yao, Nyanja, Mang'anja and Lomwe.[2] Traditionally, uncles in these ethnic groups are meant to be leaders. However, matrilineal societies are patriarchal in that in these societies it is still a man who dominates, and though a woman's father or husband is not the highest authority, her maternal uncle, who is custodian of the children, is.[3] Never-

---

[1]   See chapter 2.
[2]   Orison Chaponda, "Christian Initiation Rites in Southern Malawi," Module paper, Department of Theology and Religious Studies, Chancellor College, Post Graduate Colloquium, Nantipwiri, May, 1999, p. 1.
[3]   Isabel Phiri, *Women, Presbyterianism and Patriarchy. Religious Experience of Chewa Women in Central Malawi*, Blantyre: CLAIM-Kachere 1997, p. 13.

theless the woman's position in society is higher in a matrilineal than in a patrilineal setting. In the case of termination of marriage either through death or divorce, the children belong to the maternal side.

Though matrilineal societies have always been patriarchal, there is also a shift to more patriarchal structures within some matrilineal tribes, which has been debated. Isabel Phiri attributes this shift to the coming of missionary Christianity.[4] In this she differs with Matthew Schoffeleers, who argues that patriarchal structures were already in place before the expeditions of David Livingstone to Malawi through "cultural infiltration."[5] I argue that both factors are true but not exclusively responsible for the partial paradigm shift. The shift is due to interplay of factors. Employment opportunities such as in tea farming in Thyolo, sugar cane production in Chikwawa, white colour jobs in the urban centres such as Blantyre, Zomba and Balaka have also contributed to the growth of patriarchal aspects in matrilineal societies. However, patrilineal societies are still a minority in the southern region and are only predominant in Nsanje district with the Sena. It is women from such cultural background that form part of the Baptist Convention of Malawi (BACOMA).

The church came to Malawi largely under the influence of Southern Baptist missionaries from America, as an extension of their work in Zimbabwe and Zambia.[6] However, I do not reflect much on the history of missionary women although missionary women are a part of the history I write. A brief history of how Baptist Convention work started in Malawi is important as I reflect on the lives of women of this church in the Southern Malawi. The first Southern Baptist missionaries (SBM) came to Malawi in 1959.[7] But this was after a group composed of three Southern Baptist Missionaries, Bill Wester, Clyde Dotson and Gerald Harvey together with one Malawian and a Zambian had come to conduct a feasibility study of Baptist work in Malawi (Nyasaland) in 1955.[8] By then Baptist Convention

---

[4] Ibid, p. 48.
[5] Mathew Schoffeleers, *Religion and the Dramatization of Life. Spirit Beliefs and Rituals in Southern and Central Malawi*, Blantyre: CLAIM-Kachere, 1997, pp. 34-37.
[6] Rendell Day, "From Gowa Industrial Mission to Landmark Baptist". One Hundred Years of Baptist Churches in Malawi 1894-1994," PhD Module, Department of Theology and Religious Studies, University of Malawi, 1994.
[7] See Judy Garner, *History of the Baptist Mission in Malawi. A Rambling Remembrance of some People and Events in the History of the Baptist Mission in Malawi*. Lilongwe: Baptist Publications, 1998, p. iii.
[8] Ibid, p. 3.

work had already been established in Zimbabwe (Southern Rhodesia) and Zambia (Northern Rhodesia). Malawi was therefore the only country in Central Africa that was not touched by Southern Baptist work. After the feasibility study SBM decided to begin work in Malawi. In 1959, Bill and Blanche Wester, LeRoy (Buddy) and Jean Albright came first and were followed by Rev and Mrs Beverly Kingsley in 1961.[9]

BACOMA is neither the only nor the first Baptist church in Malawi. Other Baptist churches include: Seventh Day Baptists, Providence Industrial Mission (PIM), which is officially called African Baptist Assembly (ABA),[10] Evangelical Baptists and others. As such women in the Baptist Convention are not the only Baptist women. Further, in the reflection on women in BACOMA, I do not claim that their experiences are the same as those of other Baptist groups, although Baptists share common distinctives.

The *aim* of this study is to show through the description of the history of Baptist Convention women that Baptist doctrines and polity are liberating. The *hypothesis* is that Baptist Convention women in the history of their church have enjoyed and do enjoy relative freedoms as opposed to women in other churches, because of Baptist doctrine and polity, though even this is conditioned and at times limited by their culture and the way they read or hear and understand the Bible as well as other factors within and outside their church.

Baptist distinctives

The Freedom that women in the Baptist Convention in Southern Malawi enjoy should be seen in relation to the Baptist polity and doctrine. These women believe, firstly, in the authority of Scripture as the basis for their Christian faith and practice.[11] But Baptist women in the south do not live

---

[9]   Ibid, p. 4.
[10]   PIM was the first Baptist Church which came to Malawi in 1900 through John Chilembwe, who was sent as a missionary to Malawi by the black National Baptist Convention of America, Inc., see: Hany Longwe, "The History of Achewa Providence Industrial Mission" (APIM), MA, University of Malawi, 2000. See also: Leroy Fitts, *A History of Black Baptists,* Nashville: Broadman, p. 124; H. Leon McBeth, *The Heritage,* Nashville: Broadman, pp. 784-786 and Robert Baker, *The Southern Convention and its People,* Nashville: Broadman, 1974, p. 290.
[11]   The word "scripture" in both singular and plural is a translation of the Greek word *graphe,* which simply means "a writing." This word was used by Jesus (John 10:10)

in a vacuum. They live in a culture and are surrounded by other women such as those belonging to main line churches like the Roman Catholic Church or the Church of Central Africa Presbyterian (Blantyre Synod), or Evangelical churches like Churches of Christ or Seventh-day Adventists, or Charismatic, Pentecostal or African Independent Churches of various descriptions. These other women also claim to depend on the Bible, though in different ways. And there is always the tension between culture and the Bible.

The second Baptist distinctive is their belief in the Lordship of Jesus. This implies that Jesus is the model for Christian life and practice, not only for men but also for women in the Convention. Women in the Convention are to emulate the life and leadership styles of Jesus in church and society, who is the Lord of their lives and of the whole creation. Everything therefore is under Jesus' obedience. Because of such a claim, Baptist women may view issues of African Traditional Religion differently from women of other churches.

The third distinctive is their belief in the priesthood of all believers. Baptists believe that all are equally called to the propagation of the gospel. Whatever it takes for the gospel to be propagated, whether it is baptizing, serving Holy Communion, preaching, pastoral work, teaching, encouragement and so on, these roles are open to all.[12] Though it is usually not explicitly stated, the concept of the priesthood of all believers together with the idea of the non sacramentality of the ordinances,[13] creates room for full and equal participation in the ministry of the church of both women and men. Marriage is not one of the ordinances that Baptists believe in.[14] Thus the position of women in Baptist churches is expected to be more liberated.

---

and the New Testament writers. They all treated them as "the Holy Scriptures." See Robert Gramack, *New Testament Survey,* Grand Rapids: 1995, p. 42.

[12] See Dee Mocorn, *"What do we Stand for as Baptists and Evangelicals?" Towards a Holistic, Afro-Centric and Participatory Understanding of the Gospel of Jesus Christ,* Johannesburg: Baptist Convention of South Africa, 1995, p. 86.

[13] Baptists practise baptism and communion but refuse to call them sacraments. If pushed to use a term that comprises both (though there is no such a term in the Bible), they tend to use "ordinances".

[14] In standard Baptist theology, marriage is not an ordinance, but a divine order though in popular theology it is often perceived as an ordinance of equal or even higher quality than baptism and communion. For a discussion of these issues in Bap-

The fourth distinctive is regenerate church membership. One is a member of a Baptist congregation because one has asked Jesus to come into her life through prayer by faith. One undergoes this experience when one realizes that one is a sinner,[15] and that the wages of sin is death but the gift of God is eternal life through faith in Jesus.[16] One therefore confesses Jesus into her life.[17] Conversion is therefore very central to these women's experiences. What kind of conversion have these women had? Was it a spiritual conversion as required by their church? Or was it a change from another church to a Baptist church? Or was it both? And how does this conversion contribute to their liberation in the roles they play in church and society?

The fifth distinctive, which is an aspect of church polity, is congregationalism. This means that a Baptist congregation is not controlled by any central governing body. Although the congregations are linked to a central body (the Convention), they are not obliged to follow its decisions. The Convention can come up with suggestions, but every time these suggestions are open to the individual congregation's interpretation. This is why there is room for disparities between congregations. A congregation, for example, has the power to decide on the position of women in its local congregation without being forced by another. However, the experiences these women show depict that there is a move towards centralized governing as in other churches with centralized structures. This is possible, possibly because the old political, cultural and religious background of these women do present a challenge to their Baptist polity of congregationalism. These women—or their mothers—have been exposed to hierarchical structures under the colonial government,[18] and the end to colonial rule was not an end to the hierarchical political culture either, as Malawi Congress Party rule was not only hierarchical but oppressive too.

---

tist type churches in Africa see: Klaus Fiedler, "For the Sake of Christian Marriage, Abolish Church Weddings", *Religion in Malawi*, no 5, 1995, p. 22-28.

[15] Romans 3:23 "All have sinned and fallen short of the glory of God." (NIV).

[16] Romans 6:23 "For the wages of sin is death, but the gift of God is eternal life in Christ Jesus our Lord." (NIV).

[17] Romans 10:13 "Everyone who calls on the name of the Lord will be saved." (NIV).

[18] See A.C. Ross, *Blantyre Mission and the Making of Modern Malawi*, Blantyre: CLAIM-Kachere, 1996; also Pachai, *Malawi: The History of the Nation*, pp. 70-80.

Hierarchical structures have many times been associated with male dominance. However in the traditional culture of these Baptist women in the South, women just as men were leaders such as chiefs and spirit mediums. In the Southern region, there have been women mediums at shrines such as Thyolo Mountains, Michiru, Mwanza, Chipoka and Nsanje.[19] Even in this traditional form of leadership the structures were hierarchical. The significance of this scenario in this study is that women can also be high up in the hierarchical structures sometimes increasing the liberation of fellow women but sometimes not. Hierarchy has also been well embedded in the traditional culture.

Likewise in the villages of the Southern region, the chief—who may be a women or a man—is in control, she or he may have advisors, but the last word to the villagers remains in his or her authority.

Is it strange that this culture has been a challenge to the Baptist congregational ideas of these women? The study shows that there is such a challenge and even the General Secretary of Baptist Convention may desire to exercise such authority over the church, but he is torn between two worlds, whether he is supposed to dictate the church or be a mere servant to the decisions made by the grassroots. The same struggle results in the national leadership of the women's organisation as regards to the limit of her influence. Are she and her committee as viewed in chapter 2 supposed to dictate the running of the organisation on the grassroots women? The study shows that struggle in the lives of Baptist Convention women in relation to congregational behaviour and Centralized government structures, and this has a bearing on their liberation especially in the event that those higher in the hierarchy are men.

The reality is that although Baptist polity is congregational, the old and prevailing political, cultural and religious cultures present a struggle to Baptist women to attain such an ideal. However, Baptist polity makes women more liberated than women in other centralized churches, which cement the hierarchical culture.

Baptists believe in the separation of church and state and that the church is not obliged to follow the dictates of the state, but rather gives

---

[19] See Isabel Apawo Phiri, *Women, Presbyterianism and Patriarchy, Religious Experience of Chewa Women in Central Malawi*: Blantyre: CLAIM-Kachere 1997, p. 23-24.

freedom to its members as to whether they should engage themselves in active or passive politics.

These Baptist distinctives will play a major role in interpreting both the history and the present situation of women in the Baptist Convention in Southern Malawi.

My approach

I do not claim that I have done this study as a distanced observer; neither does this book claim for itself an "objective" approach.[20] As I research and write, I am deeply involved, and I feel it's better to tell beforehand.

I write this reflection on women as a woman. In this, I empathize with the experiences of my fellow women. To write women experiences from a women's perspective is to satisfy the desires of many modern historians who realize that most histories in the past have been written from a male perspective.[21] These men, in the pursuit of writing history, have tended either to ignore or misrepresent women's experiences. This has not always been deliberate,[22] but men have often failed to present women issues with fairness because of patriarchal tendencies and ignorance. They write as an outsider and not as an insider. There is, therefore, a need to write experiences of women not only from the women's perspective but also about fellow women.

If I write from a women's perspective, am I then a feminist? Maybe, maybe not. If to be a feminist means to complain no end that we women have been oppressed, then I am none. If it means to believe that God created women and men equal and that He put no restrictions on women's participation in the life of the church, then I am happy to be a feminist. If to

---

[20] But I do not take this disclaimer as an excuse for a sloppy approach as to facts, feelings and footnotes.

[21] Isabel Phiri, *Women Presbyterianism and Patriarchy*, Blantyre: CLAIM-Kachere, 1997, p. 13.

[22] John McCracken writes in his new edition of *Politics and Christianity in Malawi 1875-1940. The Impact of the Livingstonia Mission in the Northern Province*, Blantyre: CLAIM-Kachere ²2000 (1977), p. 16: "If I was to begin studying Livingstonia today ... I would display much greater sensitivity than is contained in *Politics and Christianity* to the position of women within the church. Much more work requires to be done on Scottish women teachers, whose role I underestimated, on missionary wives, about whom fascinating fresh new evidence has emerged and, above all, on Christian women, a silent majority in much of this book.".

be a feminist means that I believe that women are better than men, I am none, but when it means that I believe that Christ accepts female disciples as happily as male ones,[23] then I am happy to subscribe to such kind of feminism.

I also write as a Baptist. I became a Baptist in 1988 while living in Zomba town. Before then, I belonged to CCAP (Blantyre Synod). I moved out of CCAP (Blantyre Synod) because I sought a church where I would be free to serve God with the gifts that He has given me. In the CCAP I would not have been allowed to offer a public prayer, on a normal Sunday, even if I was convicted to do so. Public prayers were a domain of church leaders. I was a mere church member by then. The decision to become a Baptist was not easy because I had been Presbyterian since birth. My parents were church leaders in Livingstonia Synod, and naturally I struggled to live the religious heritage of my youth. Together with my husband I at first decided to have membership in both CCAP and Baptist. In the mornings we went to CCAP and in the evenings we went to the Baptist church. Before long, Zomba Baptist Church showered us with privileges, not only to offer a public prayer but also to preach. Since it was a smaller congregation than Zomba CCAP, it was easy for us to form meaningful relationships. We loved the Baptist church and decided to move completely to it.

Since I write as a Baptist, I have the advantage of writing from the inside. The story I write is my own story. And I am also a participant of this story. As such, this record of women's experiences benefits from my own personal experience with Baptist Convention women, especially since 1998.

I also write as a native Malawian Baptist. This means I approach the experiences of women from a Malawian perspective and not from a missionary perspective. It was the tradition of missionaries to write histories with a view that they were the first to preach the gospel to the lost tribes of Africa. As such they wrote about their own histories and experiences and in these missionaries were at the centre of the stories as main players. Malawians were often represented as their students. This record of women's experiences is written from the perspective of the grassroots

---

[23] Christ said that there is joy in heaven about one sinner who repents; he did not specify that male repentance is dearer to him than female repentance. Either leads into being his disciple.

and shows how local women received and participated in the Baptist faith. Missionary women are also part of the experiences of these women, although only from the local perspective, because they were real people who came and worked with Malawians. The advantage of this approach is that I write a current reflection on lives of these women, where the emphasis is to write from the ordinary people's view and not from that of the elite. The disadvantage is that I may minimize the position of missionary women because my focus is not on them but on Baptist Malawian women.

I also write as an Evangelical. Evangelicals can broadly be defined as those church members that call themselves Evangelicals. As such they are found even in churches that are not evangelical by tradition. Evangelicals are simply those members that are committed to a personal faith in Christ and rely on the Bible as the only basis for faith and Christian living.[24]

Since there are different shades of evangelicalism: conservative, conciliar, and with fundamentalist leanings, it is important to state from which evangelicalism I write. Mine is a conciliar evangelicalism with a conservative leaning. Not all Baptists share this kind of evangelicalism. In fact, there have been disagreements within Baptist circles because of differences in evangelical leanings applied to church issues. An example of such disagreements is the recent vote against women's ordination by the Southern Baptists of America. Since different Southern Baptist missionaries worked in different areas, they might have brought differing influences to bear.

The starting point

I seized the opportunity to conduct interviews in the South East region when I attended a regional committee meeting in Zomba Baptist Church in May 1999, to which I, as a woman theologian of the Baptist Convention, had decided to invite myself. Although I had fears that I might be asked to leave the room, I was astonished that they welcomed me as "*Mbusa wa chizimayi*" (female pastor)[25]. The regional coordinator ex-

---

[24] See David B. Barrett, *World Christian Encyclopedia. A Comparative Survey of Churches and Religions in the Modern World. AD 1900-2000*. Nairobi: OUP, 1982.
[25] "Pastor" because they were not trained. Mr Botoman was elected as chairperson of the church but was basically referred to as "pastor".

plained to fellow committee members why I did not have a congregation to pastor even though I am as qualified as any other male pastor to pastor a church. The regional coordinator told them that it was because in Baptist Convention churches, there is yet no woman pastor. For this reason, the coordinator continued, my work is pastoral work among women in Baptist Convention churches. The coordinator lastly invited me to feel at home at their meeting and make contributions during their deliberations. I was overjoyed to see that the regional coordinator's plea was put in practice during the deliberations, when I was called upon from time to time to give advice.

Chapter 1

THE HISTORY OF BAPTIST WOMEN IN SOUTHERN MALAWI 1961 - 2001

1.0 Southern Baptist missionary women defining Baptist polity

This chapter begins with how the foundation of women's work was laid in two distinct areas, mainly through the influence of missionary women: Jali in Zomba, the origin of BACOMA work in the South East sub-region and Cliccord House in Limbe, Blantyre, the origin of BACOMA work in the South South region.[1] Work in these areas started independently of each other. The aim of this chapter is to give the historical context of Convention women and show struggles these women had as they utilized opportunities offered to them by missionary women. The story is told from a perspective of the ordinary women. The argument is that although there was a high level of foreign missionary influence in the life of indigenous Convention women, given that it is the missionaries who started this work in Malawi, the local women were given the opportunity to engage themselves in the work which they felt to be important, and their engagement took note of both culture and the Bible. Isabel Phiri shows how missionary Christianity brought by the Dutch Reformed Mission in Central Malawi was often oppressive to Nkhoma Synod women.[2] I argue that this experience was not unique to Nkhoma Synod women; it was widespread. However because of Baptist polity and doctrine, among Baptist women, this oppression, even though they did not have the ad-

---

[1]   Cliccord House was the building in Limbe that was rented by the Southern Baptist missionaries for Sunday services and Bible studies as early as 1961.
[2]   Isabel Phiri, *Women, Presbyterianism and Patriarchy*, p. 69.

vantage of leadership role models as Nkhoma Synod and Anglican women of Northern Mozambique had,[3] was less pronounced.

1.1 In the beginning: Blantyre Cliccord House and New Jerusalem 1961-1966

1.1.1 Missionary women

Baptist Convention women's history in the Southern region begins with a group of élite migrant women in Blantyre, at Cliccord House in Limbe, as early as 1960.[4] The first group of the elite was the three Southern Baptist missionary women who played a major role in defining the kind of Baptist doctrine local Baptists should receive. These women were Mrs Blanche Wester, Mrs Jean Albright and Mrs Beverly Kingsley. They came to Malawi accompanying their husbands in 1960. Their husbands were on a missionary assignment to Malawi and staged themselves first in Blantyre to learn Chichewa, the national language at that time. After a while, these missionary couples were allocated to different areas of ministry. The Westers went to Zomba, to start work there. The Albrights were sent to Lilongwe to start Baptist work there in 1961. The Kingsleys were assigned to Blantyre for five years until 1966 establishing work there, after which they went to Lilongwe to work at the Bible School that had already been started in 1962 by the Albrights. According to the policy of the Southern Baptist Mission Board, these women were first to be good wives to their husbands and to look after their home and children. Secondly, they were to be supporters to their husbands' ministry.[5] It is with this kind of Christianity that these missionary women influenced the Convention women. In Blantyre the missionary women established community work in places such as Ndirande, geared to teaching women how to sew. Their work attracted the attention of many because these classes

---

[3] Van Koevering shows how two single women, Bertha Healing and Florence Seddon, were such models among the Nyanja women of the Anglican Diocese of Northern Mozambique by 1931. See: Helen van Koevering, "Dancing their Dreams. The Lakeshore Women of the Anglican Diocese of Niassa." MPhil, University of Bristol 1999. Phiri also shows how single women such as Annie Marie Declare and Martha Murray met this need. See Isabel Phiri, *Women, Presbyterian and Patriarchy,* p. 44.

[4] Int. J.M. Ng'oma, Soche Baptist Church, 25.5.1999.

[5] Int. Rev Dr Sam Upton, Southern Baptist missionary, Lilongwe Baptist Seminary, August 1999.

were free of charge as opposed to the paid services offered by the government.[6] There was no single woman missionary during this period as was the case with Nkhoma Synod and the Anglican Church.[7] As such Convention women were only exposed to the leadership of married women who majored in support ministries to their husbands. The roles that missionary wives played were accepted because they were resonate with the way culture defined women's roles in the traditional Malawian society, where a woman's place was the kitchen and in areas of teaching, women were to teach fellow women as in the traditional initiation services. It is clear that in the beginning the doctrine of equal partnership between women and men was not observed.

1.1.2 Expatriate women

The second group of the elite was wives of expatriates.[8] These came to Cliccord House neither by active evangelisation nor by the preaching of missionaries. They joined as they sought an English speaking church. A few of them were already Baptists. These expatriate women joined the church largely because their husbands did so. A few joined the church alone like Mrs Effie Cameroon. Those women who joined the church even though they were not Baptists did it because either their denomination was not represented in Blantyre or though present, did not have an English service. The missionary women attracted such women through friendship, Bible studies usually held on Tuesdays and sewing activities.[9] The role of expatriate women seems to have been well accommodated to the support ministries of their leaders, the wives of the missionaries. In this respect missionary women seemed to largely dictate their definition of the Baptist polity on expatriate women as well. The expatriate women in turn worked hard at improving their homes and families by participating in the missionary women's activities. Such role must have been fulfilling to these non-locals as it gave them a sense of contributing something

---

[6] See: Judy Garner, *History of the Baptist Mission in Malawi: A Rambling Remembrance of some People and Events in the History of the Baptist Mission in Malawi*, Lilongwe Baptist Publications, 1998 p. 8.

[7] See Helen van Koevering "Dancing the Dreams" and Isabel Phiri, *Women, Presbyterianism and Patriarchy*, p. 44.

[8] Int. J.M. Ng'oma, Soche Baptist Church, 25.5.1999.

[9] Int. Hany Longwe, Research notes. See also Judy Garner, *History of the Baptist Mission in Malawi*, p. 8.

to the welfare of the locals.[10] However, Mrs Effie Cameroon was an exception to this trend. She provided accommodation to the needy at the backyard of her house. This was a leadership role in that she acted in her own right to reach these marginalized people in this way, and invite them to her church at Cliccord House.[11] She was in agreement with missionary women to use a felt need to reach people, but then further expounded this strategy by showing that sewing was not the only felt need in the community through which people could be won to the church. She saw that providing a home to the homeless was also strategic in inviting people to the church. In this way, she redefined the interpretation of missionary women concerning Baptist polity and doctrine. She was however, not without support because at this time she did not have transport and Mrs Beverly Kingsley offered transport to take them to church. Inevitably, her ministry brought women and men of a lower social class into the church. One of these was Mrs Lazarus Malabwanya who was converted to the Baptist faith in this way.[12] She and her husband were beggars in the city of Blantyre because they were blind and did not have any trade or training for employment. Their children Samuel Malabwanya and Fanny Kwelakwela also became Baptists and as of 1964, this Malabwanya family was already Baptist.[13] In reaching this family and others of similar social status, Effie Cameroon's mission echoes an important ministry of Jesus related in Luke 4:18, 19:

"The spirit of the Lord is on me,
because he has anointed me
to preach good news to the poor.
He has sent me to proclaim freedom for the prisoners
and recovery of sight for the blind,
to release the oppressed,
to proclaim the year of the Lord's favour."[14]

Mrs Effie Cameroon's ministry made the congregation at Cliccord to be quite mixed socially and culturally. There were now low class people who had come into this congregation that was predominately white and upper

---

[10]   Sewing crafts such as quilting is very common among American women.
[11]   Int. Mrs Fanny Kwelakwela, Bangwe Baptist Church, 30.4.2000.
[12]   Ibid.
[13]   Ibid.
[14]   NIV, Jesus quoting the Servant Song from Isaiah 61:1-2.

class. However some of these people from low social status became very instrumental in the growth of Convention work in the Southern region. Mrs Kwelakwela became a pillar at the beginning of Bangwe Baptist Church later. Samuel Malabwanya became a leading pastor in the Convention. He was educated with financial assistance from Rev and Mrs Beverly Kingsley, up to Standard 8. He was then sent to do theological studies in Gweru Baptist Seminary in the later years.[15] His wife Chrissie is fondly remembered by the women in the South East region as well. She is a symbol of a time when women in this region had sewing classes in their local churches in the later years.[16]

The other two expatriate women who are also well remembered in Blantyre at this time were Mrs Klova and Mrs Bright. Mrs Klova was a Coloured, married to a white American. She and her husband were already Baptists by the time they came to Malawi.[17] Mrs Bright was the wife of the Mayor of Blantyre and she and her husband were also already Baptists before they came to Malawi.[18] It is evident that the common patterns of behaviour, even among expatriate women, was to accommodate to support roles of missionary women, but that there are always deviants who aim to bring change to the dominant culture. This was why even during the British Protectorate and the Kamuzu regime, there were political activists who worked against the political dispensations of the day to bring about change. Baptist doctrine and polity does enhance this new pattern of behaviour. The freedom to obey one's conscience is key to this. It is the same disposition that enhanced Effie Cameroon's initiative to redefine the missionaries' interpretation of Baptist doctrine and polity and gain freedom. This is a good example where dominant culture can be foregone for the sake of the gospel, which is liberating.

---

[15] Int. Fanny Kwelakwela, Bangwe Baptist Church, 30.4.2000.
[16] Int. Mrs Mwanakhu, Mpinda Baptist Church, 26.12.2000.
[17] Int. Mr J.M. Ng'oma, businessman, Soche Baptist Church, 25.5.1999; also int. Mary Galatiya, Likudzi Estate, Chipiliro Baptist Church, Balaka, 15.5.2000, businessman.
[18] Ibid.

1.1.3 Wives of migrant Malawians (machona)[19]

The third group were the *machona* women, wives of Malawian men who had migrated to neighbouring countries like Zimbabwe, South Africa and Zambia, looking for better jobs.[20] These women were not Malawians by birth. The first woman of this group was Mrs Mary Galatiya. She is South African and was born 11.9.1928 at Summerset West in the Cape Province.[21] She became part of the English service when her husband, Stephen Galatiya, met Rev Wester at Limbe market while selling *kachewere* (Irish potatoes) in 1961.[22] Mary Galatiya had become a Baptist in South Africa before she came to Malawi in 1960.[23] Since 1960 she and her husband had sought opportunities to start a Baptist church in her husband's home area of Neno in Mwanza. The effort proved futile because Stephen Galatiya's parents who were strong Seventh-day Adventists opposed the new religion of their son.[24] Even when the Galatiyas moved 30 km away from their village to Kambale in Chimchembere village in Mwanza, to begin Baptist work there, the response was negative since the place was still close to their relatives who continued to discourage people from becoming Baptists.[25]

The other *machona* woman was Mrs Ellen Ng'oma, who became Baptist in 1965 through the witness of Stephen Galatiya. She was married to a Tonga from Nkhata Bay, Mr J.M. Ng'oma. At the time of her conversion, her husband was working with Singer Company. Rev Galatiya preached first to her husband about the Baptist faith. The husband re-

---

[19] I prefer to use *machona,* although others prefer not to use it because of negative connotations that are implied in the word, that they are people who are lost and have forgotten their home country. I use it to refer to people who went to work outside Malawi for a time and came back.

[20] This tradition was well set in Malawi since the 1920s under various influences such as payment of hut tax, looking for white color jobs among others. See: John McCracken, *Politics and Christianity in Malawi 1875-1940. The Impact of Livingstonia Mission in Northern Province,* London: Cambridge University Press, 1977, pp. 149-153.

[21] Int. Mary Galatiya, Likudzi Estate, Chipiliro Baptist Church, 15.5.2000.

[22] Ibid.

[23] Ibid.

[24] Neno is a strong Seventh-day Adventist area, see Yonah Matemba, Matandani. The Second Adventist Mission in Malawi, Zomba: Kachere 2004. [MA University of Malawi 2000].

[25] Int. Mary Galatiya, Likudzi Estate, Chipiliro Baptist Church, 15.5.2000.

ceived the message with joy. He asked Stephen Galatiya to find time and explain the message to his wife as well. Rev Galatiya did just that and Mrs Ng'oma believed the message. She was later to play an important role in the Baptist women's history in Southern Malawi. Both Mrs Ng'oma and her husband had been strong members of CCAP. They had had a church wedding after being duly baptized through baptism by sprinkling. Rev Galatiya recognised the strength of their religion and thought that the best approach to win them to the Baptist faith was by pointing out the weakness of what they already had, baptism by sprinkling.[26] Rev Galatiya explained to them to believe in the baptism of Jesus by immersion and that, if they truly loved Christ, they would be willing to follow the baptism of Jesus. Both were convicted of needing baptism by immersion. This earned them membership in the Baptist church.[27] The story of Mrs Ng'oma shows how respect for individual conscience is a liberative ingredient to women and men, even in their engagement in the church. If CCAP had been willing to offer baptism by immersion to those who feel the need to have it and allow such to remain members of the church, this would provide freedom to such members.[28]

---

[26] The majority of Baptists do not believe that baptism by sprinkling is biblical.

[27] Int. Mr Ng'oma, Soche Baptist Church, Blantyre, 25.5.1999. According to CCAP you cannot be rebaptized, and so this meant that they fell out of fellowship with their CCAP. Information from Rev Dr Steven Paas, Zomba Theological College, Zomba and Mrs Fulata Moyo, Chancellor College, Zomba. 2000.

[28] There are others in the CCAP and other church traditions who have gone through such baptism in private and have not revealed it to their church leadership. Such baptisms are usually carried out by other churches. This is a an interesting development in that Baptism which is normally intended for membership becomes a private matter in the name of personal conscience. The founder of the Christian Missionary Alliance Church in America, Albert B. Simpson is one of such examples who sought private baptism by immersion in 1881, in an Italian Baptist Church, while he was already pastor of a Presbyterian church. His motivation for private baptism, which is typical for many who seek such baptism, was to avoid misunderstandings and condemnation by his friends and church. See: Robert Niklaus, John S. Sawin, Samuel J. Stoez, *All For Jesus. God at Work in the Christian Missionary Alliance Over One Hundred Years*, Camp Hill: Christian Publications, 1986, p. 43. See also: Klaus Fiedler, *The Story of Faith Missions, From Hudson Taylor to Present Day Africa*, Oxford: Regnum 1994, p. 184. Klaus Fiedler also adds that the motivation for having believers' baptism in Faith Missions was for spiritual development. In the Anglican Church, baptism cannot be repeated. In the Roman Catholic Church immersion is a possible rite, and there is a liturgy available for this, except if it is rebaptism, which is not allowed. But ordinarily members are not aware of such privilege.

The other *machona* women were Mrs Elidah Maseko, Mrs Nyirenda and Mrs Kandawe.[29] Mrs Kandawe was a Zimbabwean, while the others were South African by birth.[30] They all became Baptists through the witness of Rev Stephen Galatiya. It seems that the fact that they were all of other ethnicity encouraged them to join the Baptist church that was very diverse in ethnicity and status. The Baptist church was also receptive to women of difficult marriages.[31] Mrs Elidah Maseko and Mrs Nyirenda - who were pastors' wives even - were good examples.[32] Their husbands were sequential polygamists[33] and this had no negative implications on their wives' church office. This behaviour of the husbands would have been very restrictive to their wives in attaining or retaining church membership in other churches. In CCAP and other churches, the other wives of a sequential polygamist are normally perceived to have stolen someone's husband even in the event that either the previous wife or her husband was at fault. The fact that women of such backgrounds are accepted in a Baptist church has negative as well as positive effects on the image of their church. It is positive in the fact that it is liberating to such women who have no room in other churches. It is negative in that it is perceived that Baptists are not serious concerning issues of divorce and remarriage. This acceptance in the early period is perceived by some as a desperate attempt by early missionaries to gain enough membership, which was scarce at that time.[34] However, this accusation is not valid. The gist of the matter is that Baptist doctrine and polity does offer much freedom in the area of marriage to its members, even in America, where the missionaries came from.

Rev John Nyirenda was married twice while in the Baptist church. In the first marriage, his wife divorced him while in Seminary in Gweru and as such he came back to remarry.[35] He had been in Seminary only for a

---

[29] Int. Fanny Kwelakwela, Bangwe Baptist Church, Blantyre, 30.4.2000.

[30] Ibid.

[31] See chapter 4 for more details on how Baptist women are more liberated in the area of marriage.

[32] Pastor's wife *(mayi mbusa)* is an office in Baptist Churches, albeit an informal one, but one of perceived spiritual leadership.

[33] Married to more than one wife, but one at a time.

[34] Int. Mr J.M Ng'oma, Soche Baptist Church, 25.5.2000. The attitude of accepting divorce and remarriage has continued till today. For more details see chapter 4 on marriage.

[35] During this early period, no pastor went into training without a wife.

year by then. When he came back he remarried but unfortunately even this second wife divorced him. On his own, he left the Baptist church in his single state and joined the Salvation Army. But his membership there was short-lived and he came back to the Baptist church. He died a Baptist and single.[36] The first wife of Rev Nyirenda was South African, and the second was Zimbabwean.[37] Both left the Baptist church after divorce. The fact that these women were pastors' wives did not restrain them from divorcing their husbands.[38]

Rev Maseko also had a complicated family. He may have been married to three women, but another tradition says that he was only married twice.[39] The first wife was South African and she divorced him when one of her daughters died suddenly in Maseko's home in Ntcheu. Mrs Maseko left and went back to South Africa and left her children with Maseko. However even in South Africa she remained a Baptist till her death in 1999. Maseko, a businessman, left Ntcheu and went to live in Blantyre where he remarried. This second Mrs Maseko is well remembered as a pastor's wife who helped women to sew at Bangwe Baptist Church.[40] When Maseko died in 1985, he died as a divorcee.[41] In the case of Revs Nyirenda and Maseko, we see as liberating that Baptist churches do allow women leaders to divorce their husbands if need be. The mandate is not only in the hands of male members of the church.

The engagement of *machona* women was also tuned to roles missionary women did. In this we see that they did not try to redefine the missionaries' interpretation of Baptist polity and doctrine, which encouraged women to be in support roles. This was firstly, probably because they worked side by side with them. The *machona* women were highly literate. They read and spoke English well. Further, they knew Chichewa, their husband's language. With this versatility they became ideal inter-

---

[36] Int. Fanny Kwelakwela, Bangwe Baptist Church, 25.5.2000.
[37] Int. Mr J.M. Ng'oma, Soche Baptist Church, Blantyre, 25.5.2000.
[38] Marriage is not a sacrament in the Baptist Church. See chapter 4.
[39] According to J.M. Ng'oma, Maseko was married to Beauty Maseko, in his second marriage, who owned a restaurant where Rev Nyirenda liked to dine. According to Mr Gawaza, Rev Maseko married Elidah Maseko, who was a second wife. If Elidah and Beauty are names of one woman then he married twice, but if these are different women, then he had had three marriages.
[40] Int. Mr Gawaza, Bangwe Baptist Church, Blantyre, 30.5.2000.
[41] Ibid.

preters of the missionary women as they carried on their church work.[42] Mrs Mary Galatiya became an assistant pastor's wife when she and her husband came back from Seminary in 1965, where they had been since 1963. In her new role, she assisted Beverly Kingsley, the pastor's wife there, to teach the women sewing skills and women's work just as she had learnt in the Seminary. Secondly, *machona* women were overridden with the prevalent traditional and missionary culture that encouraged women domination. Even though Baptist polity brought equal partner-ship, they did not see that preached by their leaders, the missionary women. The fact that they did not behave differently even though they had opportunity to do that shows that some women chose to obey the culture of the day over and against their Baptist doctrine, and were less liberated.

Apart from the missionary women, *machona* women and low class Malawian women, other ordinary Malawian women also joined the church. These came largely through the witness of Mrs Galatiya, espe-cially after her Seminary days in Gweru in 1965. These ordinary Mala-wian women were the likes of Mrs Chisale (who later left for Mwanza, her home village), Mrs Wala, Mrs Pound, Mrs Chiphwephwe who left for Thyolo later, Mrs Mbandambanda, (who left the Baptist church later), Mrs Kamwendo (who died in 1996), Mrs Giver, (who became the first or-dained woman deacon in the South South region in 1970).[43] At that time the Baptist Church seems to have been an attraction to displaced peo-ple, (especially women), born in other nationalities and districts. Reasons could be many, but one possibility is that the church gave them a sense of belonging in a place where they did not fully belong. The other possi-bility is that there was no struggle to earn membership in the church, re-gardless of their social standing, as might be the case in other churches. Further, the church seems to have provided opportunities that were stra-tegic for this extraordinary section of the community. It provided an Eng-lish Sunday School, opportunities for fellowship and service which were probably seen to be more restricted in other established churches.

---

[42] Not only literal interpretation, but also bridging the gap with the locals.
[43] Int. Fanny Kwelakwela and Mr Gawaza, Bangwe Baptist Church, Blantyre, 25.5.2000.

1.1.4 The split between missionary women and local women

The church at Cliccord House could no longer use English only as a medium of exchange during its services. Some of the members could not understand English, while some from the expatriate community could not understand Chichewa. It was therefore decided in 1966 to divide the congregation into Chichewa and English services.[44] The English service took place in the upstairs room, while the Chichewa service was held in the downstairs room, which was interpreted by local people as racism. This was most likely. Rev Galatiya and his wife, Mary Galatiya, became a pastoral team over the Chichewa service, leaving the English service in the hands of the Kingsleys, the missionaries in this church then.

1.1.5. The exodus of the Chichewa congregation to Newlands

Further change came when a decision was made in 1966 to have indigenous support for an indigenous pastor. This move was undemocratically enforced by Rev Roy Davidson who replaced Rev Kingsley, strengthening the local Malawians' suspicion of missionary racism towards them.[45] Beverly Kingsley and her husband had by that time moved to Lilongwe to open the Bible School there.[46] Rev Galatiya consequently made a motion to his congregation to leave Cliccord House and establish themselves in Newlands.[47] During one Sunday service, Galatiya told his congregation that he felt that Davidson was a racist in his decision concerning indigenous support for an indigenous pastor. He told the congregation that he was going to leave Cliccord House and begin a church in his house in Newlands. He preached a sermon on Acts 3:6 where Peter, talking to the crippled man at the Temple gate called Beautiful, said "Silver or gold I do not have, but what I have I give you; In the name of Jesus Christ of Nazareth walk." From these verses he challenged the congregation that if they wanted to follow him, they should do so but that they should not ex-

---

[44] This decision was not forced on the church. Stephen Galatiya suggested it after consultations with Rev Kingsley who was the senior pastor then. Rev Kingsley agreed to the idea and the congregation adapted this. Int. Rev Galatiya, Likudzi Estate, Chipiliro Baptist 15.5.2000.

[45] Ibid.

[46] Ibid.

[47] Ibid. This story is a women's story because women were also involved in it and the decision also had implications on women's work as it is seen later in the chapter.

pect him to give them *kaunjika* (second hand clothing)[48] or money because he did not have any. The following Sunday, which is still referred
to by some of the early Convention people as Big Sunday, the whole
Chichewa congregation came to Newlands to pray in Galatiya's house.
Cliccord House was conspicuously without a Chichewa congregation
during this Sunday and thereafter.[49] This decision is a testimony to the
fact that the stand of the Baptist church to obey individual consciences
was liberating to women. Further that the women chose to be in solidarity
with their husbands and moved out of the church, even though they earlier on enjoyed close association with missionary women, shows how
Baptist women are liberated. They chose to forego status for the sake of
the gospel and attained their freedom.

1.2 In the beginning: Zomba (South East region) 1961 to 1966

By the time Baptist women's work was starting and blossoming in Blantyre, there was already a spark of Convention women's work in Zomba at
Ndalama and Chayima Baptist Churches,[50] even though this offshoot
was not responsible for the beginnings of women's work in Blantyre.
Nevertheless, in the late 1960s some women from the South East region
trickled to Blantyre. Mrs Rosebay Botoman, for example, was a member
of Chayima Baptist Church in Jali, after being forced by her husband to
join his church,[51] before she and her husband went to Blantyre and
joined Soche Baptist in 1967.[52] Her husband came to Limbe to look for
employment.[53]

---

[48] Missionaries were given such clothing by their sending churches to distribute to
those in need as a means of showing compassion and helping in the propagation of
the gospel.
[49] Ibid.
[50] Details are given below in this chapter.
[51] For details on Chayima, read later in the chapter. For details on Mrs Botoman's
forced conversion, see chapter on marriage.
[52] Int. Rosebay Botoman, Rev Botoman, Chisomo Baptist Church, Blantyre,
28.3.2000.
[53] Mr Botoman was literate but never wanted to go to seminary because he believed
God was enough to disciple him. (Int. Martha Chirwa, Zomba Theological College,
14.12.2000 and Mr. Ng'oma, Soche Baptist Church, 31.3.2000, Int. Mrs Rosebay
Botoman, Chisomo Baptist, Chilomoni BC, 28.3.2000.

1.2.1 At Ndalama: the core group

The pioneering Convention women in the South East came from Ndalama Baptist Church as part of a group conversion that happened there. Whereas the congregations at Cliccord House in Limbe grew as a result of individual or family conversions, there were group conversions at Jali.[54] But although most of women's work can be traced from Chayima village in 1962, the first church in the South East region and in Malawi was Ndalama Baptist Church in the same year.[55] The church was the result of a group conversion from Zion Church.[56] Kachasu Gama was the pastor of this church, but got disappointed by the leadership of Zion Church. He and friends therefore searched for another denomination. One time Kachasu Gama heard about Baptist missionaries in town.[57] He met the Westers in Zomba town and asked them to adopt their Zion church. The Westers agreed, in fact it was a good thing for them because they had come for that purpose, to establish Baptist work in Malawi. This agreement resulted into the whole congregation being baptised into the Baptist church.[58] This became Ndalama Baptist Church. Although Kachasu Gama was already pastor of Ndalama Zion Church, he needed to be schooled in Baptist beliefs. Fortunately, in the same year, the Bible School in Lilongwe was to begin. Rev Wester arranged that Kachasu Gama be among the first Bible School students.[59] Kachasu

---

[54] The issue of conversion in terms of moving from one church to the other, and that it was frequent in this area for a whole congregation to switch to another denomination, needs more study. For details see also appendix 1. For a detailed study of the denominational change of one congregation see: Rhodian Munyenyembe, Some Effects of Denominational Pluralism on Congregational Discords: The Case of Namadzi ZEC and Church of Christ Congregations in an Ecclesiological Perspective, BA, University of Malawi, 2001.

[55] See Research Notes, Hany Longwe. See also Judy Garner, History of the Baptist Mission in Malawi, p. 9.

[56] Judy Garner, History of the Baptist Mission in Malawi, p. 3 records this former church as Church of Christ. Hany Longwe's research notes agree with my findings that it was a Zion church.

[57] According to Judy Garner, Kachasu Gama had gone to town to look for children's Sunday School materials in Blantyre when they met the Barrs at Likhubula, who directed him to the Westers. Ibid, p. 9.

[58] Int. Rev Chisi, Ufulu Baptist Church, Lilongwe, 23.6.2000.

[59] Some of the students came from Achewa PIM. See Hany Longwe, Identity by Dissociation: The First Group to Secede from Chilembwe's Church. A History of Pe-

Gama went through the training but his wife, who was going to be pastor's wife upon his graduation, did not. Although Baptist women's work
from Ndalama did not progress to other areas, it was an important
church because it offered opportunities for theological training for Mrs
Galatiya and her husband.[60] The Galatiyas had to be part of a local
church, for them to be sent for theological training in Gweru Baptist
Seminary, and so the Galatiyas became members of Ndalama Baptist
Church, which recommended them for theological training.[61] Although, in
this initial stage, it is difficult to gauge women liberation as regards roles
they played, we see one aspect of liberation in their faith life, that of being easily accepted into the Baptist church. The women with their men
did not have to attend classes to be members neither did they have to
show their valid wedding certificates to be accepted.

1.2.2 At Chayima: the core group

The second group of women in the South East region had a more lasting
history than the pioneering group at Ndalama. This second group came
from Chayima, the second Convention Baptist church to be established
in this area. It is from this church that most of the Baptist congregations
in the South East region originated.[62] The church is in Chayima village 5
km east of Jali Trading Centre in Zomba rural.[63] Chayima church is built
on an elevated platform, characteristic of how houses are built in this
area. The valleys are left to the growing of crops like maize, tobacco and
rice. This building arrangement has created a lot of space between one
homestead and another.[64] The first women in this church were members

---

ter Kalamba and the Achewa Providence Industrial Mission (APIM), MA, University of
Malawi, 2000, p.
[60] Mrs Galatiya was later to become an important figure in the work of Baptist
women at national level.
[61] See Hany Longwe's Research Notes.
[62] Int. Rosebay Botoman, Chisomo Baptist Church, Chilomoni, Blantyre, 28.3.2000.
Mahere and his elder brother, CheMaloya fought 28.3.2000 against each other for
leadership. One Sunday the members of the church were ready for the Holy Communion organized by Che Mahere.
[63] Int. Rosebay Botoman, Chisomo Baptist Church, 28.3.2000.
[64] Int. Rosebay Botoman, Chisomo Baptist Church, Blantyre, 28.3.2000; Mrs
Mahere, Rev Maida, Mrs Maida, Chayima Baptist Church, Zomba, 10.3.2000.

of "Severe Church",[65] a branch of Churches of Christ.[66] These women together with others left their church to join the Baptist church when disagreements arose in their church centering on leadership.[67] After such a disappointment with "Severe Church," the members decided to seek another church. They went to Zomba town where they met Mrs Wester and her husband. They learnt that the Westers, too, were looking for people who could work with them. Mrs Wester and her husband spelled out to the delegates some of the beliefs to discuss them with their flock at Chayima. Some of the beliefs mentioned were: They were to refrain from drunkenness, polygamy, smoking and going to traditional dances.[68] Most importantly, they were to be willing to receive salvation in Jesus. Mrs Wester and her husband challenged the delegates to go back to their church to find out if their flock was ready to abide by these demands. When the delegates went back, the members unanimously accepted to be Baptist. Similarly, this experience shows that women were liberated but of course not without a form of oppression. The dictates against polygamy and traditional dances were oppressive. To deny Baptist women participation in traditional dancing implied that they were against initiation.

The Chayima women have a long history. Before coming to "Severe Church", they earlier on belonged to the Church of God. They moved out of that church because of leadership disputes.[69] At that time the women

---

[65] Int. Rev Maida, Mrs Maida, Anganeje Mahere, Chayima Baptist Church, 20.3.2000. Int. Rosebay Botoman, Chisomo Baptist Church, Blantyre, 28.3.2000.
[66] For the history of Churches of Christ see: C.B. Shelburne, History of the Church of Christ in Malawi, np, nd, 4 pp. (A copy is available in the Baptist Theological Seminary of Malawi in Lilongwe).
[67] "Severe Church" because the leader was Mr Severe, a Malawian.
[68] Although *chinamwali* (initiation) is not mentioned here, reference to it is implied because *chinamwali* involves traditional dancing. This stand has an implication on how missionaries defined Baptist doctrine. Were Baptist women completely to deny their cultural heritage? Was this what it meant to be regenerate? To leave everything behind including culture? This seems to be true in the sense that traditional initiation was systematically discouraged through the tradition of the booklet *chinamwali*. For more information on the subject see, Rachel Nyagondwe Banda, *Coming of Age: Christian Chinamwali for Baptist Girls in Malawi,* Zomba: Kachere, 2005.
[69] This was between Rev Chimenya and Mr Severe. Mr Severe was involved in an extramarital affair with a girl in his church. Rev Chimenya and the whole congregation thought this was unbecoming and as far as they were concerned, it was not right

worshipped in Mrs Majomboshe's house.[70] But after conversion to Church of Christ, they had a church building which they lost when they became Baptist. They went back to Mrs Majomboshe's house, after which a temporary mud house was built on her land.[71]

1.2.3 Increase in numbers at Chayima

This first group of women at Chayima did not remain static; it started attracting other women including men. These came from different places within Zomba. A few of them came from Chayima village where the church is built. These were the likes of Mrs Rosebay Botoman[72] (the niece to Abusa Majomboshe); Anganeje Tsegula (Mrs Mahere); Mrs Chimenya, whose husband was the first pastor of Chayima Baptist Church; Mrs Chipolopolo, who became pastor's wife at Chayima Baptist Church, when Mrs Emma Chimenya left with her husband and Mrs Majomboshe (an aunt to Anganeje Tsegula), who with her husband became missionaries to the Mulanje area.[73] All these women became pastors' wives without theological training. During this time, pastors' wives did not accompany their husbands to Bible School in Lilongwe to do theological studies. There were other women as well that joined the church, the majority of them following their husbands.[74] To admit women as pastors' wives without training was oppressive because in this state, they were denied access to theology, which was key to the right interpretation of Baptist polity and doctrine. As such, these untrained pastors' wives were unintentionally subjected to be obedient to the missionary interpretation of Baptist polity and doctrine, which encouraged women's subordination.

---

for them follow such immoral leadership. Int. Rosebay Botoman, Chisomo Baptist Church, Chilomoni, Blantyre, 28.3.2000.

[70] House churches are not only a reality of New Testament world, but in this period as well.

[71] Int. Rosebay Botoman, Chisomo Baptist Church, Blantyre, 28.3.2000.

[72] She followed her husband after she had been challenged by him that *m'mphuno yimodzi simulowa zala ziwiri* (two fingers cannot go into one nostril at the same time). In this proverbial saying he meant that since they were one, they couldn't go to different churches. She has been a pastor's wife in Blantyre from 1969 to the present time.

[73] Read Gazamiyala's note that Convention work started 1962; Int. Rev Davidson Lichapa, Makolije Baptist Church, 8.3.2000. Int. Mrs Botoman, Chisomo Baptist Church, Blantyre, 28.3.2000.

[74] Int. Rev Maida, Chayima Baptist Church, 20.3.2000.

Emma Chimenya, wife of Gresham Chimenya, a few weeks before she died, in June 2000

Other women came from neighbouring Mpheta village, about 1 km east of Chayima.[75] One of such women was the mother of Pastor Maida. Other women came to join the church as word about a new church spread. Word about Mrs Wester's activities of teaching cooking and sewing also spread. This drew local women from far and wide to be part of this new development. Mrs Mercy Chimbaka (nee Matewere), Elidah Fayson (who died in 1987), Mrs Tereza Jumbe (who enjoyed a long life and died aged about 100 years), Mrs Esmy Masangano (nee Mayinuka, who also lived long and is believed to have reached 110 years before she died) and Mrs Andisambula—the only woman who started a Baptist Church in those early days—came from far away. Mrs Andisambula originated from Mandawala village in Zomba rural.[76] These women had to walk long distances, which turned into a blessing,[77] since there was need later to start new Baptist churches near the localities of these

---

[75] Int. Mrs Maida, Chayima Baptist Church, 20.3.2000. Int. Mrs Botoman, Chisomo Baptist Church, 28.3.2000.

[76] Ibid. I also visited Mpheta village.

[77] Among many reasons, people also choose churches because of distance. See Henry Church, *Theological Education that Makes a Difference*, Blantyre: CLAIM-Kachere, 2001, p. 214f.

women. In this way, women's work grew to new areas. Elidah Fayson, Tereza Jumbe, Esmy Masangano and others for example, became women pillars of Makolije Baptist Church, near their home village in Jali. The sewing and cooking programmes were liberating to Baptist women because through such programmes they were empowered to be better teachers, mothers, wives or women in their homes and churches.

1.2.4 Church of Christ, fertile ground for conversion

A good number of women in the core group in this region earlier belonged to Churches of Christ. The reason seems to lie in the conversion of an influential leader of the church. At this time there were conflicts surrounding leadership in the church. This disorganized state of the Church of Christ there in the 1960s provided an opportunity for its members to leave for other churches. Pastor Chimenya's transfer to the Baptist Church influenced a lot of these conversions. The fact that he was a key leader in Church of Christ at Chayima and revolted against it brought a negative impact on members of Church of Christ in this region. Andisambula was one of the Churches of Christ members who left during this period. She was a member of another branch of Churches of Christ (Simisi).[78] She had heard of Chimenya's new church across Thondwe River in Chayima village and left her church in search for this new church. After some time the distance to the new church wore her out. She then transferred her membership to Chimbalanga Baptist Church, which had also just started. However, walking to Chimbalanga Baptist Church also proved to be taxing.[79] In this experience, it is clear that the Baptist polity of congregationalism is liberating. Women in the Church of Christ were squeezed out because of what happened in the hierarchy, so the Baptist church became a good alternative to them because they did not have to worry about a leadership hierarchy. They could be a complete church on themselves without any reference to a governing body elsewhere.

1.2.5 Growth beyond Chayima and Ndalama

Women's work grew to Thundu and Makolije villages among others and conversions came from other churches than the Churches of Christ. One of such areas where work spread was near Jali centre in Thundu village.

---

[78] See Shelburne, History of the Church of Christ in Malawi.
[79] For more details on the role of Andisambula, see further down in the chapter.

In 1964, Thundu Baptist Church was started in Mrs Malikebu's home,[80] who was the first woman convert in this church. At this time she was a chief's wife. She got converted after her husband was converted from CCAP to Baptist in 1963. Her husband found his faith when he had gone for fishing at Lake Chirwa from Mr Mbona who was a Baptist there. He shared with his wife about the new Baptist belief he had found. She too believed and became a Baptist. Before then, she had been a Muslim. She started meeting with Mrs Chagomwa and Mrs Musa who also came with their husbands. These women became Baptists through charity work by Mrs Wester and also through one to one evangelism by Mrs Malikebu. Mrs Wester and her husband brought *kaunjika* (second hand clothing) to Malikebu's home, where needy local women were given such clothing at a small price.[81] This attracted some to the Baptist faith. These activities were complimented by Mrs Malikebu's witness in the area. When the missionaries conducted meetings in the area, she would go into the neighbourhood and invite other women. Through these efforts, women's work grew at Thundu Baptist Church.[82] The combination of charity and gospel was no doubt a testimony that the missionaries were genuinely interested in the lives of local women. It was liberating for the women to receive the gospel from them.

Women's work in the 1960s also spread to Mwathanavi in Julius village in 1963 and Mpinda village in 1964. Mrs Chiwamba was one of the first women converts at Julius Baptist Church. She served as a *mlangizi* (instructor) in this church. From this church women's work spread to Chilunga in Madeya village in Mulanje in 1964.

These new branches came from the evangelistic efforts of Makolije Baptist Church. The main method of winning others to the Baptist faith in these areas was through *phwando*[83] (party) evangelistic meetings. The

---

[80]   Int. Mrs Malikebu, Thundu Baptist Church, Zomba, 28.11.1999.

[81]   This selling of second hand clothing got the Westers into trouble in the later years.

[82]   Int. Mrs Malikebu, Thundu Baptist Church, Zomba, 28.11.1999.

[83]   *Phwando* means party. This strategy of having an evangelistic *phwando* was used by Makolije Church to start new churches. Through this women's work grew. They used to ask the chief if they could have a meeting in his village. The chief usually agreed and requested the neighbouring chiefs and people to attend. At the meetings there was preaching and people believed. Women were taught about Baptist beliefs in parallel sessions with men. Women taught fellow women and it was usually

role of women at such meetings was mainly in support roles. Women did not preach at the evangelistic *phwando* meetings. They only taught Baptist beliefs after the meeting to women who had decided to become Baptists. Even this was difficult and very few locals were able to do this, as such Wester did most of the teaching. Obviously, local women needed to learn the Baptist beliefs before teaching their fellow women. The pastors' wives also lacked theological training, which their husbands had. Women were also not allowed to preach at a normal Sunday Service, as the perception was that women were unholy to stand in the pulpit and unfit to preach to men. This is a cultural issue related to uncleanness during women's menstruation.[84] It is not an American Baptist influence. Southern Baptist women have never been barred from standing in the pulpit because of any assumption of unholiness. However, since even Mrs Wester, a missionary, remained quiet in the Church and was mainly involved in support roles such as cooking, sewing and hospitality[85] the cause of women preaching to women only can therefore not be explained away by culture alone. Missionary Christianity also did contribute to this negative trend. But more so, it was the spirit of the day and in many churches women did not preach. For this reason, Baptist women, even though they were at an advantage to show liberation through their polity and doctrine, were unable to do so. Culture and spirit of the day seemed to override them

1.2.6 Problems and challenges

The history of the beginnings of work in the southern region shows that although Baptist doctrine is liberating the correct interpretation of it is important for such liberation to be realized. However in this history women were deprived of the important ingredients necessary for the correct interpretation. Two of the ingredients were education and theological training.

pastors' wives that did it. Int. Davidson Lichapa Junior, Jali Centre, Zomba rural 8.3.2000.
[84] Ibid. See Felix Chingota, "Sacraments and Sexuality", *Religion in Malawi*, no 8, April 1998, p. 34.
[85] Int. Mrs Mahere, Chayima Baptist Church, 20.3.2000.

1.2.6.1 Educational limitation and theological training of pastors' wives

While the Blantyre core group was seasoned with women of a high social and non Malawian ethnic background, with high literacy, and had a theologically trained pastor's wife, Mrs Mary Galatiya, the South East region had mostly women of limited literacy, and so were their husbands. Because of this educational limitation, there were no theologically trained women. As such they were limited in their way of understanding of their Baptist polity and doctrine. For this reason they took upon themselves the oppressive interpretation of the doctrine done by their missionary counterparts who, by their way of life, taught subordination of women in the church and encouraged sexism through their division of roles women played in the church in the same patterns laid down by their culture. In the initiation ceremony, for example women teach girls and women and so even in the church, women teach fellow women. There were two problems related to literacy. The limitation on theological training were inevitable firstly, because their husbands were uneducated, they were ineligible for theological training abroad. Secondly, even though such husbands went for Bible School in Lilongwe, they were not allowed to bring their wives along with them. Paradoxically so, there was no such provision during this period, even though upon graduation, their wives were expected to be good pastors' wives in their churches.[86] This had a negative consequence on the position of women in the local churches. Because of their lack of understanding of their Baptist heritage, which was liberating, in addition to inadequate educational background, culture was another challenge to the engagement of women in the church.[87] Cultural limitations and lack of theological training made it impossible for pastors' wives in the South East region to be effective. The first victim of such circumstances was Mrs Kachasu Gama of Ndalama Baptist Church. Others include Mrs Chimenya of Chayima Baptist Church and Mrs Majomboshe, who both later became pastors' wives in Mulanje. Even though the Bible School in Lilongwe had excluded women in training, it is surprising enough that in the later years those who went for

---

[86] Int. Mrs Mary Galatiya and Rev Stephen Galatiya, Chipiliro Baptist Church, Likudzi Estate, Balaka, 15.5.2000.
[87] Int. Mrs Mary Galatiya and Rev Stephen Galatiya, Chipiliro Baptist Church, Likudzi Estate, Balaka, 15.5.2000.

training abroad took their wives with them.[88] Beginning with Stephen Galatiya, the first qualified candidate from Malawi to go to a seminary abroad in 1963, every pastor was sent with his wife. Surely it was a more expensive venture as compared to sending Mrs Kachasu Gama and others to Lilongwe. This sheds light on the perception of Southern Baptist missionaries in Malawi concerning what was more important to the local ministers' wives, that they should foremost be good wives to their husbands. They were to be supporters of their husband's ministry but not in the context of church work, rather in submission to and agreement with their husbands.[89]

1.3 The importance of women in the South East

1.3.1 The role of pastors' wives

History shows that there has been little influence of these pastors' wives in the South East region. This is because lack of theological training meant that they did not have the basic ministry skills such as those their fellow pastors' wives acquired from theological colleges abroad. The only possible role for these women was that of being mlangizi.

1.3.1.1 Mlangizi (instructor)

Mrs Kachasu Gama, for example, apart from being a local *mlangizi* in her area, also served on women's committees as *mlangizi* for the whole South East region. The role of *mlangizi* was plausible because it is more a cultural than a theological one and is usually accorded to any woman who is considered to be culturally qualified to do the job.[90] Even in the church therefore, for any *mlangizi* to be effective, she needs to be accredited in her society as worthy of such a role.

---

[88] These colleges abroad are Gweru Baptist Seminary and Lusaka Baptist Seminary. They were both Southern Baptist seminaries. This signifies a change in the approach of the Southern Baptist missionaries as regards theological training.

[89] This would be in line with a conservative hermeneutics of Ephesians 5:22 "Wives, submit to your husbands as to the Lord" (NIV).

[90] For one to qualify as a *mlangizi* she must have gone through the initiation at which she is a *mlangizi*. For one to be chosen as *mlangizi* at this time, she must have gone through all the initiations. For more details, see chapter on initiation.

1.3.1.2 Custodians of culture and religion

In the history of the Baptist Church, one of the occurrences that is peculiar to this church and that is rare in most churches is the accordance of pastorship to chiefs.[91] This means chiefs' wives become pastors' wives. The pastors' wives in the South East who were also chiefs' wives became a bridge between church and society because they had a significant influence in both circles. Mrs Kachasu Gama senior is an example of a pastor's wife who was also a chief's wife *(akazi a mfumu)*. The tradition of chiefs as pastors started with the congregations that originated from Chayima Baptist Church in 1962. Before then, no congregation was led by a chief. Some of the pastors' wives in this category are: Mrs Lichapa, of Makolije Baptist Church whose husband has had two marriages because he lost his first wife through labour complications,[92] Mrs Linly Chauluka of Chauluka Baptist Church, Mrs Malikebu of Thundu Baptist Church and Mrs Mahambuwa of Emau Baptist Church.[93] Through the church's accommodation of according pastoral duties to chiefs' wives, the church becomes liberating to the women in this church. It affirms that traditional leadership is not pagan, and can be maintained even when women in this leadership occupy a church role. However the chiefly roles of such women sometimes negatively affected their pastoral roles. As pastors' wives they were shepherds of the flock but because of the demanding responsibilities of being chief's wives, their influence in the church was being limited. Usually they recognized themselves first of all as custodians of their culture in their villages, than shepherds of the flock. However even though such ineffectiveness was seen, the church found it difficult to replace such leadership, because to do so would imply that you are against the chief's wife and the chief. It is apparent that the Southern Baptist missionaries did not have any theological problems regarding chiefs being leaders of the church. The other hindrance of having chief's wives as leaders of women's work in a congregation was witchcraft accusations, which were one of the problems to their spiritual

---

[91] These are local traditional chiefs and not Traditional Authorities (TA's). There are still pastors' wives in the South of such backgrounds.

[92] Her husband has recently left the chieftaincy to his nephew to have more time for his church.

[93] See Rendell Day, Emau Baptist Church, MA module, Department of TRS, University of Malawi, 1995.

ministry.[94] For example, there were witchcraft accusations regarding three pastors and pastors' wives in this category. In two cases the pastor's wife is accused of bewitching the first wife of her husband in order to marry him. In a second case, there was a witch hunting exercise in the village and the pastor's wife with her husband were found with a concoction of traditional medicine for bewitching others. Such accusations can be made against any person but they are more detrimental to the life of the church if they are related to a church leader, in this case, a pastor's wife. It is also always a challenge to hold both roles at the same time because, as custodians of tradition, there are times when, in the name of tradition, one may forgo her basic Christian beliefs. The challenge to the Baptist Church is how such women leaders at congregational level can be maintained without tarnishing the gospel.[95]

1.3.1.3 Master piece of Baptist faith to women

Pastors' wives during this period were not always active in their local congregations. One of the reasons was that it was their husbands that were called to ministry and not them. Though not all were in prominent positions in church and society, nevertheless just being consistent members of the church was an encouragement to women members. But this was not without disadvantages. The husbands of these pastors' wives preached the Baptist beliefs every Sunday, and male members of the congregation could easily identify with the sermons but women members also needed a fellow woman to speak to them about this faith, and this was not provided through these pastors' wives. These pastors' wives only relied on theology acted by missionary women as they faithfully attended the services, and certainly this was not enough. Jesus would have been the best example to teach through theology acted because he was perfect but he also preached. It is therefore important that, as Jesus did, theology should be both acted and said if it is to benefit the believing community. This is not to claim that theology acted alone is useless. Mrs Kachasu Gama for example, is only remembered as a faithful attendant

---

[94] All the pioneering pastors with their wives have stories of witchcraft accusations surrounding them. However this does not mean that they were indeed involved in witchcraft. Traditionally chiefs are associated with witchcraft. Again traditionally, even though the wife may not be involved in witchcraft, she is always perceived to be collaborator with her husband.
[95] See chapter 2 on *Umodzi* concerning the role of a pastor's wife.

of her Baptist church and in this she encouraged other members.[96] But she is also remembered through her daughter in law, wife to her son (widely known as Kachasu Gama junior), who started Zomba Baptist Church in town. Her daughter in law became the first woman to receive theological training under very lucky circumstances. Her husband Kachasu Junior was employed as a cook by the Westers. As he worked there, he learnt how to read and write English and even started a Baptist Church there. When the Westers went on furlough, he started Bible studies with other domestic workers around Old Naisi where the Westers lived. His wife was also with him. He held these Bible studies in the garage. When the Westers came back, they found this group meeting in the garage every Sunday for church services. The Westers were very comfortable with the arrangement until one day Rev Gama decided to treat his congregation to a traditional drink (*thobwa*), prepared by his wife. The Westers were not happy with that and decided to rent a room at Zomba Community Centre for Sunday Services. This is what later on turned into Zomba Baptist Church.[97] However his literacy was not enough for him to be admitted into Theological Seminary but at that time there was no one literate enough in the whole South East region that would qualify for the training. For this reason Kachasu Gama Junior was later chosen by the missionaries to go for training, to fill that gap.[98] His wife also went for theological training and became the first trained pastor's wife in this region. However the area was too wide for her to be effective. Mrs Kachasu Gama's (junior) role was short lived due to the fact that Ndalama Baptist Church changed to another denomination. They left Zomba Baptist Church and changed to another denomination 1994. The church still remembers her for what she did up to 1994. The reason why she left BACOMA was that Kachasu Gama became one of the founders of Hope Church, after a leadership struggle in both the Convention and Zomba Baptist Church.

---

[96] Int. Mrs Malikebu, Zomba Baptist Church, 28.10.1999; Int. J.M. Ng'oma Soche Baptist Church, 25.5.1999 Int. Rosebay Botoman, Chisomo Baptist Church, Chilomoni, Blantyre, 28.3.2000.
[97] Int. Rev Chisi, Ufulu Baptist Church, 12.3.2001.
[98] Int. Rev Malikebu, Thundu Baptist Church, 19.5.2000. Also Int. Rev Chisi, Ufulu Baptist Church, Lilongwe, 12.3.2001.

1.3.1.4 The role of missionary women: Blanche Wester

Because of lack of trained pastors' wives in this region, Mrs Wester intensified her ministry activities in this area. Before Mrs Kachasu Gama, she was the only woman discipler during the early period covering many areas in the region.[99] To achieve this she had to visit congregations at that time.[100] Her husband used to show Jesus films and through this way many became Baptists. The film was normally shown every evening from Monday to Friday. As her husband taught men, Mrs Wester taught the women concerning Baptist beliefs. The difference in their subjects was that Mrs Wester did not teach women about leadership (udindo).[101] This was deliberate because women were not envisaged to become leaders in the church in accordance to the culture and zeitgeist of the day.[102] By this time, she was able to speak Chichewa with the local women. She was also culturally sensitive. For example, she used to put on chitenje (two meter piece of cloth women wrap around their waist), just for the sake of identification locals and in this she was well accepted by the local people. Mrs Wester used her domestic skills to empower women in other methods of cooking as well as sewing. These activities also drew women to the church. They offered opportunities for women to socialize with others and vent out their feelings and frustrations. This also gave them opportunity to break off from the monotony of their every day chores. Moreover they were able to learn skills that could even be used for generating income in their homes. No wonder these activities drew women to her Baptist church.[103] But even though her work was good, it was difficult to sustain what she was doing because she did not have able local leadership who would catch her vision. Nevertheless, Baptist women were offered opportunities that most women in other churches did not have. This contributed to their liberation in society and church, because such programme boosted their self worth and image.

---

[99] Int. focus group, Ntokota Baptist Church, 19.3.1999.
[100] Her children were at Sir Harry Johnson Private Primary School in Zomba town, Int. Mrs Marylyn Upton, Area 36 Baptist Church, 5.1.2001.
[101] Int. Rev Lichapa, Makolije Baptist Church, 19.3.1999.
[102] Int. Rev Chimkwita, Lilongwe Baptist Seminary, 12.3.2001.
[103] Int. Rosebay Botoman, Chisomo Baptist Church, Chilomoni, Blantyre, 28.3.2000.

1.3.1.5 The ministry of the church to women

Although Mrs Chimenya was a pastor's wife, the women in Jali area re-member her husband's activities among them more than hers.[104] Mrs Chimenya mainly remained in the background and rarely attended joint meetings. This was the same with other pastors' wives such as Mrs Gazamiyala of Ntokota Baptist.[105] However they are remembered for their dedication to hospitality and for encouraging other women. Rev Chimenya was renown for his ministry to the women. Others remember him as clever.[106] But for some, he is remembered in a much deeper way through his ministry among women. To these women, Chimenya became famous because he was revolutionary. He visited the women in *chikuta* (seclusion after giving birth to a child).[107] In this way he went against the cultural taboo that women are unclean when they have just given birth. The women felt respected and were affirmed of their dignity in this way. Chimenya also held these women's babies in *chikuta* and prayed for them.[108] In this way the women got encouraged with this act that showed that children were full human beings and loved by God even at a tender age, when culturally they were not considered to be full human beings. In this instance, Baptist polity became liberative by denying cultural over-tones that were oppressive to the women. This is an example where Baptist women choose the gospel in the event that culture is against it.

The women also received medical attention from pastor Chimenya. When Mrs Mahere got a deep cut on her leg, she was overwhelmed by her pastor's care.[109] This is a testimony that women were cared for in this church, proving that they were taken seriously as important members of the church. Such church attitude is liberating because it affirms that women are created in the image of God just as men are.

---

[104] Ibid.

[105] Int. focus group, Ntokota Baptist Church, 19.3.1999.

[106] Int. Rev Maida, Mrs Maida, Chayima Baptist Church, 20.3.2000.

[107] *Chikuta* is a place of seclusion where women stay soon after delivery. According to Chewa culture, there is to be no contact to men.

[108] Int. Rosebay Botoman, Chisomo Baptist Church, 28.3.2000; Anganeje, Chayima Baptist Church, Zomba, 20.3.2000. Even though the church started in Majomboshe's home and the building is also on late Majomboshe's land, it is pastor Chimenya's name that is famous at Chayima Church.

[109] Pastor Chimenya used to come every morning to wash her wound and put on traditional medicine.

1.4 Local identity and women's status 1966-1970

1.4.1 Blantyre: 1966-1970

That the Chichewa congregation moved out of Cliccord Building in 1966, meant that the local church was independent of missionary influence.[110] This was possible because of the autonomy of the church as understood by Baptists. Since the two congregations were independent, each congregation was free to do things as determined by themselves. This gave the women a chance to attain their own local identity and much liberation from the missionaries' interpretations. The activities that local women did at Newlands in Rev and Mrs Mary Galatiya's home depict just that. There was now a paradigm shift from support roles to leadership roles and towards equal opportunities for male and female members of the congregation. Local women were more liberated in sharing their Baptist faith with others. This shows that it was not the local culture that inhibited women's leadership roles in church and society, but rather local missionary Christianity.[111] This in the missionary church, women continued to stick to support roles, as affirmed by missionary women. The theological orientation of the Galatiyas contributed to women's liberation in the local congregation. Mary Galatiya and Rev Galatiya had just come back from seminary training in Zimbabwe. While in Zimbabwe Dr Lockert, one of the Southern Baptist missionaries who lectured there, influenced Rev Galatiya to involve women in leadership just as men. Dr Lockert had taught in Nigeria for a long time and the Nigerian church was already progressive in women's issues at that time. Rev Galatiya brought this influence to his New Jerusalem Church in Newlands.[112] This is a clear testimony of the different evangelical leanings among Baptists ranging from more conservative to more progressive. Women in the local congregation did benefit from the progressive evangelicalism brought by the Galatiyas.

---

[110] This was the case with Mrs Linly Mauluka at Mauluka Baptist Church, Mrs Malikebu at Thundu Baptist Church, Mrs Gazamiyala at Ntokota Baptist.
[111] Anthropological studies have shown that women have traditionally been accepted as leaders in matrilineal societies.
[112] Int. Rev Galatiya, Likudzi Estate, Chipiliro Baptist Church, 15.5.2000. Rev Galatiya and Rev Davidson did not meet for a whole year from 1966 to 1967 although they were in the same city of Blantyre. Even after they met, the Chichewa congregation operated independently of the English speaking church.

1.4.1.1 Door to door preaching

Rev Galatiya taught women in his congregation how to do "door to door evangelism." Women, together with men, would go out to their neighbourhood to preach the gospel using the strategy of an evangelistic dialogue with people. Rev Galatiya taught them key questions, which would encourage the dialogue, such as: Which church do you go to? Are you a Christian? How do you know that you are a Christian? From people's responses to the last questions the women would find a niche where to begin to share the gospel.[113] This strategy reinforced equality between men and women members of the congregation as they saw themselves playing the same roles. This was different from the order of things at Cliccord House and showed a move towards liberation.

1.4.1.2 Preaching

Rev Galatiya also encouraged women to preach on a normal Sunday.[114] This was impossible not only in the missionary Baptist church but also in other churches in those days. During the first weeks at Newlands, Mrs Ng'oma would sing choruses together with her pastor in the evenings, attracting people to the house. Many in the neighbourhood came to listen to the singing. Someone would then preach. Mrs Ng'oma and Mary Galatiya sometimes preached at such gatherings,[115] a proof that when the church is enlightened about women's position, it provides an avenue for women's liberation. The church members begin to critically look at the zeitgeist and the cultural teaching of church and society and are able to do what they believe is the truth.

Women preaching was, at that time, only permitted in this Chichewa congregation. This was never done in Cliccord House even after the Galatiyas came back from Seminary. Although Rev Galatiya was enlightened about women's position in the church, he was under Kingsley and Davidson, whom he had to obey.[116] This is however not in line with Bap-

---

[113] Int. Rev Galatiya, Likudzi Estate, Chipiliro Baptist Church, 15.5.2000.

[114] Preaching on a normal Sunday refers to preaching on a Sunday other than that which is traditionally allocated to women in a church calendar.

[115] Int. Mrs J.M. Ng'oma, Soche Baptist Church, 25.5.2000.

[116] For example even though Rev Galatiya was a pastor and brought Mrs Ng'oma and her husband to the Baptist faith, he could not baptize them. Up to 1995, only missionaries conducted baptism. Int. Rev Galatiya and Mrs Galatiya, Likudzi Estate, Chipiliro Baptist, 15.5.2000.

tist doctrine and polity that encourages democracy. The Galatiyas were free to discuss this issue with the missionaries. The Galatiyas reluctance to reinforce women's liberation in this church could have been because he did not want to cut the hand that fed him. But when he broke off, he knew he had nothing to loose, and hence promoted the liberation of women in this church. The missionary women in Cliccord building never preached. If ever they did something at all during a normal Sunday service, it was to sing a song, do a drama or pray and give a testimony. The missionary women were also involved in children's Sunday school. As good mothers, they were the right people to teach children good Christian behaviour. This was not wrong, but if women who were gifted to do more than this and were barred to do that, such women were oppressed.

1.4.1.3 Support roles

Apart from leadership roles Convention women engaged in support roles. They did that out of their own choice, not because they were restricted from leadership roles as was the case in Cliccord House and in other church cultures. And this should be permitted. Women's liberation should neither aim at forcing women who don't feel called to be in leadership a position to be leaders, nor should women's liberation be limited to the occupation of leadership roles. It is about women attaining their full potential as God has equipped them.

Some of the support roles included singing, praying and giving. Singing was not only restricted to the Sunday service. Many people came to a Baptist church because of attending a funeral where they heard this Christian singing and the preaching of Rev Galatiya. The Baptist women did not only sing at the funeral of their own church member, but even at that of a non-churchgoer.[117] This attracted those who were rejected by their own church. They felt the compassion of Jesus through these Baptist women. Rev Galatiya also encouraged women to pray for him as he preached at the funerals. Prayer was one of the support roles of these women in their congregation. Mrs Malabwanya was instrumental in giv-

---

[117] This would not be done in other churches. I have witnessed three times, at a funeral of a Seventh-day Adventist, a CCAP Blantyre Synod member, and a Roman Catholic where the deceased who were supposed to have been members of their churches were refused a church funeral, because the deceased did not satisfy some conditions of membership like consistent church attendance in one, lack of disjunction certificate in the other and not paying church dues in the third.

ing financial support to the Galatiyas. Such support roles were liberating to women, because they did them not out of being oppressed but out of choice.

1.4.2 Expansion from New Jerusalem

The church in the house of the Galatiyas grew to such an extent that the house became too small to accommodate the members. Therefore Rev Galatiya pulled down his house and converted it into a church hall. This hall was named New Jerusalem Baptist Church. They chose this name from Acts 1:8,[118] and to them, Newlands was their starting point (Jerusalem).[119]

In 1967, after New Jerusalem was started, Soche Baptist was started under the same leadership of Rev Galatiya. The church was in Naperi where the present Living Stones Baptist Church was started.[120] In 1968 another offshoot from New Jerusalem, Bangwe Baptist Church, grew. It was started in Chief Mwamadi's village, where Rev Maseko, who was a member of New Jerusalem, purchased a plot.[121]

Mary Galatiya, as pastor's wife, supervised women's work in all the three congregations. She was assisted by laywomen like Mrs Ng'oma, Mrs Klova and Mrs Elizabeth Njolomole.[122] They would visit women in the three churches alternatively and also organize joint meetings where women from all the three congregations would come and learn Baptist beliefs and fellowship with one another.[123] Mrs Galatiya continued to teach these women what she had learnt at the seminary. This development gives a background to the philosophy of organizing women's work into associations and regions as discussed later in this chapter. The main reason was to facilitate women's work.

While the local women in the congregations enjoyed much freedom in ministering in the church, women at Cliccord House in Limbe continued

---

[118] "But you will receive power when the Holy Spirit comes on you and you will be my witnesses in Jerusalem, and in Judea and Samaria, and to the ends of the earth." NIV.

[119] Int. Rev Galatiya and Mrs Galatiya, Likudzi Estate, Chipiliro Baptist Church, Balaka, 15.5.2000.

[120] Int. Mr J.M. Ng'oma, Soche Baptist Church, 25.5.1999.

[121] Int. Fanny Kwelakwela, Bangwe Baptist Church, 30.4.2000.

[122] For more information on Elizabeth Njolomole, see chapter 1.

[123] Int. Mrs Galatiya, Likudzi Estate, Chipiliro Baptist Church, Balaka, 15.5.2000.

to serve in support roles only. However this trend drastically changed in later years, as shown in the participation of women in Chichiri Baptist Church.[124] Did the missionary women redefine their earlier definition of Baptist polity and doctrine that encouraged women's subordination? or what factors led to such a transition? The answer seems to rely on cooperate involvement between missionary women and locals as will be seen in the later discussion in the chapter.

1.4.3 Jali, Zomba 1966-1970: Mrs Andisambula begins a congregation

During this period women in this region began to enjoy other forms of leadership apart from being *alangizi* and pastors' wives. They learnt well that Baptists are called to the priesthood of all believers. Lay women just as pastors' wives and even men, had the same mandate by God to preach the gospel. An example of such lay leadership was Mrs Andisambula who started a church in 1966, and thus became the first woman in Malawi to start a Baptist congregation.[125] Mrs Andisambula attended Chimbalanga Baptist Church only briefly. Because of long distance, and having to cross Thondwe River on her way to the church, she decided to bring the Baptist church to her home area. She was a wise woman and studied the times. She was aware of the struggles the Church of Christ had in the area. She decided to talk to some members of the Church of Christ in her village to consider becoming Baptists. The people took her seriously and asked her if they could go with her to Chayima and study what the Baptist people did in worship. She took them to Chayima. The people were impressed and decided to become Baptists. Mrs Andisambula together with these new Baptist members came back to the village and convinced other Church of Christ members to become Baptists too. The result was that there was a mass exodus of members of Church of Christ in Mandawala village to the Baptist church, which was established under Mrs Andisambula's mango tree. Her husband was not a Baptist;

---

[124] Some hold the opinion that this church in Cliccord House never spread. It is the same church which in history has been referred to by different names, eg. Limbe Baptist Church, Chichiri Baptist Church. Int. J.M. Ng'oma, Soche Baptist Church, Blantyre 15.5.1999. I disagree with this view because membership has changed over the years, with new members coming into the congregation.
[125] Int. Rev Gowelo, Mandawala Baptist Church, 9.3.2000.

he continued to be in the Church of Christ.[126] The liberation that Mrs Andisambula shows in the area of leadership is against the flow in her area of influence - the South East region. However, what she did is not unique. Throughout history, we have seen courageous women going against the flow, whether their immediate contexts allowed it or not.

With the same activities as in the earlier period, Mrs Wester continued to help in the strengthening of women's work at Mandawala Baptist Church. At this church, Mrs Wester is fondly remembered by the earliest members of the church. When Mrs Wester heard of this mass exodus of Church of Christ women in Mandawala village to join the Baptist Church, she visited the place to teach the women about the Baptist faith. She did this several times under that mango tree. The local women were encouraged by her humility to mix with them and eat with them. She also slept in the village at times and showed women how to cook and sew. She also provided medication to women that were sick.[127] These activities made her to be well in touch with women's needs. At this time, Andisambula was elected leader of the women. She deserved to be pastor of the Church but since the teaching of the day was that women were to be silent in church, the church could not be left in her hands.[128] Rev Wester appointed a male deacon to be leader of the church instead. According to Southern Baptist missionary Christianity, a woman could not be leader of a church.[129] They believed in the priesthood of all believers but not in a woman being head over a man, and being pastor of a church is to ascend to the highest rank in a local church. The circumstances that led to the rise and fall in leadership in Mrs Andisambula's life have something to say about women's liberation. It depends on who is in the final authority and how available grassroots support is. In her case Rev Wester had final authority, and in his theology a woman was not to be pastor of a church. She also did not have enough support whether from fellow women or men to vote for her against the missionary's decision. In Bap-

---

[126] Ibid. There was a leadership struggle between the leader of Church of Christ and the founder of the church - Mr Severe. Int. Anganeje, Chayima Baptist Church, 20.3.2000.

[127] Int. Rev Gowelo, Mandawala Baptist, 9.3.2000.

[128] Ibid. Int. Rosebay Botoman, Chisomo Baptist Church, 28.3.2000. Rosebay was about 70 years at the time of the interviews and still pastor's wife at Chisomo Baptist Church.

[129] Ibid, and also Rosebay Botoman, Chisomo Baptist Church, 28.3.2000.

tist polity, power rests in the hands of the grassroots and voting is permitted.

1.4.4 Women deacons and treasurers in the South East region: 1966 to 1970

The other key area where laywomen found room to minister was as deacons. This was the case in all Baptist congregations in the South East region at that time. At Ntokota Baptist, for example, Esmy Mayinuka (Mrs George) and Bessy Jameson (Mrs Kankhani) were deacons.[130] However in the South South region in Blantyre, the first woman deacon only appeared in 1970, Mrs Giver.[131] To be a deacon as a woman was not a small achievement. In other churches at this time no woman was a deacon. Even among Southern Baptist missionaries, no woman was a deacon. It is not true that being a deacon is another kind of support role, it is a leadership position. In the Baptist Church deacons are part of the church council, which is the leading body of the local church.[132] The office of a deacon is not restricted to hospitality work and visitation as it may be implied in other church traditions..[133]

Women were also involved in other power positions in the local churches. One of such roles was the role of treasurer. Mrs Kankhani was treasurer in 1967 at Ntokota Baptist Church, apart from being deacon of the church.[134] It is not true to suggest that a woman was chosen to be the treasurer because it is a woman's job as men easily misuse money. Women just as men do misuse money and if a woman is chosen to be treasurer, it is just because she is qualified to do the job.

---

[130] See Journal by D.J. Gazamiyala, 21.8.66.
[131] Int. Rev Chisi, Ufulu Baptist Church, Lilongwe 23.6.2001.
[132] It is the same as the "session" in CCAP.
[133] In many Baptist churches, there are no elders as leaders, only the pastor (elders) and the deacons. This is the pattern in BACOMA as much as in the Southern Baptist tradition.
[134] See Journal by D.J. Gazamiyala, 21.8.66.

1.5   The growth of women's work and the position of Convention women during the period of revival: 1970 to 1985

1.5.1 Introduction

Even though the ground for women's work was laid in the earlier period, much growth in the work and its organization took place during this second period. Much of the growth was due to a revival that started in the late 1960s and lasted into the mid 1980s. Looking at the developments within the Baptist church, this revival was sparked by factors both within and outside it.[135] The fruit of this revival was a cooperative spirit among Baptist women from different regions, congregations and ethnic groups. Women from such diverse backgrounds would come together to disseminate their Baptist beliefs, sometimes even in cooperation with interdenominational organizations such as New Life for All,[136] within Malawi or other mission groups from outside Malawi. The latter was more prominent during the *Chitsitsimutso cha 1970* (Revival of the 1970s) which had the slogan *"Chidzachitika ndi Chiyani 1970?"* (What will happen in 1970?).[137] This revival crusade was led by a Harvey from America, starting from Blantyre and from there it spread to other districts within Malawi.[138] This period shows that women were more liberated as local women became more involved, even those with low literacy levels in the South East region. The methods of propagating their Baptist beliefs also diversified as they got exposed to methods of evangelism during the revival meetings. The organization of this women's work however was laid down by women who went abroad for theological training and missionary women. There was much cooperation between missionaries and nation-

---

[135] This revival spread all over Malawi. See: Klaus Fiedler, "Even in Church the Exercise of Power is Accountable to God", in: Kenneth R. Ross (ed), *God, People and Power in Malawi*, CLAIM-Kachere: Blantyre, 1996, pp. 187-224.

[136] For one of the main participants see: Jack Selfridge, *Jack of All Trades Mastered by One*, Fearn: Christian Focus, 1989.

[137] Int. Rev Malikebu, Thundu Baptist Church, 19.5.2000. See also Hany Longwe, Identity by Dissociation; Int. Rev Chisi, Ufulu Baptist Church, 23.6.2001. Different people were organized in a committee comprising of locals and those from abroad. Harvey was one of the white men and a prominent leader, these crusades in the south in the 1970s were referred to by his name as Harvey Crusades.

[138] Int. Rev Malikebu, Thundu Baptist Church, 19.5.2000.

als in this endeavour, and seems to have contributed positively to women liberation.

The aim of this section is to show growth and organization of women's work that took place in different areas because of the revival in terms of the position of women during this period. The argument is that women's work grew out of Jali and Blantyre to other places within the districts and outside them, as far as Lower Shire, Thyolo, Balaka, Mulanje and Mozambique border. This revival did not affect areas evenly, however it had an impact on the position of women in church and society providing much liberation to women, albeit in some places women were still restricted.[139]

1.5.2 Women at Limbe Baptist Church (opposite Chichiri Stadium)

The Christians at Limbe Baptist Church moved from Cliccord House to opposite Chichiri Stadium where the BACOMA offices are now. Women had by then increased in number, and a second service in Chichewa had been reintroduced. At the beginning of 1970, Rev Galatiya and Rev Roy Davidson were reconciled, but they still maintained separate congregations, a very necessary step during the time of revival. This meant that the women in the Chichewa congregation and those in the English speaking Limbe congregation could cooperate in disseminating their Baptist beliefs to others.[140] But how did this cooperation affect women's liberation in their church? It is evident that there was much adjusting in terms of roles women played from both sides. Missionaries in the South such as the Westers, the Davidsons, Rebecca and Dudley Phiffer and Glandor and Charles Middleton[141] who were missionaries in the Lower Shire continued to worship and be involved in support roles at this church.[142] The Middletons and the Phiffers chose to live in Blantyre in-

---

[139] Klaus Fiedler argues that revival blurs distinctions between men and women and therefore increases the power of women in the church (Klaus Fiedler, *Story of the Faith Missions*, pp. 112-124; 292-318).
[140] Int. Rev Galatiya, Chipiliro Baptist Church, 15.5.2000.
[141] Because Dudley Phiffer died and his wife Rebecca married Charles Middleton when Glandor died in a car crush in Lesotho, it should be noted that this Mrs Middleton is different from the current one who is Rebecca.
[142] Int. Mrs Marylyn Upton, Area 36 Baptist Church, 5.1.2001.

stead of Chikwawa, their mission field because of the many mosquitoes in the Lower Shire.

Women's meeting in 1973 led by Mrs Phiri

They were afraid of getting frequent malaria attacks if they stayed in the area.[143] Rev Dudley Phiffer could not even come back to Malawi for his next assignment because he was diagnosed with leukemia and was at a high risk if attacked by malaria.[144] In the case of the Middletons, it was Glandor who was in ill health and as such they could not stay in Lower Shire and in fact they also could not come back to Malawi for their next missionary assignment. Both the Middletons and Phiffers were reallocated to Transkei where there was no malaria.

---

[143] Int. Rev Wilfred Kalenga, Nsomo Baptist Church, 28.9.2000.

[144] Int. Rev Malikebu, Thundu Baptist Church, 19.5.2000, Int. Mrs Marylyn Upton, Area 36 Baptist Church, 5.1.2001. Dudley died with leukemia in America in 1981. He went to Transkai in 1981 but after only 11 months there he got sick from leukemia. When he was advised by the doctors that he had only a few days to live, he made only one request, that his elderly parents at home should see him alive. He was told that he would not be able to survive the plane but he insisted to be flown to America so that his parents should see him. He survived the flight and died 7 days after his arrival in a hospital in America.

Although missionary women continued to be involved in support roles in their local church, this was not without exception. Glandor is remembered in the South among Baptists as an able public speaker, not only in Baptist circles but also at the interdenominational level. With her talent she was even invited as a speaker at a Keswick Convention in Blantyre. Although she spoke at women's meetings she was part of the leadership team at this convention. Her public speaking role was also complimented by active women's work in the rural areas among Baptists of Lower Shire and Chiradzulu District.[145]

Limbe Baptist Church became known as Chichiri Baptist Church. It still remained ideal for the missionary families in the South, because their children needed an English Sunday School. There were congregations established in their areas but the services were run in Chichewa. Because of the missionary influence, the white community working in the diplomatic missions and other jobs were attracted to this congregation. The English services and the higher social level were an attraction to the members. Even the few black women members of the congregation in the 1970s were upper class Malawians who could easily identify with the white community.[146] The only black women in the 1970s were Mrs Douglas Banda, Mrs Chipembere, Mrs Banda, Mrs Lillian Jonga and Mrs Margaret Nyika.[147] The spirit of revival was really with this congregation in that new members joined the congregation without being explicitly evangelized. Mrs Margaret Nyika, for example, became part of the church when she saw the church as she was going to her former church, CCAP. At that time she was on discipline because she did not bring her disjunction certificate from Austria, where she had gone for studies.[148] When she visited the Baptist congregation, which by then had moved from Cliccord House to opposite Chichiri Stadium, she liked it. She also thought that it was unnecessary for her to go through the discipline while there was that Baptist church which was very welcoming to her.[149] The

---

[145] Mrs Fanny Kwelakwela, Bangwe Baptist Church, Blantyre, 30.4.2000; also Mrs Marylyn Upton, Area 36 Baptist Church, 5.6.2001.
[146] Int. Rev Galatiya, Chipiliro Baptist Church, 15.5.2000.
[147] Mrs Margaret Nyika, Blantyre Baptist Church, 26.5.1999: Int. Mrs Fanny Kwelakwela (nee Malabwanya), Bangwe Baptist Church, 30.4.2000.
[148] Ibid.
[149] Ibid. See also Klaus Fiedler, "Even in the Church the Exercise of Power is Accountable to God", in Kenneth Ross (ed), *God, People and Power in Malawi*, p. 208.

Baptist church tradition was more liberating to women in such circumstances and was able to accommodate them.

Mrs Lillian Jonga also became part of the congregation on her own because of her children. Since her children spoke English only, it was difficult for her to take them to the Chichewa service. She also liked the Sunday school classes in the English service.[150] Unlike in the earlier arrangement where all in the English service were white, during this time of revival, this service was attended by blacks as well and some of the missionaries were even part of the Chichewa service. Even though Lillian Jonga became a Baptist through the witness of the Westers, she chose to attend the English service even though the Westers were members of the Chichewa service.[151] The first wife of Aleke Banda, a renowned politician in both the one party and the multiparty dispensations in Malawi, was a member and got wedded in this church.[152] She was married in church by Rev Kingsley.[153] At her wedding, a government official from outside Malawi and his wife were in attendance,[154] at this time, her husband was already in politics. She and other local women in this congregation were not involved in leadership roles. A few women did sometimes visit and teach women in rural congregations in the South South. Mrs Lillian Jonga was one of them. She helped Mrs Davidson with translation as she visited local women,[155] in the Lower Shire. Even after she left the Baptist Convention in the later years, she continued to work among PIM women in Chiradzulu, where she was well received. This was at the time she was the president for the Baptist Women Union of Africa (BWUA).[156] Under this organisation, PIM women were members, apart from Seventh-day Baptist women, Baptist Convention women and Evangelical Baptist Church women.[157] Naturally she felt welcome among fellow Baptists.[158]

---

[150] Int. Mrs Margaret Nyika, Blantyre Baptist Church, 26.5.1999.
[151] Int. Mr William Jonga, South Lunzu Baptist Church 12.11.1999.
[152] Int. Mrs Margaret Nyika, Blantyre Baptist Church, 11.11.1999.
[153] Int. Rev Chisi, Ufulu Baptist Church, 23.6.2000.
[154] Ibid.
[155] Int. William Jonga, South Lunzu Baptist Church, 12.11.1999.
[156] BWUA is a branch of BWA (Baptist World Alliance) which has three branches: the Youth, Women and the general section.
[157] Representatives from these churches meet under this umbrella every five years in different countries.
[158] Ibid.

1.5.2.1 Cooperation between Limbe Baptist Church and Chichewa congregations in Blantyre

Because of the reconciliation between the Davidsons and the Galatiyas, the distinctions between the Chichewa congregations that were started by Rev Galatiya and Limbe Baptist Church were blurred. This was seen in the fact that local Malawian women were free to join Limbe Baptist Church, which was mainly an option for the white community after the split. Mrs Ng'oma who was an influential member of New Jerusalem was even willing to work with Mrs Davidson as a housemaid. Her association with Mrs Davidson also helped in the support of Rev Galatiya. When the Galatiyas struggled materially, she would tell Mrs Davidson who usually sent the Galatiyas some material help.[159] The other way how this cooperative spirit was shown was in the way local women teamed up with missionary women in preaching the gospel during the revival crusades. This cooperation was not restricted to fellow women because the evangelistic teams during the revival were composed of both women and men.[160]

The revival crusades started in Limbe market and other markets. They would usually erect banners at such places that read "Chidzachitika ndi chiyani 1970". Then Harvey, a visiting missionary, would preach and someone would interpret. This is where women also took an active role. Mrs Ng'oma helped to translate in the South East region.[161] Such crusades usually lasted for three days. Many people came to such crusades and got converted. However, not all became Baptists. It is this time when Limbe Church, now at Chichiri again introduced a Chichewa Service as well. Liberation is seen in that women were taken seriously as partners in the propagation of the gospel.

Apart from the revival crusades of the early 1970s, there was another one in the 1980s. This crusade was aimed at evangelizing different districts in the country, not so much different from the Harvey Crusade.[162] The main preacher was Rev Maxiditon, but women still were involved in interpretation and teaching fellow women.[163] However, women did not

---

[159] Int. Rev Steven Galatiya and Mrs Mary Galatiya, Chipiliro Baptist Church, 15.5.2000.
[160] Rev Malikebu, Thundu Baptist Church, Zomba, 28.11.1999.
[161] Ibid.
[162] Ibid.
[163] Ibid.

preach in these new congregations, in this missionary Christianity seemed to overtake local identity which had allowed women to preach. The teams of these revival crusades were mixed in that they were not dependent on where one came from. As such, women from different regions would come together to preach the gospel in one region. This is how Mrs Galatiya and Mrs Ng'oma of Blantyre, Mrs Elizabeth Njolomole of Mzuzu and Mrs Hilda Mallungo of Lilongwe went to Lower Shire to preach the gospel. One of the notable woman converts from the second revival is Molly Longwe. She is married to Hany Longwe. She was converted to the Baptist faith in 1980. She was formerly in Blantyre Synod together with her husband and children. However even though she was a committed member of her church she did not invite Jesus into her life. Her life was spiritually dry. Her journey to the Baptist faith started with joining a women's prayer group in Blantyre and attending church services at Chichiri Baptist Church. One time the women's prayer group was held in her home and her husband even joined them, although he was not a Baptist at that time. When Chichiri Baptist Church, held a revival service in the church in 1981, Molly and her husband invited Jesus into their lives.[164] She was baptised together with her husband, and her husband attributes his conversion to the faithful prayers of his wife Molly.[165] The banners raised at this revival of the 1980s had captions that read "*Muli Moyo mwa Yesu?*"[166]

Even though revival crusades were in process, and many activities were happening outside congregations, work at congregational level continued. The position of women in the area of preaching during this period seemed to decrease. Mrs Ellen Ng'oma and Mrs Mary Galatiya who had been very active in preaching in the earlier Chichewa congregations, declined in this role in the late 1970s.[167] One possible explanation would be that Galatiya's influence declined and with the restored cooperation with missionaries, there was more influence from the missionary side, which did not encourage women preaching. But another observation is that as

---

[164] Int. Rev Hany Longwe, Lilongwe Baptist Theological Seminary, Lilongwe, 6.1.2001.
[165] Ibid.
[166] Ibid.
[167] Int. Mrs Agnes Maya, Zomba Baptist Church 28.10.2000. By the time Mrs Agnes Maya and her husband came to Blantyre in 1979, Mrs Ng'oma and Mrs Galatiya were not preaching on a regular Sunday.

churches get more established the leadership roles of women begin to diminish. This is also seen in the case of rural women pastors in the South East region. After some time, Mrs Nasimango and Mrs Makina as pastors were replaced by men.[168]

Women were however still involved in other leadership roles. Mrs Molly Longwe was teaching a Sunday school class of the little boys and girls. At this time she had no theological training and little ministry experience. Her teaching skill was by the Spirit and her experience in her teaching role at Mpemba Management Training College.[169]

More churches were started, within Blantyre, and this time not only through Rev Galatiya but other locals. The revival programmes continued as well. Chisomo Baptist Church was one of the churches started independently of Galatiya. The church was started in Michiru hills of Chilomoni suburb[170] by V.W. Chitsukwa and his wife. The Chitsukwas were originally members of old Soche Baptist Church, but they had found a plot in Chilomoni suburb, as such it was far to walk to Soche for church services. They therefore decided to start a Baptist church in their new suburb. With the revival spirit of the day, it was not difficult to open a new church there. All they did was to sing in their house Christian choruses and the neighbours would come to listen to their singing and then Mr Chitsukwa or some man would preach. In this way some would join the church. Mrs Chitsukwa's role was to welcome people in her home. At times she offered food to the members of the congregation after the services. Her husband became the pastor of the church even without theological training, and Mrs Chitsukwa became the pastor's wife.[171] This is typical in Baptist churches where the leader of a church is labelled as such regardless of theological training. A pastor is just a leader of the church not necessary one who has gone for theological seminary training, as it is the case with other churches.[172] Wives of such leaders are also called pastors' wives.

Later, the congregation felt that they needed a trained pastor. This is how Mrs Maya became a pastors' wife at Chisomo Baptist. Mrs Maya

[168] For more details on women pastors, see chapter 4.
[169] Her husband Hany Longwe also taught a youth Sunday School class in the same church. Int. Hany Longwe. Lilongwe Theological Seminary, Baptist, 6.1.2001.
[170] Int. Mrs Fanny Kwelakwela, Mrs Gawaza, Bangwe Baptist Church, 30.4.2000.
[171] Int. Rosebay Botoman, Chisomo Baptist Church, 28.3.2000.
[172] Int. Rev Chimkwita, 12.3.2001.

was already a Baptist when she came to Malawi. She was already a trained pastor's wife by 1963. She and her husband got trained at the Baptist Seminary in Lusaka, and had already served in a Baptist congregation in Zambia.[173] However, she and her husband found it difficult to work in Chisomo Baptist Church because the Chitsukwas did not feel comfortable with them. It is them that struggled to start the church, and why would someone replace them? The Mayas therefore left the congregation and started new work in Che Musa village in Blantyre rural.[174]

1.5.3 Women in Baptist churches in Thyolo

The first Baptist church in Thyolo was started during the time of the revival crusades. Baptist work could no longer remain in Blantyre. The revival crusades had been targeted at every district and brought conversions in many districts including Thyolo.[175] Mpando Baptist church was the first congregation to be established in this area in 1975.[176] The first women in this church, including the chief's wife, Mrs Estere (Esther) Mpando with her daughters, came from a mass conversion of a Lutheran Church in that area.[177] In the year it started, there was a leadership struggle in the Lutheran Church and this created a fertile ground for conversion to the Baptist message. When Kantunda and other church members, who were all men,[178] went to Blantyre, they believed the Baptist

---

[173] Int. Mrs Agnes Maya, Zomba Baptist Church, 28.10.2000; also Int. Fanny Kwelakwela and Mrs Gawaza, Bangwe Baptist Church, 30.4.2000. For more details on Mrs Maya, see chapter 3.

[174] Ibid. Also int. Mrs Agnes Maya, Zomba Baptist Church, 28.10.2000.

[175] Thyolo is dominated by the Sena and Mang'anja as well as other tribes who come to work in the tea estates. Int. Mrs Martha Kholomana, Mpando Baptist Church, 26.7.2000.

[176] Rev Green J. K. Kantunda started this church with the help of Rev Sibley who was based in Blantyre and doing missionary work in this district. Int. focus group, Mpando Baptist Church, 26.7.2000; Int. Rev A.G. Kantunda, Mpando Baptist Church, 7.8.2000.

[177] Int. Mrs Martha Kholomana, Mpando Baptist Church, 26.7.2000. Rev Kantunda was a pastor of a Lutheran church in Mpando village in Thyolo at that time.

[178] These were such as Mr Mandawala, Mr Mcloundi, Mr Muhuta and Mr Khaula. They heard about the activities of Baptist Church in Blantyre, and decided to go to Blantyre where they attended some of the leadership classes that were taking place at the old Soche Baptist Church, which was at Kamba in Blantyre, where Rev Nkhata was doing pastoral work. After a three days training these delegate, became Baptists. They met Rev Sibley and inquired about how he could start a Baptist church in

message and became Baptists. Although their wives did not go with them to Blantyre, they had their support and in turn they also joined the church encouraging other women to join. The church later attracted more members, mostly smallholder farmers. Most of the women members of this church were wives of smallholder farmers,[179] and multi cultural, as these came from different parts of Malawi.[180]

The engagement of women at the start of the congregation was mainly in support roles. Preaching was restricted to the pastor of the church. Mrs Macloundi became a key leader to the women. She was helpful in teaching women about the Bible. At this time women did not preach on a regular Sunday. Mrs Mary Kantunda was the first to preach on a regular Sunday in 1977 when her husband was too sick to preach.[181] Since then no woman preached in this period.[182] Otherwise able women such as Mrs Chitseko only preached to fellow women. She is currently living in Blantyre and worships at Blantyre Baptist church with her husband who is an accountant.[183] The majority of women were restricted to singing in the choir and a few gave *ulangizi* (instruction) to young girls.[184] Mrs Estere Mpando has been *mlangizi* at this church since her conversion.[185] As a chief's wife, just as was the case with chief's wives in the South East, she was well suited to this role that demands thorough mastery of the culture to which the initiates belong. Even though the role of a deacon was common in the rural, South East, there was no woman deacon in this rural church, during this period.[186] It is unlikely that this situation was a result of missionary influence because even in the South East, there were also Southern Baptist missionaries.

---

his area. They went back to their old church and preached to their congregation about their new faith. Many decided to leave the Lutheran church for a Baptist church.

[179] Int. Mrs Kholomana, Mpando Baptist Church, Thyolo, 26.7.2000.

[180] Ibid.

[181] Int. Mrs Kantunda, Mpando Baptist Church, Thyolo, 26.7.2000.

[182] The second woman to preach was Mrs Chrissy Chikwakwa, a member of the church in 1994.

[183] She was in Thyolo because her husband was working as an accountant in the Tea Small Holder Company. Int. Mrs Martha Kholomana, Mpando Baptist Church, 26.7.2000.

[184] Int. Martha Kholomana, Mpando Baptist Church, 26.7.2000; Int. Rev K.A.G.J Kantunda, Mpando Baptist Church; Thyolo, 7.8.2000.

[185] Ibid.

[186] Ibid.

Neither can it be because the church was just starting because in the South East region even in the early beginnings of Baptist work in the 1960s, women deacons already existed. It is more likely that patrilineal society more dominant in this church was a cause for the situation.

The other place where women's work started in this district was at Mambo Baptist Church in 1985.[187] The women in this church were a fruit of an evangelistic campaign that was planned by members of Mpando Baptist Church. They went to the chief and requested permission to hold a crusade in his area. After the pastor preached, many were converted to the Baptist faith. Mrs Mary Kantunda also went to this crusade together with other women from Mpando Baptist Church.[188] The women's role was to sing choruses at the beginning of the crusade. At this particular meeting Mrs Makuwa, a church member from Mpando, was even asked to offer a prayer.[189] At Mambo women did not preach on a regular Sunday during this time. The first woman preached in this church in the later period.[190] Since Thyolo was still under Blantyre Association during this time, the women in this church continued to receive teaching from women leaders at association level. Most of these women came from Blantyre churches. These were the likes of Mrs Annie Kawamba of the current Soche Baptist Church, Mrs Kayiya and Mrs Chitseko of Chichiri Baptist Church, Mrs Kwalira, who was by then a member of Mpando Baptist Church, was also very helpful in teaching women in this church. She actually by this time attended the church regularly alternatively with Mpando Baptist. Her idea was to encourage women's work there.[191] Women's work grew much more in the later period.[192]

---

[187] Int. Rev A.G.J Kantunda, Mpando Baptist Church, 7.8.2000; Int. Mrs Martha Kholomana, Mpando Baptist Church, 26.7.2000.

[188] During this time, Baptist churches from Mpando, such as Ndalama Baptist Church, Chididi Baptist Church, Saopa Baptist Church, Chimiko Baptist Church were started in this way. Int. Rev A.G. Kantunda, Mpando Baptist Church, 7.8.2000.

[189] Int. focus group, Mpando Baptist Church, 26.7.2000.

[190] This was in 1987, and it was a woman from Blantyre who first preached in this church. Int. Mr Philmon Kambalame, Mrs Olive Kambalame, Ntokota Baptist Church, 26.7.2000.

[191] Mrs Kwalira was very instrumental in strengthening women's work in the district even in the other churches, which were founded later. Ibid.

[192] Many churches were planted in the 1990s, and many preaching points were started in 2000. Churches and preaching points with date of establishment from Mpando Baptist are; Ntokota Baptist in 1992; Tembenuka Baptist Church in 1998 in T/A Chimaliro; Ntchulo Baptist Church in 1999 in T/A Chimaliro; Savala Baptist

1.5.4 Women in Baptist Congregations in Lower Shire

The first congregation in the Lower Shire was Chikwawa Baptist Church in 1969 led by Rev Sweetie.[193] He started a second church, Kulima Baptist near Ngabu in 1970. The third congregation was Nchalo Baptist Church in Chikwawa, and the fourth was Nsomo Baptist Church in the same district.[194] Although Nsomo was started later, it is from here that most of the congregations in Chikwawa and Nsanje trace their origin.[195]

These first churches were founded by the missionaries in Blantyre with the cooperation of Rev Sweetie of Domasi village, T/A Mlilima in Chikwawa district. He was a pastor of Evangelical Nyasa Mission[196] and decided to join the Baptists, when he got dissatisfied with his church. When he went to Limbe to meet Southern Baptist missionaries there, he was told that he needed to prove his worth if he was to be pastor in a Baptist church, by starting a church. When he came back to Chikwawa he was approached by two other pastors of Evangelical Nyasa Mission who also wanted to leave their church. Rev Sweetie told them of the missionaries' challenge to start churches.[197] These were Rev Pompi and Rev Kangulama in Chikwawa district. Their major way of converting others was through open air preaching.[198] In this both men and women were involved. This strategy was probably patterned after the revival crusades that had reached many districts.[199]

The first pastors' wives in Chikwawa were therefore Mrs Sweetie, Mrs Pompi and Mrs Kangulama, wives of the men that started Baptist

Church in 1999 in T/A Chimaliro; Waruma Baptist Church in 1999 in T/A Nchiramwela; Namadzi Baptist Church in 1995 in Chimaliro Baptist Church (Namadzi was born out of conflict at Ntokota Baptist Church due to issues relating to land ownership). These preaching points have also been started: Namilonje in 1999; Chimiko in T/A Nchiramwela in 2000; Ndalama in T/A Mchilamwela in 2000; Thyolo Boma (the word Boma is district) in T/A Kapichi in 2000; Ngamwani 2 in Thekerani in 2000; Mwabvu in T/A Chimaliro in 2000; Namilonje in T/A Chimaliro in 2000. In most cases the traditional method that the late Rev Kantunda used of going to the chief first was used. Int. Rev A.G. Kantunda, Mpando Baptist Church, 7.8.2000.

[193] He died in 1999. Int. Rev Jim Kalenga, Nsomo Baptist Church, 28.7.2000.
[194] Int. Mrs Kalavina, Nchalo Baptist Church, Chikwawa, 27.7.2000.
[195] Rev Longwe refers to the churches as the nucleus of Lower Shire congregations. See Rev Longwe's unpublished field notes.
[196] Nyasa Mission was started in 1893 at Likhubula as an Industrial Mission.
[197] Int. Rev Kalenga, Nsomo Baptist Church, 28.7.2000.
[198] Ibid.
[199] Int. Mrs Malikebu, Thundu Baptist Church, Zomba, 19.5.2000.

Churches in this area. All these did not go for Baptist theological training. Their husbands' education was too limited to enable them to go to Baptist Seminary abroad.[200] However these women already had some pastoral experience in their former church. But even then, they were limited to be involved in leadership roles. This shortfall was complimented by abilities of some laywomen. In the case of Mrs Kangulama, for example, because she was illiterate, it was Mrs Kong'a who helped her to teach women the Bible.[201] Mrs Pompi, also known as Nambewe, was the pastor's wife then at Nsomo Baptist in Chindoko village.[202] She also was illiterate and was helped by Mrs Christina Kalemba in teaching women. Since her husband died in 1981, she remained single. Throughout the 1970s, she was a *mlangizi*. In this capacity she advised women during women's weekly meetings about Christian marriage but also organized *ulangizi* for girls.[203] Mrs Pompi was being assisted in this role by Anasefu (Mrs Kudzala).[204] The involvement of lay leadership in these Baptist churches also shows much liberation among Baptist Convention women as compared to women of other congregations where clergy connections are key in defining women's leadership position.

Whereas there were women preachers in the first Chichewa congregations in Blantyre, there were none in these congregations in the Lower Shire, just as was the case among missionary women in Limbe Baptist and Chichiri Baptist. This was probably because these congregations in Chikwawa were started independently of Rev Galatiya who was the only local leader that encouraged women to preach during this period. Rev Nkhata, who was at Soche Baptist Church and the missionaries started churches in these areas. These may not have encouraged women to preach. In fact in the whole South South region, there were no women deacons. The first and the only woman deacon was ordained in 1970 in Chichiri Baptist Church.[205]

---

[200] Details on conditions to enter theological college are discussed later in the chapter.
[201] Mrs Kong'a left the church in 1975, when her husband was transferred to Blantyre.
[202] Int. Mrs Kalavina, Nchalo Baptist Church, 27.7.2000; Rev Kalenga and Christian Kalenga, Nsomo Baptist Church, 28.7.2000.
[203] Focus group, Nsomo Baptist Church, 28.7.2000.
[204] Ibid.
[205] Ibid.

However even though the majority of women in Lower Shire were mainly involved in support roles such as collecting water and cooking at funerals,[206] some were also involved in leadership roles, even apart from preaching. Women were involved in starting churches, together with men. The growth of women's work also shows that the revival spirit blurred the distinction between women and men and often encouraged openness to the Baptist message, and churches were easily organized, usually in a week. Women were involved in starting churches through door to door evangelism.[207] They would go into an area, for a week together with men, to begin Baptist work there. The men would ask permission from the chief to hold meetings in her or his area.[208] Then beginning the first day they would spread into the village homes inviting people to the meeting or a Biblical film that night. They would also tell others about their Baptist faith. Some women and men would believe the Baptist message.[209]

While women in Chikwawa were involved in this way, in Nsanje women usually followed after the churches were started by men.[210] The main reason for women not going with men on the first trip was probably transport problems. The key women who were involved in starting congregations in Chikwawa were Mrs Pompi, Mrs Christina Kalenga, Mrs Ntchona, Mrs Sagonja and Mrs Samu among others,[211] who were all members of Nsomo Baptist church at that time. These women were also responsible for teaching women in Nsanje Baptist congregations. Since the congregations were the result of Nsomo Baptist member efforts, they felt responsible to supervise church work there.[212] Such activities were possible regardless of the fact that pastors' wives in this region did not have any theological training. These women were also assisted by women from other districts such as Mrs Ellen Ng'oma, Mrs Elizabeth Phiri and Mrs Mallungo from Lilongwe.[213]

---

[206] Ibid.

[207] Int. Christina Kalenga, Nsomo Baptist Church, 5.5.2000.

[208] In Lower Shire, chieftaincies are either female or male, because the area constitutes of both matrilineal and patrilineal societies.

[209] Int. Christina Kalenga, Nsomo Baptist Church, 5.5.2000.

[210] Int. Jim Kalenga, Nsomo Baptist Church, 28.7.2000.

[211] Int. focus group, Nsomo Baptist Church, 28.7.2000.

[212] Ibid; In 1977, congregations was opened at Kalonga near Mankhamba in T/A Ndamela in Nsanje, Reno and Mtondo in T/A Tengani, Sankhulani among others.

[213] Int. Christina Kalenga, Nsomo Baptist Church, 5.5.2000.

There was the desire to accept women in the Baptist churches regardless of their marriage status. For example, there are two women known as Mrs Sagonja in Nsomo Baptist Church, both married to the same polygamous husband. The senior Mrs Sagonja was involved in starting congregations in Chikwawa. She originally came from Nsomo village and was the first disciple of Mrs Pompi. She was very good at visitation and teaching fellow women Baptist beliefs. Because she knew how to read and write, she could easily use the women's Bible study materials then. She also served as an instructor of GAs,[214] even at the regional level. The fact that she was married to a man who never went to church and was polygamous did not have a negative effect on her ministry and acceptance in her church. The junior wife is also well accepted in this congregation and is involved in leadership positions in the church.[215]

Even though women's work was being supported by lay women leaders, there was need for women with theological training. Mrs Christina Kalenga of Nsomo Baptist Church had such an opportunity in 1979.[216] Mrs Kalenga was not the first woman to go for theological training in this area. Mrs Kanyemba and her husband went to Tanzania for theological training earlier than the Kalengas but this earlier couple was dismissed from Baptist Convention, when her husband wrote a letter while in Seminary, challenging church leaders that at the time of his arrival, he would change the order of running things in Malawi. This gesture was interpreted as pride and as such he and the wife were told to leave the Baptist upon their return.[217] There was also Mrs Mponya, whose husband died soon after seminary. She worked with the women in Chikwawa briefly and she also died in the late 1970s.[218]

---

[214] GA is a short term for Girls Auxiliary group. This voluntary group is composed of girls ranging from 12 years. They learn the Bible and are led by Umodzi women. For details of Umodzi, see chapter 2.

[215] She is currently serving as a Sunday School teacher. Int. focus group, Nsomo Baptist Church, 28.9.2000.

[216] Ibid.

[217] Int. Rev Jim Kalenga, Nsomo Baptist Church, Ngabu, Chikwawa, 28.9.2000. The other tradition says Kanyemba was arrogant at the Annual General Meeting. His arrogance was seen in his constant raising of hands, asking questions and comments during this meeting. Rev Makhaya was the Convention leader who dismissed him, Int. Rev Chisi 14.10.2001.

[218] She is fondly remembered as a talented woman in ministering to woman, Int. Rev Chisi, 14.10.2001.

Mrs Christina Kalenga therefore, was the third pastor's wife to go for theological training in this area. However, she was the first trained woman to serve in this area for a longer time. Just like the others she went on her husband's ticket to Zambia Theological Seminary in Lusaka in 1978 and came back in 1980. When Christina came back from training, she became very instrumental in training women in this area.[219] At the Seminary, she had been in the men's class. Apart from the women's course, she also studied New Testament, Old Testament, Sewing and First Aid. The women's course was basically about the Women Missionary Union, and ideas on how to teach fellow women scriptures, and distinctives about the uniform. While in training, Christina got a uniform in 1979, after successful memorization of the verses.[220] With this training she has worked hard among women in the Lower Shire.

After this theological training, she strengthened women's work in the region. Her return from theological college coincided with the second revival crusade, which started around 1982. During this revival, apart from disseminating Baptists beliefs, she had a challenge to organize women's work in the area. After all women's work had already started to grow with the revival of the 1970s. It was now time to give in depth training to the local women as well as organize the work.

She began to meet this challenge of organizing women's work by beginning informal joint meetings at a particular congregation, which later became the foundation for associational meetings.[221] Christina Kalenga helped to begin the first association in Chikwawa in 1982. This was easy because she had the privilege of seeing how the associations in Zambia were organized while she was in training. This first association in the Lower Shire was composed of nine churches.[222] The first leaders of the association were herself, Mrs Patrishu Nambewe, Mrs Ntchona and Mrs Samu.

Christina Kalenga's conversion to the Baptist faith had not been easy. She was challenged by the drastic change of her husband, Jim Kalenga to the Baptist faith. Christina had eight children, two of whom died. She was born into a Seventh-day Adventist family; as such she did her primary education at Malamulo. When she married her husband Jim in

---

[219] Int. Christina Kalenga, Nsomo Baptist Church, 5.5.2000.
[220] For information on verses and uniform see chapter 2.
[221] For knowledge of association, see introductory chapter.
[222] An association can have as many as a hundred or as few as eight congregations.

1961 by church wedding she moved with her husband to the Evangelical Nyasa Mission.[223] However, her husband drifted away from church life. Even in these circumstances, she remained committed to her faith. In 1970, at the time of the revival crusades in Baptist churches, she was surprised when her husband drastically changed his attitude towards the church. This change had started when he read a tract that was being distributed during the crusade meetings that Rev Pompi and his friends organized. Kalenga was awakened to spiritual things and together with his friends decided they would join that church to which Rev Pompi belonged.[224] However, Christina was very skeptical about her husband's new interest in another church especially after her experience with him dropping from church life and his drunken behaviour. She decided that she would continue going to Evangelical Nyasa Mission where she was well established. By then she had a uniform of the women's group in that church.[225] In fact all the wives of the founding members of Nsomo Baptist Church resisted joining their husbands' new church.[226] Their husbands were drunkards and the women had no trust that their change was genuine. After a month, the women saw that an incredible thing had happened in their husbands' lives. They were not the same drunkards any more and were truly zealous for the things of God. Mrs Christina Kalenga joined first and all the other women followed her. There were also conversions from Zion Church. They started meeting at Ntondo village in Nsomo T/A Ngabu. Their services were first held under a tree for two years.[227] In 1973, Rev Charles Middleton and Rev Galatiya came to open the church and baptized the members there.[228]

Mrs Patrishu Nambewe is remembered as a strong member at Nsomo Baptist Church. She was a convert from Evangelical Nyasa Mis-

---

[223] Int. Rev Jim Kalenga, Nsomo Baptist Church, Chikwawa, 28.9.2000.
[224] Ibid.
[225] The uniform was sky blue dress, which is currently changed to blue skirt and white blouse. Int. Mrs Christina Kalenga, Nsomo Baptist Church, Chikwawa, 5.5.2000.
[226] The founding members included Mr Bwanali who had the idea of starting a Baptist church, Mr Jim Kalenga, Mr Fresor Kudzala, Mr Fredson Kalenga- Jim Kalenga's elder brother, Nelson Kachule who died in 1975 and Mr Sostein Chafudzika. Int. Jim Kalenga and Christina Kalenga, Nsomo Baptist Church, 28.7.2000.
[227] Jim Kalenga was the main preacher during these years. He was doing the same before he left Nyasa Mission. Ibid.
[228] Ibid.

sion after marrying a heathen (*wakunja*). Even with such a marriage background she was well accepted by local women and her church. She became key at assisting women greatly in the Lower Shire in memorizing verses. She was a very dedicated woman in her church and was among the first women to have a uniform in Lower Shire, because she was exposed to the idea of a uniform much earlier than her friends in the congregation. This was because she usually was among the delegates going to Lilongwe for the national meetings that happened every year at which issues of the uniform were discussed.[229] She was later widowed. As a single woman she was able to attend such long distance meetings and to be involved in a lot of women activities without being constrained by a husband.[230] At the congregational level, she was just as busy. She was the chairperson of the women's group of her church for a long time.[231] Even though Christina Kalenga had theological training by this time, it was Mrs Ntchona who was elected to be the first chairperson of the association. In Baptist churches, theological training does not necessarily give a leadership position in church. In the second term, Mrs Samu was the chairperson, again a laywoman. She was chosen to this post because of her talent to lead fellow women. During her term of office she was very successful in organizing and leading women's meetings.[232]

Mrs Samu was married; she came into the church after Christina Kalenga was already there. She got converted when she visited Nsomo Baptist Church and believed the Baptist message. At that time Jim Kalenga was a deacon in the church. Christina, his wife had been secretary of the church from 1976 to 1977.[233]

The spirit of revival did not only remain with Nsomo Baptist Church. Since then other churches were started within Chikwawa and Nsanje districts. These churches were opened basically through tract distribution by Middletons and Phiffers and local Baptists. In addition, local Baptists in conjunction with the missionaries conducted evangelistic crusades in different places. Through these efforts, many were converted to the Baptist

---

[229] For more details on women's national meetings see chapters 2 and 3.
[230] She herself died in 1985. Int. focus group, Nsomo Baptist Church, 28.9.2000.
[231] Ibid.
[232] Int. Christina Kalenga, Nsomo Baptist Church, 5.5.2000.
[233] Ibid.

faith.[234] However other conversions to the Baptist faith happened without an initiative from these leaders. There were often times when people from different places would come to Nsomo and request them to start a Baptist church in their area.[235] The spirit of revival in Nsanje district was very imminent in 1977 when most of the conversions took place.[236] The women in this district were taught by Christina Kalenga and other local Malawians including the efforts of Rebecca Phiffer and Glandor Middleton. They used to organize seminars for women together with the local women leaders where women would learn about their Baptist beliefs. Mrs Rebecca Phiffer would sometimes take her four children when doing such training.[237] Such trainings were key to women's liberation.

At the congregational level, women were also active. Apart from Mrs Sagonja junior there was Mrs Pitison who was also a Sunday school teacher. Mrs Pitison died in 1977. Although she was involved in this role, her husband was not a churchgoer, he was a drunk. This would not happen in Blantyre Synod where, if the husband is not a Christian, the wife is unlikely to be a leader in the church.[238] Baptists believe in individual choices, which is more liberative.

1.5.5 Women in Baptist churches in the South East

Even in this region, the spirit of revival was prominent, though not all areas were visibly affected by the revival. Nevertheless there was a great openness to the Baptist faith in many areas and this led to growth of

---

[234] In 1974, Bile Baptist Church, Mangadzi Baptist Church and Makande Baptist Church, were started. In Nsanje several churches were also started mostly with the help of Dudley Phiffer. His financial support helped the leaders of Nsomo Baptist Church to open Baptist churches in Nsanje. The first Baptist church to open in Nsanje was at T/A Malemia. They went to Chief Malemia and asked him permission to start a church in the area. They held a crusade for 4 days. A few were converted but these were only young girls and boys. Low numbers of conversion in this area were due to the fact that this area already had lots of other churches. The second Baptist Church was started at Mbang'ombe and Kwanjobvu in Nsanje. Ibid.

[235] These were the likes of Nyenyezi Baptist Church and Reno Baptist Church. Ibid.

[236] In this same year, the following churches were started: Kalonga Baptist Church, near Makhamba Railway Station, Nchacha Baptist Church, In Nchacha village in T/A Mlolo Ntalika Baptist Church in T/A Mlolo, Mphamba Baptist Church in T/A Ndamela, Nangalembe Baptist Church, near Sankhulani Railway Station. Ibid.

[237] Ibid. Also Int. Mrs Marylyn Upton, Area 36 Baptist Church, Lilongwe, 5.1.2001.

[238] Int. Rev Jim Kalenga and Christina Kalenga, Nsomo Baptist Church, 28.7.2000.

Baptist women's work from Jali to other districts such as Mulanje and Balaka and even as far as Mozambique borders.[239]

This growth was also visible within Jali area,[240] where not all areas had been affected by the two revival crusades. In the case study of the growth of women's work from Makolije Baptist Church to Mphyuphyu area near Lake Chirwa, this trend is real. In 1969, Linly Kachingwe (Mrs Linly Mauluka) with her husband walked two hours to `Makolije Baptist Church to hear the Baptist message at one of the *phwando*[241] evangelistic meetings[242] organized by the church.[243] Linly together with her husband was converted to the Baptist faith.[244] This shows that the wind of revival probably started earlier than the 1970s. In fact preparations for this revival crusade started in 1967 and finished in 1969. During this preparation period, time was spent on making posters and training counsellors to teach those who would become Baptist then.[245] Linly Mauluka and other converts from her village attended Makolije Baptist Church for two years after which they requested their church to start a new congregation in their village. When they had been granted permission, they went back home and told people one to one about their Baptist faith.[246]

Among the first women who believed the Baptist message were: Mrs Nchadza, together with her husband, Mrs Mindano, who together with her husband were in the Church of Christ; Mrs Stenala Matako, who with her husband belonged to the Assemblies of God; the mother of Mrs

---

[239] Int. Rev D. Malikebu, Thundu Baptist Church, 19.5.2000.
[240] This area at this time included a wide section of Zomba rural from Mayaka to Mphyumphyu area.
[241] The word *phwando* is a Chichewa word referring to a party. As is normal for all parties there is eating or/and drinking. At these *Phwando* meetings the main attraction was meat either goat meat, or beef or chicken. Int. Rev D. Lichapa, Makolije Baptist Church, 20.3.2000.
[242] These meetings were evangelistic in that after the eating, there was the preaching of the gospel. Ibid.
[243] Int. Mrs Nellie Nanthambwe, Mrs Linly Mauluka, Rev Mauluka, Mauluka Baptist Church, 24.3.2000.
[244] With them were Mr Mawonga, the uncle of her husband, Mr Che Khula, from Chifisi village. These also were converted at that meeting. Ibid.
[245] Int. Rev Chisi, Ufulu Baptist Church, Lilongwe, 23.6.2000.
[246] Int. Mrs Nellie Nanthambwe, Mrs Linly Chauluka, Rev Mauluka, Mauluka Baptist Church, 24.3.2000.

Stenala also became Baptist;[247] as did Mrs Nyalugwe Kwanda.[248] These first converts together with others formed Mauluka Baptist Church. Even though this was the time for the first revival crusades, women's work from this congregation only grew in numbers and not in terms of geography. Growth of women's work into other places only took place during the second revival crusades of the 1980s. However in the 1970s new women continued to join the church.[249]

From 1974 to 1976, the following women were converted to Mauluka Baptist Church: Née Edah Kalonga (Mrs Makha), Née Esnala Kalonga and Née Lyda Kalonga, all three from one family. As matrilineal women they stayed in their village. Upon marriage, it is customary that their husbands join them. Adjustments to this role are also possible, for example if they are working husbands[250] in which case they would go with them to places of employment. Other new women converts were Mrs Phoebe Makaye[251] and Nellie Chitedzi (Mrs Nanthambwe).[252] Mrs Nellie Nanthambwe has been key to women's work in the South East region.

In the 1980s women's work spread from Mauluka Baptist congregation to other areas. Firstly to Kataya Baptist Church, which is the first daughter church of Mauluka, started in 1980. The church was started when a woman in this village married Mr Mindano,[253] a widower who had been a key member of Mauluka Baptist Church. The wife of his second marriage Mrs Mindano together with other women such as Mrs Pandamalata and her husband and Mr Katunga, who also left Mauluka Baptist due to distance, became the first members of Kataya Baptist Church.[254]

Women's work also went to Khanda Baptist Church in 1981 because some more members left Mauluka Baptist Church because of distance. In the same way, women's work started in Kandulu Baptist Church in

---

[247] Mrs Stenala lived in her village with her husband together with her mother. (Ibid.) This is typical for matrilineal societies. The husband stays in a wife's home.
[248] Her husband died in 1989, but she is still a Baptist. Her husband came from Khanga village in T/A Mkutumanje because of marriage. Ibid.
[249] Intervals at which the churches were formed show this trend.
[250] Working in the service of employment in the formal sector of the economy.
[251] She was converted together with her grandfather James Makaye. (Ibid.).
[252] Nellie became Baptist on 9th Sept 1977 (Ibid).
[253] Mr Mindano came from Kumbila Village in T/A Mkutumanje. He married in Kataya village in the same T/A Mkutumanje.
[254] Ibid.

1983. Unlike at other new branches of Mauluka Baptist Church, at Kandulu a revival crusade was held. Both women and men were sent to conduct the crusade in Kandulu village. Mrs Mbulanje with her husband, Mrs Gwede with her husband, were among the team. The crusade was successful and some became Baptists. Among the women converts from the crusade were Mrs Gonani and Mrs Nashoni, who became first members of the church.[255]

Women's work spread to Ramus 1, an area very close to Lake Chirwa. The first women of this church were a result of a revival crusade that took place along Lake Chirwa in 1984. The shore of this lake is characterized by fishermen, boats (both with engines and manual although the majority are manual), fishing nets, buyers and sellers of fish. There are also traders in maize, only that this maize comes all the way across the lake from Mozambique. The maize is deposited at this shore by a motorboat. Often there are other people who come to visit the place, a majority of whom would be in transit to a beautiful Island, Chisi Island on which are huge trees of Kachere, yellow fever trees as well as baobabs.

In 1984, Mrs Blanche Wester and Bill Wester together with other members of Mauluka, organized a revival crusade along this lake. Women as well as men sang choruses to invite others to come to the meeting. After the choruses, Rev Wester preached and at the end of the sermon a song (known among Baptists as *Nyimbo ya Mayitanidwe*) intended to invite people to make a decision for Christ was sung.[256] After this song, some believed, some of whom became Baptists. During the meeting there was also the distribution of tracts of different kinds. One of the common tracts was *Khasu Loswela Mphanje*.[257] This growth of women's work from Mauluka Baptist continued geographically even after the revival crusades.[258]

---

[255] Ibid.
[256] This song is no. 81 in *Nyimbo za Chigonjetso*, a Chichewa Baptist hymn. Song number 79 in the same hymnbook is also sung for this purpose.
[257] The English version is *Four Spiritual Laws*, produced by LIFE Ministry, an interdenominational Christian organization.
[258] Int. Rev Mauluka, Mauluka Baptist Church, 24.3.2001. In 1982, Ramus 2 Baptist Church was started along Lake Chirwa, Chirima Baptist Church was started on Chisi Island across Lake Chirwa due to the evangelistic campaigns along the Lake; Kango Baptist Church was started in 1991 near Likangala river in T/A Mwambo; In 1992, Chimwayi Baptist Church was started in T/A Kuntumanje; Khumba Baptist Church

Such growth in this region was not only from Mauluka Baptist; it was from other congregations as well even though it was not uniform. Some congregations grew more than others. Women leadership was also more prominent in some congregations than in others. Mina Baptist Church, for example, was born during the revival in 1979. The people in Mina village heard of the Baptist Church at Thundu and asked Rev Malikebu to open a branch in their area. Mrs Malikebu taught the women at Mina Baptist Church because Thundu became a supervising church for Mina Baptist.[259] Rev Gowelo also started Namachete Baptist Church, a branch of Mandawala Baptist Church[260] in 1977. Women did enjoy positions of leadership at this time.[261] Some of such women were from Mauluka Baptist Church. These were the likes of Mrs Nellie Nanthambwe, Mrs Linly Mauluka, Mrs Samang'anda, who often served as *mlangizi* in the area, and Mrs Vuta.

Makolije Baptist Church did contribute to spreading women's work outside Zomba. One of the major ways of establishing this work was through *phwando* meetings. *Phwando* meetings were crowd pullers because people could eat meat that was a rare delicacy in their homes. It was also a chance to socialize with friends. Davidson Lichapa and Rev Kalayitoni Banda in Mayaka often used this method.[262] At such *phwando* meetings only men preached and women were involved in cooking food as well as teaching fellow women who had become Baptists about Baptist beliefs. With this strategy women's work spread to Mulanje and even to Balaka.[263]

During this period, Mrs Wester was assisted in teaching women by local women from other regions such as Mrs Ellen Ng'oma from Blantyre,

---

was started in 1994 again through evangelistic campaigns along Lake Chirwa. Rose and Dison Chigwede were first members of this church. They both died with Rose dying in 1997; Tala Baptist Church was started in 1996, because of distance; Nanchengwa Baptist Church was started in 1998, led by Mr Belo. Other Churches that were not traced from Mauluka Baptist that were started during this period were the likes of Songani Baptist Church in 1985 and Thunga Baptist Church. Both are in T/A Mkutumanje.

[259] Int. Mr Gowelo, Mandawala Baptist Church, 25.11.2000.
[260] Int. Mrs Gowelo, Mandawala Baptist Church, 25.11.2000.
[261] Some were pastors even. For more details see chapter 3.
[262] Int. Rev Kalayitoni Banda Namachete Baptist Church, 3.8.2000.
[263] Int. Rev Davidson Lichapa, Makolije Baptist Church, 20.3.2000.

Mrs Elizabeth Njolomole Phiri and Mrs Chrissie Malabwanya.[264] Mrs Malabwanya is well remembered in this region as someone who assisted Mrs Wester in teaching the South East women. She is the daughter of Rev and Mrs Galatiya. She went into Seminary in 1973 and came back in 1975. Although she originally comes from Neno in Mwanza, she served as pastor's wife in Blantyre. However her church role as pastor's wife did not restrict her to her congregation only. She also spent time teaching women in the rural South East.[265]

Women's work also continued to spread in Mayaka area in T/A Chikowi, Zomba. Gunde Baptist Church was opened in 1972, Emau Baptist Church in 1974,[266] while Nachiswe Baptist Church was planted in 1977. All three congregations were a result of revival crusades conducted around these areas, after a crusade that took place at Jali Trading Centre in 1972. This crusade was attended by people from Mayaka area who in turn went to start Baptist work in the same way in their respective areas.[267] The first women convert to Nachiswe Baptist Church was Mirriam Banda, whose husband Samson was also a Baptist. Mirriam Banda came from a Catholic background and joined the Baptists because of her husband. When her husband Samson later became pastor, she became a pastor's wife. Only later did she go for some theological training at Lilongwe Bible School.[268] Coupled with the fact that she was not very literate, it meant that for a few years she depended on other local women leaders to train women in her congregation. This area was still part of Jali association at that time: women such as Mrs Nanthambwe from Mphyuphyu would come to assist in women's work in this area.[269] The members of Nachiswe Baptist Church came from crusades that were conducted in these areas: Mwanyula village, Taibu village, Kotokosa village, Atamiteche village and Mlemba village. The engagement of women at revival crusades in these areas was to invite fellow women to the meeting and cooking. No missionary women came to these revival meet-

---

[264] Int. Mrs Mwanakhu, Mpinda Baptist Church, 2.9.2000.
[265] Int. Mrs Christina Kalenga, Nsomo Baptist Church, 28.7.2000.
[266] Int. Rev Mwanakhu, Mpinda Baptist Church, Zomba, 3.7.2000. For a study of Emau Baptist Church see Rendell Day, Emau Baptist Church.
[267] At the crusade of 1972, Rev Thomson preached. Int. Rev Kalayitoni, Nachiswe Baptist Church, 3.8.2000.
[268] She went to Bible School in 1986. Int. Mrs Mirriam Banda, Nachiswe Baptist Church, 3.8.2000.
[269] Ibid.

ings that were held around Nachiswe Baptist Church.[270] At Emau Baptist Church, the first women converts were Miss Mahambuwa,[271] the sister to Rev Mahambuwa and Mrs Chitsulo. Since there was no able women leader in this congregation, women's work was assisted by women from Mpinda Baptist Church in Mikuyu area near Mikuyu Prison. These women leaders from Mpinda were: Mrs Chiwamba, Mrs Chawona and Mrs Tambula Mwanakhu. These women mainly travelled on foot to this area. When going for training, they would take with them flour and *ndiwo* (relish) for food. Such training sessions would normally last for three days.[272]

At the same time, women's work also spread to Mikuyu area.[273] At Rita, the first women converts came from Jehovah's Witnesses background. A man from Rita village approached the pastor at Mpinda Baptist Church to come to his village and preach about their Baptist beliefs. He did this for three weeks at the end of which there were 20 converts, women and men. Women's work from Mpinda went as far as near the Mozambique border when in 1985 Chimbalanga Baptist Church near Nswang'oma was started.[274] The women from Mpinda went to these churches to teach fellow women about Baptist beliefs. Some of the women that went were Mrs Nankwenya, Mrs Samu and Mrs Tambula. At the revival crusades some of these women also went. Their role was singing choruses and teaching fellow women Baptist beliefs.[275]

From Chayima Baptist Church, women's work also spread to Mulanje during this period of revival. The first Baptist Church in this area was Malambo Baptist that was started in this period in 1976 when Rev Majomboshe and his wife left Chayima Baptist Church to be missionaries in

---

[270] Int. Rev Kalayitoni, 3.8.2000. More Churches were started later in 1986, 1987, 1989, and 1990 and the same methods of conducting crusades were used.

[271] She is different from Mrs Mahambuwa who is talked about in chapter one. Ibid.

[272] Int. Rev Tambula Mwanakhu, Mpinda Baptist Church, 3.7.2000.

[273] Some of the churches opened in Mikuyu at this time were: Namwera Baptist Church in 1975 in T/A Mwambo and Rita Baptist Church in 1977.

[274] At Nswang'oma, a man had come across a tract "*Ndichite Chiyani Kuti Ndipulumuke?*" and when he looked at the address, he found out that the owner was residing in Zomba. He decided to meet the person in Zomba where he met Tambula, the pastor of Mpinda Baptist Church. He invited Tambula to bring his church to his village. Tambula agreed and decided to have a revival crusade in that area. Men and women from Mpinda went. Int. Rev Tambula, Mpinda Baptist Church, 3.7.2000.

[275] Ibid.

Mulanje at her husband's home, against their cultural practice of a husband staying in his wife's home. Their going to Mulanje was also necessary because of the size of their family and their livestock. They needed a bigger space to live.[276] Mrs Majomboshe spent time teaching women in Baptist beliefs even though she was illiterate. In 1976, the women at Chayima continued to increase in number. Mrs Maida and Mrs Nashoni became the main teachers among women. These had the advantage of knowing how to read and write. Mrs Nashoni could even read and write English. She was a migrant from Zimbabwe and had come to Chayima to stay with her husband.[277] Even at this time the women had the privilege of teaching local women in biblical truth as well as sewing.[278]

Women's work also spread to the Mozambique border but not through revival crusades. This work silently seeped into the area mainly because of migration of Baptist members from the Malawi side. One of the reasons for this migration was marriage. This is how Naminkhaka Baptist Church was started in 1976; Chipinimbi Baptist Church was started in Kazimbi district in 1985, and Mlombwa Baptist Church in 1982 in T/A Makoya.[279]

From some of the historical accounts above, it is clear that women's roles were still limited to dealing with fellow women even during this time of revival. The missionary teaching and culture seemed to override the principle of the priesthood of all believers making women to be less liberated. It is also clear that the culture of the husband staying in the wife's village in these matrilineal societies is changing. It is possible that leadership in these matrilineal societies is also moving somewhat from women to men and this also may affect the position of women in the churches in these societies.

1.5.6 Politics and revival

Even though there was revival, there was also opposition to Baptist women's work. The major opposition was the political environment of the day. Women's work grew numerically and in the South East especially

---

[276] Int. Rev Maida, Mrs Maida, Chayima Baptist Church, 20.3.2000.
[277] Ibid.
[278] Ibid.
[279] Int. Rev Ntuwe, Rev Paulo Sabola, Rev Mosses, pastors' meeting, Zomba Baptist Church, 19.5.2000.

women enjoyed learning how to sew with Mrs Blanche Wester. However, Mrs Wester's ministry activities sparked a political strife with MCP (Malawi Congress Party)[280], which in turn led to a division within the Convention,[281] threatening the missionaries' stay in the country.[282] In the 1970s, Blanche Wester taught women how to make bags made of sackcloth (*matumba a ziguduli*).[283] This came at a time when some of the local Baptists wanted to get rid of the missionaries. The Convention group that was against missionaries conspired that they would use these bags to set up missionaries against MCP functionaries so that the missionaries would leave and then they would inherit their worth invested in church buildings, cars and the like.[284] One day Mrs Wester was called into the MCP office in Zomba where she found Mr Mussa Gama, in Zomba, Mayi Makwinja, a member of the Women's League[285] then and Mr Mpunga, one of the MCP functionaries.[286] In the office were also other Convention leaders and the sackcloth bags. Mrs Wester was accused by the party officials of demeaning Ngwazi's *mbumba* by making them sew bags from sackcloth. She defended herself by arguing that the bags were just samples and that the real bags were to be made later.[287] The party officials also expressed concern that the women were dancing for her husband as *mbumba* dancing for the Ngwazi.[288] When the party officials insisted on the case, Rev Lichapa and friends challenged them that since the Westers were given permission to work in Malawi by the Ngwazi; it was

---

[280] For more details see Emily Mkamanga, *Suffering in Silence*, Edinburgh: Dudu Nsomba, 2000. A similar incident also happened in Lilongwe someone was accused of tearing Ngwazi's picture by Rev Makhaya with the same intention. Int. Rev Chisi, 12.3.2000.

[281] In this Rev Kanowa, Rev Galatiya, Rev Malabwanya and Rev Malikebu among others were for instigating the government that Wester and his missionary friends should be deported by the government as was common in that day if one offended the Ngwazi. Rev Lichapa and Rev Mauluka were defending the missionaries so that they stay in the country. Int. Rev Galatiya, Chipiliro Baptist Church, 15.5.2000; also Int. Rev Mauluka, Mauluka Baptist Church, 24.3.2000.

[282] Int. Mrs Linly Mauluka and Rev Mauluka, Mauluka Baptist Church 24.3.2000.

[283] Int. focus group Mwanafumu Baptist Church, 21.3.2000.

[284] Int. Rev Lichapa Makolije Baptist Church, 20.3.2000.

[285] For details on Women's League see Mkamanga, *Suffering in Silence*.

[286] Int. Rev D. Lichapa, Makolije Baptist Church, 8.3.2000.

[287] Ibid.

[288] In Baptist Church, women dance and sing choruses even in a regular Sunday Service.

only the Ngwazi who could deport them. The party officials later on decided to drop the issue and cautioned those that were against Wester to
go back to their churches and do church work instead of quarrelling with
the Westers. Even though the issue was settled on the side of the party
officials, those that were against the Westers still wanted them to leave.
They leveled against her other allegations relating to ministry, for example that at joint meetings in Lilongwe women were given little tablets of
soap. This was interpreted as mean behaviour (the western mind
clashed with the local perspective, with the western mind looking at efficiency, easy storage for example, while the African mind looked at suffi-
ciency, that is to be able to use it even after the conference). The other
allegation was leveled at her husband.[289] A meeting was called by the
Convention leadership to decide the fate of Mrs Wester and her husband
at Chongoni, a lay training center for Nkhoma Synod near Lilongwe and
it was decided that the Westers should stay.[290]

Baptist women in the Southern region did portray their Baptist doctrine and polity of separation between church and state. However in certain cases their Baptist freedom was hampered by the dictatorship of the
day. This was shown when Baptist women were not allowed to make political decisions that were commensurate to their individual consciences.
Women, for example, could not hold their meetings in church without being disrupted by party supporters, usually MYP (Malawi Young Pio-

[289] That he was selling suits to the pastors, which were donations and supposed to
be given free. Int. Rev Malikebu, Thundu Baptist Church, 19.5.2000.
[290] Rev Mauluka recalls an interesting story that happened on his way to Chongoni
for this meeting. They were not aware that this meeting was to take place at that day.
Their friends who were against Wester did not want them to be at the meeting because they would defend Wester. But fortunately the missionaries alerted them. They
took the bus and went to Lilongwe, and arrived late and so they could not proceed to
Chongoni. They decided to sleep at one of the pastors who was shocked to see
them. Their host devised a plan of how he would start off very early without the
knowledge of Lichapa and Mauluka. He did that but unfortunately Mauluka heard his
steps out. Mauluka quickly alerted his friend to wake up and go. The two decided
they would walk to town. By God's grace, one of the missionaries who was also going to the meeting saw them and gave them a lift. They arrived earlier than their host
who was so much in shock to see them already at the meeting. The situation was
tense but they defended Wester and Wester stayed in Malawi till it was time for them
to go back home. Because of this defence, the Westers built churches for Lichapa
and Rev Mauluka. These churches are the largest in Jali area and are of the same
design. Int. Rev Mauluka, Mauluka Baptist Church, 24.3.2000.

neers),[291] if their meeting coincided with their party meetings. In Jali for example one time when women had such a collision of meetings, the party supporters came and told the women to stop their church meeting and go for the party meeting. They shouted at them saying *Tchalichi, Tchalichi, Tchalichi chani? Tiyeni kwa Ngwazi* ("Church, church, church, what? Let's go to the Ngwazi.")[292] The call to go to the Ngwazi did not imply that the Ngwazi was in the area, but because his[293] Mbumba were in the area, it meant that the Ngwazi was also invisibly present at that meeting in that area.

Baptist women sometimes could not refuse political involvement. In Blantyre for example, Mrs Ellen Ng'oma was chosen as the women's league chairperson of the area, in her absence.[294] Even though she did not want the post she was obliged to take it to avoid wrath from the government, which might include jailing her husband or worse.[295] In Jali area, Mrs Makina, who was pastor of Mwanafumu Baptist at that time was one day forced to go and dance at a party meeting in the area. When they discovered that she did not have a party uniform (a cloth with an imprint of Ngwazi's face on it), they forced her to wet her clothes and put them on and go to the meeting.[296] Had they inquired about a party card, they would not have found her with it because she had none.[297] The experience of Mrs Makina was a typical one among Baptist women who had come from a Jehovah's Witnesses' background. Mrs Makina and her husband had been Jehovah's Witnesses before they joined the Baptist faith. As such they carried with them the beliefs of their former religion, which forbid them to buy a party card and the Ngwazi uniform, among other things. Baptists accommodated such women because they respect individual consciences. Mrs Kanichi, a widow of Makolije Baptist was also a convert from Jehovah's Witnesses. She too did not own the Ngwazi uniform or the party card.

---

[291] For details on MYP see Mkamanga, *Suffering in Silence.*
[292] Int. Mrs Malikebu, Thundu Baptist, 19.5.2000.
[293] Usually written with a capital letter H, even when this possessive pronoun is in the middle of the text, to signify Ngwazi's divinity.
[294] Int. Mrs Mary Galatiya, Chipiliro Baptist Church, 15.5.2000.
[295] For punishments given to crimes such as these, see Mkamanga, *Suffering in Silence.*
[296] Int. Mrs Makina, Mwanafumu Baptist Church, 21.3.2000.
[297] Ibid.

On the other hand, some women who were not from Jehovah's Witnesses' background were also opposed to the buying of party cards and Ngwazi's uniform including going to the party dances. However they had to be tactful to achieve this. When there was a Ngwazi dance or a party meeting in the area, they would pretend as though they were going to that place of meeting only to return on the way.[298] However if they did this, they had to make sure to tactfully find out what was said at the meeting so that in the event that a party functionary inquired of them of the deliberations at the meeting, they would not be known to have missed the meeting.[299] They would also try to give towards the forced contributions collected by the party functionaries in the area so as to look supportive to the party. These contributions were in form of, for example, eggs, money, even a cow or any livestock if they were demanded of them. These gifts were often not given freely but forced.[300] Such tactics would work but sometimes they would not, especially when discovered to be in such habits.

This was true in the experience of Mrs Kanowa of Balaka. She was a pastor's wife at this time and was fond of such tactics. Little did she know that some women were spying on her. She did not own the Ngwazi uniform and did survive in this way for a long time. One time a church member who liked to go for the party dances happened to discover a wicked plan her fellow dancers were about to execute on Mrs Kanowa.[301] They were to go to her place the following evening and demand that she produce the party uniform for them to see. They planned that if she did not have it, she would be reported to party officials. Fortunately this church member alerted her pastor's wife about the delegation that was to come. When the delegation came Mrs Kanowa was able to produce the uniform, which she had borrowed from a church member. Even though this crisis was over, the chairperson of the women's league in that area was not satisfied. She continued to spy on Mrs Kanowa. However, this woman became a good friend of Mrs Kanowa when she was involved in a car accident, which cost her an eye. Mrs Kanowa took this opportunity to offer friendship to this lady by constantly visiting her in the hospital. When she came back from hospital, she became a good friend of Mrs

---

[298] Int. Mrs Chisi, Ufulu Baptist Church, Lilongwe, 23.6.2000.
[299] Mrs Mary Galatiya, Chipiliro Baptist Church, Balaka, 15.5.2000.
[300] Ibid.
[301] Int. Mrs Mary Galatiya Chipiriro Baptist, Balaka, 15.5.2000.

Kanowa and always defended her when it came to party matters.[302] Some women suffered psychologically, Mrs Mary Galatiya for example suffered in this way when her husband was imprisoned in the early 1980s.[303] And there are probably many cases like this because in these days, men easily got into trouble. They were blamed, for example, if their wives did not patronize party activities. If the wife did not have a party uniform, the husband would be blamed for not buying it for her. However the church allowed every woman to follow her individual conscience as regards their political engagements in their society. As such some were in active politics at this time, while some were not. Even in the later political dispensation, women were free to choose any political party, even UDF (United Democratic Party) that was led by a Muslim, Bakili Muluzi.

As a body of believers Baptist women tried to clear themselves from political hardships by inviting party officials to some of their meetings. In fact in 1972, when Baptist women in Malawi hosted the BWUA meeting in Blantyre, the government was invited and asked to give a speech.[304] At this meeting Bakili Muluzi, as minister without portfolio for the Malawi Congress Party, gave a speech and represented government.

---

[302] Ibid.

[303] Her husband Rev Stephen Galatiya went to Chikwawa for a crusade meeting. He was the preacher there and preached on Acts 4:12. The theme of his message was "There is no Salvation in man, Jesus is the only saviour, apart from Him no one can save." This was seen to be against Ngwazi, because he was the Saviour. This term was frequently attached to his address. In the evening after the sermon, he was visited by a group of people at his home. They grabbled him and took him away not telling him where he was going. On the way they met a group of drunks who even though they were in a terrible state recognized Galatiya. They knew that he was in trouble, because they recognized some of his company as being young pioneers (Ngwazi's underground army). They pleaded with them that the man of God should not be taken at night in that way but that they should surrender him to them and that they would keep him at the chiefs and then would bring him to them in the morning of the following day. This they did and in the morning Galatiya was taken to the police where he was taken to Chichiri prison. Int. Rev Galatiya, Chipiliro Baptist, 15.5.2000.

[304] Int. Mrs Marylyn Upton, Area 36 Baptist Church, 5.1.2001.

Convention women cared for the Ngwazi, as such they even went to cheer him. See photo below showing the official hostess to Dr Kamuzu Banda, Mama C. Kadzamira welcoming the women delegation to BWUSA meeting who came to visit the Ngwazi in 1972.

1.5.7 Single missionary woman

It has been argued that revival tends to increase involvement of women in leadership positions. This is also shown in the history of Southern Baptist missionaries to Malawi in that for the first time in 1970, a single woman missionary came to Malawi. Her name was Mary Chandler. She mainly worked with the women as a women's worker.[305] Although she did this very successfully, it was not exactly what Mary Chandler intended to do in Malawi.[306] She wanted to work as a social worker with local churches.[307] It is interesting that local Malawian women even remember her as *mayi wa chitukuko*[308], *which* is a literal translation of de-

---

[305] Int. Mrs Hilda Mallungo, Mtendere Baptist Church, Lilongwe, 14.3.2000. In the later years she mainly did accounting work for the Mission. She started as an assistant treasurer when Howard Rhodes was a fulltime treasure and became full time when Howard Rhodes left Malawi for a new missionary assignment in Kenya. Int. Marylyn Upton, Area 36 Baptist Church, Lilongwe, 5.1.2001.

[306] She is remembered among local Malawians widely as a women's worker.

[307] Int. Marylyn Upton, Area 36 Baptist Church, Lilongwe, 5.1.2001.

[308] Mrs Hilda Mallungo, Mtendere Baptist Church, Lilongwe, 14.3.2000.

velopment worker. Through Mary Chandler's involvement with the women, she became a model for single women in leadership.[309] Mary Chandler was involved in leading women not only in Southern Malawi, even though she was based in Blantyre. She was often called to train women in other regions as well and even at national meetings. Her theological training was helpful in fulfilling this role. She was also talented at crafts work and taught women this skill.[310]

1.5.8 Theological training

The other new development was that pastors' wives whose husbands did not have academic qualifications to go to theological colleges abroad went for theological training with their husbands at Lilongwe Bible School. This was an improvement from what was happening in the earlier period.[311] However, women spent only 12 weeks in training as opposed to their husbands 9 months training, during the 4-year course. The perception of the day was that women needed less training than the pastors, because it was the men that were going to be leaders in the church.

Since the work was growing, it was time to get organized. This needed competent local leadership. This was simplified because by 1970, Mrs Galatiya, Mrs Makhaya and Mrs Elizabeth Njolomole had come back from theological training. The Southern Baptist missionaries had been keen to train local leadership in theology since the beginning of Baptist work in Malawi. It is the conditions for this training that marginalized some interested women from the training.

Literacy was very important if one was to be trained, therefore, in the South East region, no one was trained in theology by 1970. The accepted literacy levels were defined by an English proficiency test administered at either Zimbabwe Baptist Seminary in Gweru or Zambia Baptist Seminary in Lusaka.[312] This did not imply that any woman who would pass the exam would be admitted for theological training, the woman had to be first a wife of a pastor to go for training. The missionary women themselves were all wives. There was no single woman among the early

---

[309] Int. Liddah Kalako, Ufulu Baptist Church, Lilongwe, 13.12.2000.

[310] In the later years she even collected some materials on history and although she was not a historian some do refer to her as such.

[311] This trend has continued to today. Int. Mrs Marylyn Upton, Lilongwe Baptist Seminary, Lilongwe, 5.1.2001.

[312] Int. Rev Galatiya, Likudzi Estate, Chipiliro Baptist Church 15.5.2000.

missionaries who came to Malawi although among them were wives who had done theological training, like Blanche Wester and Beverly Kingsley who had theological training independently of their husbands. They actually met their husbands while in Seminary.[313] But largely even among missionaries, the official training was restricted to men for pastoral work. For local men, as they went, their wives accompanied them. While there they would be trained in women's ministry skills that the missionary women used in ministry. This training included sewing skills and cooking skills apart from the WMU manual.[314]

The second condition was that the husbands of these wives should pass the English proficiency test.[315] It was therefore advantageous for women who were called into ministry to be married to literate husbands if they were to have any theological training. Key Convention women in the South East region such as Mrs Majomboshe, Mrs Chimenya, Mrs Masangano, Mrs Deliya Lichapa[316] did not go for this kind of training because their husbands did not have the academic qualifications to be admitted into theological colleges abroad.[317] Their husbands went through the Bible School in Lilongwe and became pastors; as such they were also pastors' wives. This is not strange among Baptists because even among pastors, not all are necessarily trained in either Bible School or seminary. This situation does limit women's liberation because of lack of correct interpretation of Baptist polity and doctrine that is enhanced with theological training.

The women who were able to go for theological training abroad were faced with the challenge of which subjects they would do. The wife would sit for the same English proficiency test as her husband. If she passed, she was admitted into a regular class with her husband and other male trainee pastors. In this class she did all the courses except Preaching and Ethics. Church History was optional. Apart from these courses, it was mandatory that she learnt the wife's course. The wife's course com-

---

[313] Int. Mrs Marylyn Upton, Lilongwe Baptist Theological Seminary, 5.1.2001.

[314] Int. Hildah Mallungo, Mtendere Baptist, Lilongwe, 14.3.2000.

[315] This test is no longer compulsory. It is administered only to those who are less educated and there is doubt in their knowledge of English. Int. Martha Chirwa, Zomba Theological College, 9.1.2001.

[316] See chapter 1 for the names.

[317] Int. Mrs Botoman, Chisomo Baptist Church, Blantyre 28.3.2000; Davidson Lichapa, Makolije Baptist Church, Zomba, 8.3.2000; Both were among the first core group at Chayima.

prised sewing and cooking skills and an overview of the Baptist Women's Organization (WMU).[318]

The nature of the training offered to local women was accommodated to the policy, which guided the missionary wives. They did not have to learn preaching because their ministry was not to lead but to support. They were however to master home management skills which would help them in their support ministries to their husbands. With these skills they could be hospitable and attract others to the Baptist message. Although the reason why they were not offered to do an *Ethics* course is not clear, it is possible that they thought that the course was not appropriate to women who were intended to be silent in the Church as opposed to being argumentative as is characteristic of dealing with ethical issues. This may symbolize some form of aggression, which is perceived to be appropriate for males only.

Even though pastors' wives could go for the 12 weeks training at Bible School in Lilongwe, there was still much dependence on women who had gone abroad for training in the organization of women's work in the South. While the Lower Shire benefited from Christina Kalenga, women in the South East benefited from Mrs Mary Galatiya from the Southern region, Mrs Njolomole Phiri and Mrs Makhaya from the Central region.[319] These worked hand in hand with the other local women as well as missionary women at that time.

Mrs Elizabeth Njolomole and Mrs Mary Makhaya were born in the Central region and were converted there. They become important in the history of women in the Southern region because they were influential figures at the national level. Mrs Elizabeth Njolomole was even an assistant pastor's wife at old Soche Baptist Church in Blantyre during this period, but she later on moved to Lilongwe, then to Mzuzu. During this period of revival these women helped to organize work in the South East region and even as far as Lower Shire where Christina Kalenga was.

One important means of organizing work at this time was the introduction of associations. The missionary women Mrs Wester and Mrs Kingsley were cooperating with these local women who had gone abroad for training with their husbands in achieving this. The missionary women

---

[318] WMU means Women's Missionary Union. Int. Hilda Mallungo, Mtendere Baptist, Lilongwe, 14.3.2000.
[319] Mrs Elizabeth Njolomole was in the North also during this period.

were already familiar with the concept of associations in the United States, but also in other African countries where they had worked.[320] The local women who had gone for theological training abroad also had observed how associations were organized in other countries.

Until 1972, women's work in Zomba and Migowi was coordinated from Jali. When the concept of associations started, the first association in the South East region was Jali. The women in the South South region and from the Centre that were trained abroad became instrumental in implementing this decision in corporation with the missionary women.

Mrs Elizabeth Njolomole was one of such catalysts. She became a Baptist during the early period, in 1964. In this year Leroy Albright went into the rural areas of Ntcheu district. Since the political climate was unfriendly to Europeans then, he usually asked for a police escort for his meetings. Elizabeth Njolomole's husband became the escort. Mrs Elizabeth Njolomole became a Baptist following her husband who was converted at such a meeting. She then joined Falls Baptist Church in Lilongwe, which was meeting in Mr. Kadango's store for Bible Study.[321] In the same year of 1964, Elizabeth Njolomole and her husband were sent to Blantyre to wait there as they prepared to go to Seminary. They worshiped at Cliccord House briefly and then left for theological training in Zimbabwe at Gweru Baptist Seminary in 1965.[322]

Elizabeth Njolomole has a Junior Certificate of Education; as such it was not difficult for her to pass the English proficiency test at the Seminary. She therefore was in the same class with her husband although she did not do ethics and preaching. Her studies were distracted by illness, she was ill most of the time of their training from 1965 to 1967.[323] She is a typical example of women who were converted to the Baptist Church first before being converted to Christ. She only got converted to Christ while in Seminary through the witness of a Baptist pastor there. When they came back, her husband became pastor of Soche Baptist Church. This meant that Elizabeth was to be the pastor's wife there. By this time, Rev and Mrs Galatiya were reconciled with Davidson whom they had not seen for a year. But even though there was such reconciliation, Mrs Davidson and her husband were not supervising the work in the

---

[320] Int. Hildah Mallungo, Mtendere Baptist, Lilongwe, 14.3.2000.
[321] Int. Elizabeth Njolomole, Mzuzu Baptist Church, 5.5.2000.
[322] Ibid.
[323] Ibid.

Blantyre Chichewa congregations. The coming of Elizabeth Njolomole, therefore, was a relief to Mary Galatiya who by this time was pastor's wife at Soche Baptist Church as well as at New Jerusalem Baptist Church.[324]

Mrs Makhaya also becomes an important figure in the history of women in the Southern Region, in that her husband was the first local person to direct the Bible School established in Lilongwe, to which some of the pastors in the Southern region went for their pastoral training. Through a biblical film shown around Ntcheu, Mary Makhaya and her husband were converted to the Baptist faith. She was converted from Zambezi Evangelical Church. She went to Gweru Baptist Seminary in 1965 and because of advanced age, she and her husband were there only for a year up to 1966.[325] Mary Makhaya had no direct ministry in the Bible School since during her time the pastors who went for training went without their wives. Even though she had restricted influence in the men's world of theological training, she was influential during this period when women's work was being organized on the national level.

The second association in the South East Region was Migowi. As work grew out of Jali to Mulanje, Migowi Association was formed to increase efficiency in church work. The third association was Chingale.[326] The concept of associations was not restricted to the South East Region, but was introduced also in the South South. The joint meetings in Blantyre organized by Mary Galatiya were formalized into Blantyre Association. Apart from Blantyre churches, Thyolo and Lower Shire churches were part of this association.[327]

1.5.9 Conclusion

During this period Convention women were less liberated than their Baptist polity and doctrine could permit, because of zeitgeist, culture and the way missionaries defined Baptist polity and doctrine.

Convention women in the South East region enjoyed comparatively limited freedoms as opposed to the South South region in leadership

---

[324] Int. Rev Galatiya, Chipiliro Baptist Church, 15.5.2000.

[325] Int. Elizabeth Njolomole, Mzuzu Baptist Church, 5.5.2000.

[326] Int. Mellia Makina, Mwanafumu Baptist Church, 21.3.2000. Also South East Executive, Zomba Baptist Church, 2.2000.

[327] The size of associations between the South South and the South East greatly differed with the South South associations having more churches.

roles in this period in spite of the fact that matrilineal society gives liberty for such roles. This is mainly due to the negative effects of missionary influence, especially in the theology acted of the missionary women, for example, in their policy of excluding pastors' wives from the theological training at Lilongwe Bible School. The attainment of more liberty for women in the South South region in New Jerusalem after the split is a testimony to this. However this lack of freedom the women had during this period cannot be blamed entirely on missionary Christianity. The other reason was probably because of their former church background which was restrictive as such they needed time to unlearn their past; learn and internalize the Baptist distinctives, which are potentially liberating. However the reasons why women in the South East and South South still remained in support roles might have been due to an interplay of factors which are hard to state at this stage.

The revival of the 1970s and 1980s influenced growth of women's work numerically and geographically with some places having more pronounced growth than others as more congregations were being planted. The position of women during this period was enhanced as regards equal opportunities of service especially during revival crusades. Nevertheless, there was a marked difference between the roles women played and those played by men. This was again mainly due to local women yielding to missionary influences as revival increased cooperation between missionary and local women. This shows that even though revival does increase women's power of service, this power is sometimes obstructed by other factors. Some women are overcome with such factors, but some choose to live above them and exhibit much freedom. For the latter, they need a church that will accommodate them, and Baptist doctrine and polity do allow this. As such it would be interesting to investigate whether such liberation of women influenced conversions of women from restrictive church traditions to Baptist during this time of revival.

The revival spirit enforced co-operation locally and externally and this became useful in the organization of work in Southern Malawi. However the Baptist Church should reckon with the influences on church growth that are typically western as seen in the methods utilized in the propagation of the gospel during this period. Such influences are carried on even in the next period as seen in chapter four. The fact that these influences have achieved much growth during this period may indicate their relevance to Southern Malawi. But there seems to be a reduction of growth in terms of geographical spread of women's work over time as these methods are utilized. This is seen in the leveling of growth in this chapter in some areas where such methods were used earlier as well as in chapter four in areas where such methods were utilized later. Chapter 2 and 4 therefore, are a contribution to analyzing the relevance of these methods.

Chapter 2

UMODZI WA AMAYI IN MALAWI AT THE GRASSROOTS

The story of *Umodzi wa Amayi* in Malawi is important to describe because it shows how Baptist women have responded to the lack of optimum freedoms they enjoyed in their church. Further, the story shows how women have capitalized on consolidating leadership over fellow women to show their worth in the church. Again the story shows the freedoms Baptist women enjoy in the absence of centralized structures that tend to impose their rules on their members. This is shown in the disparities as seen in the actualization of the organisation at grassroots level.

Unlike the women's organizations in other churches such as *Mvano* of Blantyre Synod, *Umodzi* does not conform to uniformity as regards its obligations and rules. This chapter shows how different congregations in the South have actualized the prescribed dictates of the organization. Since the inception of *Umodzi* in 1975, the founding members stated the rules and regulations of the organization and have since then attempted to reinforce them on member congregations through trained leadership and booklets.[1] The argument of this chapter is that these prescriptions have not always been received, and that even where they have been received, there are disparities between congregations, a testimony to the fact that Baptists believe in the autonomy of a congregation and follow the individual consciences of its members and as such are not forced to conform to uniformity, except in matters concerning major issues of doctrine. This is an expression of freedom as opposed to the more restrictive regulations in more centralized church traditions, where decisions made at the top have to be followed to the letter by the people at the grass-

---

[1] They carried forward the rules and regulations stipulated in the WMU manuals produced in Zimbabwe and Zambia. These booklets were translated into Chichewa.

roots.[2] To achieve this, I will give a brief overview of the organization and then discuss the realities at the grass roots.

2.1 History and rationale of the organization

The history of *Umodzi* can only make sense if the position of women before its institution in Southern Malawi is highlighted. The argument in this chapter is that the organization was an option for women's engagement in church and society, in view of the fact that men dominated positions in church and society.

Convention women in the earlier period were mainly involved in support roles. Although this was highly supported by missionary women, Convention women saw a chance that by organizing themselves into an organization, they could capitalize on their meager opportunities to consolidate power and prove their worth in the service of the church. This tallied with the experiences of the missionary women. They were also sidelined by men in their engagement in the church not only in Malawi but even in their home church in America. This is probably why they instituted their Women's Missionary Union (WMU) and sought to translate it to Malawi. The other motivation for missionary women to start this organization was probably to appease local Malawians in the event that their *theology acted* did not suggest women leadership in the church. The creation of this organization was to fill this gap.

The symbols of the organization became keys in consolidating this power. The foremost was the uniform. By using the uniform in some of the activities in church, they separated themselves from the non-members of the organization and gained power over them in those areas where non-members could not participate. One of such instances was in the ministry of the church at funerals. Before the organization was started, the women just stayed near the coffin while the body was in the house. There were Christian songs, but it was mostly men who led them, while women joined in the singing. Preaching, even in the house, was only done by the male members of the church. There was also no organized procession at funerals, so women were not so much valued. The men would prepare the coffin, dig the grave, bury the dead, preach, and lead songs while women remained in the background.[3] Women were not

---

[2] This is also true with some Baptist churches such as PIM.
[3] Int. Rev Ntuwe, Rev Paulo Sabola, Rev John Moses, Zomba, 19.5.2000.

even allowed to pray at funerals. At Chipinimbi Baptist Church in the South East region, for example, women only started to pray at a funeral in 1997. Since the beginning of this church in 1985, this had not been possible.[4] The reason for low involvement of women at funerals was that before the organization, women were not taught what roles they could play apart from the culturally prescribed ones like cooking and collecting water and firewood. However even though women do get involved significantly at funerals, with the beginning of the organization there are still other roles that only men can do. These are digging the grave for an adult person and burying him or her.

However the women only became organized into an organization in the South East region in 1967. At the beginning of the organization, there was no uniform and even the organization itself was defined broadly as inclusive of all women in the Convention. This was in accordance with the WMU guidelines in America. However adjustments to such guidelines have been made to suit the Malawian context, where women belonging to such an organisation are usually those with the uniform. One of such adjustments has been the inclusion of a uniform in the organization.

The institution of the uniform was in line with the cultural demands from some of the women. In the South East, for example, women had to keep their head covered by putting on a headdress.[5] Long hair was not considered as a covering for a woman's head.[6] Therefore women with long hair were also required to put on a headdress. If a woman was seen without a headdress, she was taken to task by the church authorities.[7] Therefore it was proper that the women's uniform should include a headdress.

However with the beginning of women's organization, *compared to the earlier period*, took an active role in other church activities, even apart from preaching during a Sunday service. It should be noted that the organization was not embraced by all women at the same time. This was because information about the women's organization was not disseminated to all the churches at the same time in view that Baptist Churches do not rely on a central government. Ntokota Baptist Church in Jali, for

---

4   Ibid.
5   Int. Mrs Mahere, Chayima Baptist Church, 20.3.2000.
6   Cf. 1 Cor. 11-16, "For long hair is given her as a covering".
7   Int. Mrs Mahere, Chayima Baptist Church, 20.3.2000.

example, only started the organization in 1968, a year later.[8] As a result, women by then did not have a uniform nor did they play a major role at funerals.[9] The uniform took time to be implemented in the churches. At Chirima Baptist Church Chisi Island, by 2001, there was no one with a uniform. By 1967, there was still no uniform at Soche Baptist Church, the first mother Church in Blantyre, no wonder the uniform was introduced even much later in the rural churches.[10]

Umodzi is not an extraordinary women's organisation. It follows the wind of women's organisations both locally and internationally. Over the centuries, there has been a deliberate move by church women to con-solidate power in the churches by organizing themselves into an organi-sation. Through such organisations, women have influenced the life of their churches, which are dominated by male leadership.

Umodzi as an organization is distinct from the general Baptist women's work that occurred in the early period. During this early period, there were indeed missionary women and a few local Malawians, but enough ground work had to be done, for the women to organize them-selves into an organization. As they got organized, the nature of activities changed. Women were not only involved in promoting their Baptist be-liefs but also aimed at delivering information on their identity.

2.2 Definition of the organization

The organization is in short and officially referred to as *Umodzi* and is an organization of all women that are rightful members of Baptist Conven-tion churches. *Umodzi* is not an original creation by Malawians; rather it is a derivation from the Women's Missionary Union (WMU), an organiza-tion that started in the United States of America in 1888.[11]

A survey of congregations in the south has shown that the name *Umodzi* is not used neither in all Baptist Convention congregations in the south nor by every member in a particular congregation where it is used.

---

[8] This is an organization, which was introduced later in Malawi. Int. Mrs Malikebu, Zomba Baptist Church, 28.11.1999; Hany Longwe, Baptist Theological Seminary, 14.3.2000. The organization is similar to Mvano. See Rachel Banda, A Comprehen-sive Study of Women's Organizations in the Southern Malawi, Module 3 paper, MA, University of Malawi.

[9] Journal by DL. Gazamiyala, 11.7.68, Zomba.

[10] Int. Rosebay Botoman, Chisomo Baptist Church, 28.3.2000.

[11] WMU Manual, Zimbabwe Baptist Church, 1979, p. 2.

Often, *Umodzi* is referred to by other names such as *Mvano*, *Chigwiri-zano* and *Umanyano*.[12] This is because by the time the organization was formed, there were already other women organizations operational in churches such as Blantyre Synod, Livingstonia Synod and Churches of Christ among others. In addition some of the members who are in Convention churches in the south belonged to such organizations before they became Baptists. These members were too used to these other terminologies to forget them.

Although *Umodzi* is an unfamiliar term in other churches, it is a well-known name in Baptist Convention churches. In a survey conducted in Zomba, Mayela and Songani, all interviewees who were asked "What is *Umodzi*?" affirmatively indicated the knowledge of the group.[13]

2.3 The aims of the organization

2.3.1 Official aim

Delegates attending first leadership training at Baptist Bible School in Lilongwe

---

[12] A survey of pastors' wives at Jerusalem, Misesa, South Lunzu, Mpinda, Zomba, Makolije for example found that such names were used in referring to *Umodzi*. (Int. pastors' wives, Lilongwe Baptist Seminary, 13.3.2001).
[13] See Rachel Banda, "*Umodzi* uniform and its implications", forum paper, post graduate colloquium, Dept. of Theology and Religious Studies, University of Malawi, 1999.

The official aim of the organization is to preach Christ to others, originally stipulated by the founders of the mother body, WMU in America, which was started primarily as an answer to the women's quest to share Christ with others in the community.[14] Just as WMU in America was designed to fulfill this aim through Bible study, preaching, giving and sharing, fellowship, training and prayer, Umodzi was officially designed to do the same.[15] However, interviews show that women in the south perceive this aim differently. This is shown in the activities of the organization.

At the beginning of each woman's local, associational, regional or national meeting, for example, Umodzi women remind themselves of the aim of their organization.[16] The aim is contained in a recital from 1 Corinthians 3:9a "For we are God's fellow workers". This recital is always recited in Chichewa, "Pakuti ife ndife amodzi ogwira ntchito ndi Mulungu". This recital is supposed to be memorized by every member who becomes part of the organization. Added to this short verse are other three phrases, not from the Bible: "Chirimo cha Mulungu, Chimango cha Mulungu, ndife". These additional phrases are however not known to all members in the Southern region. They are a later addition.

2.3.2 Perceived aim of the organization by the women

Practically, women perceive themselves as "soldiers for Christ". This is translated into a popular chorus "Ndine msilikali, ndine msilikali, ndine msilikali wa Yesu". At most national, regional, associational and local meetings, women sing this song with enthusiasm and occasionally use it as one of the marching songs in the neighbourhood of the venue of the meeting. While singing and marching, they salute and stump their feet like police or army officers, to the glory of their God.[17] In this way, it is clear that Umodzi women perceive themselves to be soldiers and workers for God. All Umodzi women are supposed to memorize the seven prescribed aims of the organization with the verses related to them,[18]

---

[14] Its sister organization WMU was also designed to include all Baptist Convention women.
[15] WMU manual, 1979, p. 2.
[16] Ibid.
[17] At local, regional, associational, national meeting that I have attended, this was done.
[18] For an outline of the aims and the verses see later in the chapter.

however not all women do that, basically because of lack of literacy, but also lack of knowledge of this prerequisite.[19]

2.4 Training

2.4.1 The history of training

Since the missionaries had facilitated the training of women leaders at Gweru Baptist Seminary and Lusaka Baptist Seminary, they generated leaders who were able to train local women in the practices of the organization. In the early period such women were few, missionary women organized joint women's meetings in Lilongwe to which delegates from the South region as well would go for the training in the organization. The trainings were well patronized by women from the Southern region because missionaries paid for transport, accommodation and food for the delegates to the meeting which were always held at Bible School in Lilongwe until the 1990s. Although such training sessions were done impromptu, they later became yearly events. Women would go to Lilongwe for a weekend and learn home craft skills, as well as the regulations of the organisation. Other programmes included listening to preaching, testimonies and drama.[20]

2.4.2 Training and indigenization

Attendance at such meetings went down with the indigenization policy of the late 1980s, when missionaries removed subsidy for such training costs. Even though the Convention had already been formed in 1975, it did not have enough funds to sponsor such women's activities. The only sponsorship was reserved for the national executive committee members who would travel to such meetings to teach. Ordinary women at grass root level had to raise their own funds to pay for transport, food and accommodation. This was affordable by those in paid employment or

---

[19] The three women at a South East region meeting on 29.10.2000 who were going through the tradition of putting on a uniform could not even recite one of these verses. Women at Mpando Baptist Church in Thyolo put on uniforms without memorizing verses and were rebuked by the Convention leaders.

[20] Interviews with early women such as Mrs Nanthambwe of Mauluka Baptist, Mrs Makina of Mwanafumu Baptist, testify to this fact.

whose husbands worked for an income. Most of the rural women in Jali, Thyolo and Lower Shire could no longer afford such meetings.

Missionaries did not only withdraw funding for transport, accommodation and food, they also stopped the free distribution of booklets for training, including those on WMU in Zimbabwe and Zambia. Such booklets had to be bought. In the early years, the costs were very affordable, as a result a lot of the congregations were able to purchase them. However, the prices on the booklets have since increased and very few people can afford them. There are, after the missionaries' withdrawal, also hardly any centres left where such books can be stored for sale. This means that few congregations can have such booklets.

2.4.3 Training and decentralization

Although associations existed in the early period, it is the decision to conduct training at the regional level that boosted the number of women trained in women's work. The creation of regions took place in 1993.[21] Women could then get together in their regions or associations to receive training. Even though there were still transport and accommodation costs to be met, these costs were less than those needed to attend training meetings in Lilongwe. Accommodation was free because delegates usually slept in church buildings. Some places such as Jali and Mayaka had even special buildings known as "training centres" for this purpose. At such places, delegates enjoyed free accommodation, and many women would attend such meetings.[22] Even now, the number of women to attend regional meetings is much higher than previous numbers at the national level.

However, this decentralization of training meant that regions that lacked trained women leaders became a burden on a few leaders elsewhere. The South East region was an example, as women leaders from Blantyre in the south and Lilongwe in the centre had to visit such places to conduct training. Mrs Mary Galatiya, Mrs Makhaya, Mrs Elizabeth Njolomole among others were involved in this way. In the current years Baptist women in the South region are able to train local women without reliance on women from elsewhere.

---

[21] Int. Mrs Martha Chirwa, Zomba Theological College, 12.1.2001.
[22] The attendance at regional meetings was much higher than at the national meetings in Lilongwe. Ibid.

2.4.4 Literacy and training

The other problem with training was the use of WMU booklets. Congregations with no women who could read the booklets could not use them. This is probably why different messages about the organization have been transmitted to the grass root women in the Southern region. The result is that the Southern region has always done things differently from women in other regions. The regulations and rules concerning the usage of the uniform in this region for example vary very much from what is agreed upon by the organization and is practiced. This liberation is because each congregation is autonomous and has the power to make its own decisions

Mrs Mary Galatiya, Mrs Makhaya and Elizabeth Njolomole in attendance at a BWUSA meeting

2.5 Weekly meetings

2.5.1 The situation

Although Baptist Convention women perceive themselves and are perceived to be women of the Bible, they face a lot of challenges in this area. Not all women have access to a Bible as they read it only at a

Sunday service and at their weekly meetings. Weekly meetings are a valuable resource for their Bible reading because in most congregations that is the only place where women hear fellow women explain the Bible to them. Sunday services are important but it is usually men who preach. As such women do not have the privilege of listening to the experiences of fellow women with God.

2.5.2 Time table for weekly meetings

Umodzi women traditionally hold their meetings once a week. However, not all congregations in the south do have such meetings. A survey of seven congregations in the region showed that two congregations did not hold a weekly meeting. These were Chirima Baptist Church on Chisi Island in Lake Chirwa, and Ntokota Baptist in Zomba rural. Chirima Baptist does not have weekly meetings because it is cut off from the mainland influences and lacks encouragement from the supervising church, Mpinda Baptist.[23] The women in this church are not aware of such programmes and do not have booklets to guide them in Bible study.

Ntokota Baptist Church in Jali has often suffered leadership crises and this has discouraged women from active participation in the church even though one of their members was the regional secretary of *Umodzi* in the year 2000. Since the death of the founder of the church, Rev Gazamiyala, there have been constant struggles on ownership of the church between the children of Gazamiyala and some church members. Because of such conflicts the church is now split and two additional congregations, Holy Mount Baptist Church and Jali Baptist Church have been formed from it.

On the other hand, some congregations do have weekly meetings. In the sample of seven congregations five held meetings every week. Some congregations hold meetings more than once a week. Two out of the five did this. South Lunzu Baptist Church in Blantyre holds its weekly meetings on Thursdays and Tuesdays. Zomba Baptist Church also holds its meetings on the same days. The additional day is reserved for visitation or charity work. This extra day has been necessary because it is difficult to combine Bible studies with visitation and or charity work in rural areas where travelling is mostly on foot.

---

[23]   Int. focus group, Chirima Baptist Church, 28.1.2001.

Not all *Umodzi* groups hold their meetings on Thursday. Some have changed the day of meeting because of collision with market days. Women in urban churches go to work during weekdays and have changed their day of meeting to the weekend. Blantyre Baptist Church for example meets once a month on a Saturday for this reason.[24]

2.5.3 Source of Bible reading materials

At a regular Bible study meeting, the custom is to follow booklets which were originally produced every three months. Liddah Kalako largely wrote these booklets.[25] A few booklets were also produced through a special writer's workshop organized by missionary women. At such workshops, women who had the ability to write, not necessarily with theological training, were called together.[26] Such workshops were either held in Malawi or abroad. In 1993, Martha Chirwa and Teresa Day went to Nairobi on such business.[27] Contributions from participants at a workshop were compiled together into a booklet. Such booklets were translated into Chichewa. This was not because Chichewa was the national language, but because in some churches, there were church materials in other local languages. It was likely because Baptist Churches started in the Southern region where Chichewa was the dominant language.[28]

2.5.4 Availability of Bible study materials

These study materials were plentiful in the early period because they were distributed free. In the later years, they became expensive and not available to the grassroots people. The price is increased by transport costs for congregations which are far away from Blantyre where BACOMA offices are or Lilongwe where Baptist Publication House is, since these booklets can only be purchased at these places. In many congre-

---

[24] Int. Mrs Martha Chirwa, Zomba Theological College, 15.3.2001.
[25] Int. Mrs Liddah Kalako, Lilongwe Baptist Seminary, March 2000.
[26] By the time Liddah Kalako was writing the booklets, she had no theological training, she was not even a pastor's wife. Liddah Kalako became the first woman to graduate from Lilongwe Baptist Seminary on 24th June 2000. She died a month after graduation.
[27] Int. Mrs Martha Chirwa Zomba Theological College, 15.3.2001.
[28] An attempt to translate these booklets into other languages such as Tumbuka is a recent development.

gations far from these places, such as in Jali, Mayaka, Thyolo, Chikwawa, there is an outcry for such Bible study materials.

2.5.5 Relevance of Bible study materials

The other issue concerning the relevance of the booklets is the literacy levels of the audience, especially in the South East. However some of the early missionaries tried to address this problem. Mrs Blanche Wester, for example, used to teach local women about the Bible through Chichewa songs, and even now she is fondly remembered for the biblical songs she taught women in the South East region with the aim of helping local women to memorize Scripture.

Some of such biblical songs were based on Romans 10:9, 10, Romans 10:13 and Mark 1:17.[29] The advantage of this method is that the oral communicators can easily learn biblical verses. Since the majority of the women in the South were functionally illiterate, this became an effective way of teaching the Bible. This tradition has stood the test of times, and even now it is widely used in Baptist congregations.

It is a method not only used by the functionally illiterate but by the literate as well. Both the literate and the illiterate are encouraged to memorize certain verses through songs. Most of the verses for memory are related to the aims of the organisation already outlined above, but there are also verses which are designed to help them tell others about Christ.[30] These verses show clearly how one can be saved through Christ, like Romans 3:23, Luke 13:3, showing the need for repentance; John 3:16 showing the importance of believing in Christ; Romans 10:13 and Romans 10:9-10, encouraging them to confess Christ as Lord. Every woman who owns a uniform is supposed to have memorized these verses. Nevertheless, it should not be assumed that woman who own a uniform have a personal faith in Christ, some do not.[31]

---

[29] Int. Mrs Mwanakhu and Mrs Nankwenya, Mpinda Baptist Church, 2.9.2000.
[30] These verses are widely referred to by these women as "the steps to salvation" verses. Indeed they are logically relayed, to lead someone to a personal faith in Christ. See 1961 *Umodzi wa Amayi a Baptist a ku Malawi*, BCM, p. 1.
[31] Still a few women in the South East region have confessed Christ into their lives for the first time, even though they had a uniform, during my practical ministry with them.

2.5.6   Other activities

Even though Bible reading is a major activity during the weekly meetings, other activities are also included during this meeting. A typical example of a weekly programme would include choruses, opening with prayer, a women's song, preaching, discussion and announcement of weekly women's activities. The meetings close with further choruses and a closing prayer. Just as the verses relating to the aims of the organization and the steps to salvation, the women are supposed to memorize the women's song. It is customary that at each *Umodzi* meeting this song is sung as an anthem. Women stand at attention while singing this song, probably borrowing from the tradition of how the national anthem in Malawi was sung during the Kamuzu era. Below is the women's song in Chichewa and English.

Idzani azimayi	Come women
Konse lalikirani	Preach everywhere
Muyimbire	Sing
Khristu ndiye Mulungu	Christ is God
Khristu anauka	Christ is risen
Khristu ndiye Nyali	Christ is the Lamp
M'tamandeni.	Praise Him.
Idzani ana onse	Come all children
Ndi Alongo onse	With all your sisters/brothers
Phunzitseni	Teach
Kuli wodwalatu	There are sick people
Akufoka mtima	They have a weak heart
Akukhala mdima	They are in darkness
Pempherani	Pray.
Gwirani ntchito zanu	Do your work
Limbikani ndi mphamvu	Persist with strength
Mupatseni	Give
Chikondano chanu	Your love
Mtima idzakondwa	Your heart will rejoice
Ndi chikondi chache	With His love
Yembekeza.	Wait in anticipation
Ngati tidzazituta	If we bring them
Mulungu atipatsa	God will give us
Mu zambiri	In many things
Khristu ndi wofatsa	Christ is gentle
Onse adzamfuna	All will want him

Ali mphoto yathu	He is our gift
Ndi chotsata.	To follow Him.

However there are small variations to the order of the weekly meetings within different congregations, also depending on the circumstances of the day. For example, in some congregations, not every weekly meeting includes Bible reading. Other activities such as homecraft lessons can be included. This programme of women's organization is typical to other church women groups as well like at Dorcas meetings in the Seventh-day Adventist Church.[32] In any case, there is no prescribed order of these weekly meetings in Baptist Convention churches. The order has been passed on orally and can always be adjusted. However the women's song is a constant at every women's meeting.

A survey of some congregations shows a general trend of other pro-grammes that are included in *Umodzi* weekly meetings. When asked about what programmes the women had at their *Umodzi* meetings, most Baptist congregations such as Mpinda in Mikuyu association had no other programmes apart from Bible reading.

Sewing and cooking programmes were present during the era of the early women missionaries. In Jali area for example, in the era of Mrs Janet Malabwanya and Mrs Blanche Wester, many congregations had such programmes. During the period of indigenization, such programmes could not be maintained because they are expensive. It is clear that out-side funding is necessary to maintain these programmes. This has been seen in the South East region where the reintroduction of sewing lessons with congregations has only been possible with a continued supply of sewing materials.[33] However, such programmes are important to church growth because they help to pull women to the church. Further, such de-velopment activities empower women in their homes and the church.

2.6 *Umodzi* women and funerals

Apart from fulfilling the above roles, *Umodzi* women play a significant role at funerals. Women at a local congregation teach each other on how to minister at funerals of their church members and others. Some of the

---

[32] See Rachel Banda, "Comprehensive Survey of Women's Organisations in South-ern Malawi", module 3, MA, University of Malawi, 2000.
[33] This has been my experience from March 2000 to November 2000.

things they learn are how to wash a dead body for burial, how to arrange flowers for decoration at the grave site,[34] special songs to be sung at the funeral and duties to be done before and after burial. The women also teach each other about procedures during the funeral procession. In this they have to coordinate well with each other and the male members at the funeral.

2.6.1 Determinants for roles Umodzi women play at funerals

The roles *Umodzi* women play are conditioned by the regulations and rules of the organisation. Such prescriptions are not written down but are transferred orally and through minutes. However, Baptist women unlike other church groups show much freedom in that they do not always follow such dictates and even when they do, not to the letter. Each congregation is free to adhere to their own rules and regulations.

2.6.1.1 Leadership position

According to prescribed norms relating to funerals, *Umodzi* women can only put on a uniform at a funeral of a deacon, pastor and pastor's wife or of an *Umodzi* member. They are not allowed to put on a uniform at the death of their child or spouse who is not in this category. However, this prescription is not followed in the Southern region. *Umodzi* women put on a uniform at a funeral of every member of the church including their children.[35] This has always been met with resistance at the national level, albeit without success. In the Southern region, even the children do get the honour of *Umodzi* women putting on uniforms. However in the category of children, only children above a certain age have access to such a privilege of a uniformed funeral. In most cases, a child aged about 4 months and below does not have such a privilege.[36]

2.6.1.2 Kutenga mwana

The time at which the ritual of *kutenga mwana* is done can be shortened or lengthened depending on the congregation. It also depends on whether the parents of the child *"anatenga mwana"* (have "taken" the

---

[34] Flower arrangement lessons are only in places where such traditions are followed.
[35] Almost all congregations in the rural areas I interviewed follow this custom.
[36] Int. Mrs Elias Emmanuel, Mauluka Baptist Church, Mphyuphyu, 13.7.2000.

child). Although the expression suggests the lifting of a child, it does not mean that, and in any case the parents do already lift the child many times. This custom refers to the parents resuming sexual intercourse after the birth of a child. This has to be done ritually. The parents take the child on their mat or bed and perform sex in her or his presence. The husband smears his sperms on the forehead of the child and bounces the child in the air a few times, to give strength to the baby.[37] This dramatized activity symbolizes that the child is now a full human being. Before this ritual, the child is not.

If death occurs before then the child can only be buried by women. No man including the husband is allowed to go to the graveyard. The grave and the burial of the body is all a woman's activity. At such a death Umodzi women in the South region put only on the headdress of the uniform. A prayer is offered before going to the grave and at the grave site. Otherwise, the women go to the grave without singing Christian songs.

The time for "kutenga mwana" is supposed to come with the child beginning to smile. Therefore it is not unusual to have a husband force a child to smile faster, in order to win sexual favours from his wife. Again, a wife in some cases hides her child from the husband in case he/she smiles at him earlier than she desires to resume sexual relations. At the death of the child, the church leadership asks the couple privately as to whether the child has gone through "kutenga mwana". When the parents have done that, men are also involved in the burial of the child. The question as to whether all Baptist women practice kutenga mwana or not is important. At a women's meeting in Balaka in May 2001, women gave different responses to this question. The majority seems to practice this custom seriously while a few do not. Those who don't, claim their liberation from this cultural phenomenon through the Lordship of Jesus in their lives.

2.6.1.3 Umodzi women and "nthayo"

Umodzi women do not put on a uniform at a funeral of nthayo (still birth). This child is also buried by women alone. The fact that the church has complied to this cultural practice raises a key theological question on

---

[37] The details of kutenga mwana differ considerably from society to society. For information on a Chewa version of the ritual see: J. van Breugel, Chewa Traditional Religion, Blantyre: CLAIM-Kachere, 2001, pp. 179-183.

what the church believes to be the time "when a human being is a full human being." Is it at conception or later? This is because burial of a full human being is usually done by both men and women and even in the case of a child, a headdress of the uniform is usually worn.

2.6.1.4 Funerals and conversion

Members in Baptist congregations take church involvement at funerals very seriously. In fact some have left churches because they were denied a church burial. At Malirano Baptist Church in Zomba for example, Mrs Chiwaya left her Four Square Gospel Church for this reason. While in that church, she lost a child and because her church did not provide a church burial for her child, she joined a Baptist church.[38] Umodzi women seem to be mindful of this need, and occasionally assist at funerals of people who have been denied a church burial.[39]

Although they do not put on a uniform at such funerals, they sing and give spiritual support for the bereaved. Some Baptist pastors also freely preach at such funerals. Through this, some have been converted to Baptist churches. Such a practice is not done by women in other churches such as CCAP and the Catholic Church. To the latter, only the faithful members of their church deserve their singing and spiritual guidance at funerals.[40]

2.7 Do Umodzi women Christianize funerals?[41]

Although Umodzi women have actively participated at funerals, they still struggle between being true to their Christian faith and their culture. They have indeed added a Christian perspective to funerals among Baptist churches although they have not Christianized them. This is evident in a typical procedure of funerals in the South East region. In this procedure, the women are faced with some cultural practices that may be contrary to their Christian faith, but not always.

---

[38] Int. Rev Mtuwe, Rev Mosses Chipinimbi Baptist Church, 19.5.2000.
[39] Rev Ng'oma, Mayela Baptist Church, 20.5.2000.
[40] Observations at two funerals of Blantyre Synod and one Catholic funeral in Zomba.
[41] The issue of Christianizing funerals is also a concern among other churches. See Sebastian S.W. Mwenembako, Funeral Customs, BA, University of Malawi, 2001.

When a person dies, the *Umodzi* women wash the body, even if it was already washed by the hospital staff, if it is the body of a woman. If it is the body of a male member of the church, men wash the body. This act is referred to as *"kusambika maliro"* (washing the dead body). The washing of the body is done not only for the sake of cleanliness but also to make sure that the body is well set (for example no twisting of limbs). If such deformation takes place, except in an accident, those who are washing the body may even pay a fine for this misconduct.

In the morning, the women dress the body. If the woman had a *Umodzi* uniform, she is dressed in her uniform. Other dresses or pieces of material can be added in the coffin only as cushions. The body is then laid in a coffin or wrapped in a mat (coffins can be expensive especially in rural areas and some cannot afford them). Other congregations make contributions to buying wood for the coffin.

The coffin is left in a house, usually in the sitting room on a mat. Women sit around the coffin, singing till it is time to go to the burial site. The following procedure is followed when it is time to go to the grave-yard.

2.7.1 Procedure for the procession of the body to the gravesite

2.7.1.1 In the house

While in the sitting room, a master of ceremony, usually a man begins by saying. "Now we are starting off on our journey" (to the grave site). When it is a woman's body, the *Umodzi* women carry the body to the doorsteps of the house where they are assisted by the male members to carry the body to the outside yard of the house. All the people, church and non-church alike sit outside around the yard. Men usually sit with fellow men and so do the women. Children do not sit in this crowd, unless very closely related to the dead.

2.7.1.2 In the yard of the house

When the body is taken to the graveyard, the master of the ceremony asks one person to pray. The prayer is about placing the bereaved in the hands of God so that they should mourn as those with hope. He or she prays that God would help the bereaved to seek God so that they should also find the dead person alive in heaven. The challenge that the church has at this juncture is to say the truth concerning a member who was obviously not following God. The church usually would commend even such a person as going to heaven. Culturally it is considered rude to say anything bad about the dead.

After the prayer, the church leads the congregation at the funeral in church songs. It is usually a man who leads such songs. While the body was in the house, some of the *Umodzi* women were outside arranging flowers to put on the coffin. This tradition is new and is still not a common practice in all congregations in the South East region. Originally flowers were not used because the missionaries discouraged people to use them at such a sorrowful occasion. To missionaries, flowers were a symbol of joy and were not appropriate at funerals. However, this missionary culture is breaking down because of influences from other church traditions. Many Christian churches use flowers at funerals and Baptists have also conformed to such a practice. However, there are still some congregations in the South East such as in Mikuyu and Jali areas, which do not use flowers at funerals. Zomba and Chingale Associations in the same region do use flowers. They collect flowers and put them in an orderly manner and place them on top of the coffin or mat (if the body was wrapped in a mat). As they bring flowers, the congregation stops singing and at this time it is only the *Umodzi* women that sing their special song for putting on flowers. This song is usually a secret to the *Umodzi* women. They learnt it well at their weekly meetings, and they also rehearsed the order of putting the flowers on the coffin or mat during such meetings.

2.7.2 Speeches at the graveyard

After this singing, and the flower custom, the master of ceremony calls on different people to speak while all are seated in the graveyard. It is usually a representative from the political parties in the area,[42] the chief, a relative, a church member or someone from the work place, if the de-

---

[42] The parties sometimes take this as an opportunity to campaign for support but these days they often do not show up.

ceased was employed.[43] A dead person is still considered to be part of his/her home community of the living. It is therefore isolating the dead, if he or she is buried away from his/her home area. In inevitable circumstances such as lack of transport, if the dead body is buried elsewhere, there is a ritual of collecting the spirit of the dead to his or her home area. People go to the graveyard and invite the spirit of the dead to come home in prayer. Those carrying such a spirit are not supposed to speak to anyone till they reach the home of the deceased. In patrilineal societies, as among the Sena of Nsanje, the wife is traditionally supposed to be buried in the husbands home, although, upon agreement, the wife can also be buried in her home area. In the event that the wife is buried in the husband's home, the spirit of the wife is not considered to be alien since she already was part of her husband's community before she died.

Such rituals are practiced among Baptist women, but not all follow them. Among those that do not, some claim that interacting with the spirit of the dead is idolatry. It is worship of the dead and God at the same time. This minority group enjoys such liberation because of their relationship to and faith in Christ. The church, however, does not punish someone, even if she is involved in this spirit ritual. The church leaves the decision to the member concerned based on her individual conscience.

2.7.3 Preaching

When the speeches are made, one or two songs are sung and then a church leader, usually a pastor, reads the Bible and preaches to the congregation. Many preachers take this opportunity to sensitize people about the need to go to church. Although many people do not go to church, most of them go to funerals and preachers recognize this and take preaching very seriously at such an occasion. There are women as well as men who have become Baptists even through such funerals sermons.

2.7.4 Procession to the graveyard

After preaching, a song is sung and the body is carried to the graveyard. If it is a woman's body, the *Umodzi* women carry the coffin or mat a little

---

[43] In Malawi it is very uncommon to bury the person in town when one dies there. Even in the event that she or he died outside Malawi there is usually an attempt to bring the body back to Malawi.

distance from the yard but are later helped by the men. The carrying of the body over the few first meters is just a symbol that women are burying their fellow woman. However the men recognize that a dead body is heavy and so they help women to carry it over the bigger part of the distance.

In the procession to the grave, *Umodzi* women lead the songs and usually are in front of the dead body with their uniform. The women indeed add colour to the funeral and become an inspiration to others to join their church. To women who are in the church, this encourages them to join the women's organisation.

2.7.5 At the graveyard

When the procession reaches the gravesite, the coffin or mat is laid near the grave. One person prays (usually a man). The people, who made the speeches at the house, do them again at the gravesite. A leader of the church, usually a pastor, leads the liturgy of burying the dead person. After the liturgy, as *Umodzi* women sing choruses, the men help to lower the body into the grave, and then some men begin to cover the grave with earth. It is always men who cover the grave of an adult person. The church leader preaches again and closes with a word of prayer. After this, most people disperse to their respective homes. However, it is customary that close relatives and the church people go back to the house of mourning.

2.7.6 Back to the house of mourning

Often before people reach the funeral house, there is a container of water where people from the graveyard are offered water to wash their hands. In most cases, this water is mixed with traditional herbs to chase away the evil spirits of the dead. It is believed that if one does not wash in these herbs, he or she or family members would get sick. Some church people ignore this ritual because they either believe that evil spirits cannot be washed away by this herbal mixture or do not believe that a dead person leaves them with evil spirits. Such people are sometimes taken as proud because they are violating culture and sometimes they are confronted and even forced to comply to this tradition. But the truth is that these are liberated because they take seriously the Lordship of Jesus Christ. They are Evangelicals, who believe that if culture is against the gospel, they will opt for the gospel.

2.7.7 Umodzi women at the house of mourning

The *Umodzi* women perform their last chores on that day once they reach the mourning house. They sweep the house of the deceased person and smear the inside floors with fresh mud. After this, they disperse to their respective homes.

2.7.8 Second visit to the graveyard

In certain congregations such as Bongwe, Mpinda and Liwonde Baptist in the South East region, the *Umodzi* women together with the relatives of the dead, and some male folk of the church go to the grave early next morning. This can also be done a few days after burial. In cases where this early visit is done a few days after, there is a high vigil the night before and it is culturally referred to as *tilowa lero* (we are entering today).

The following morning the people go to the graveyard. This act of going to the grave is culturally referred to as *kuzonda manda* (to check the graveyard). In this ritual, the group really goes to check the graveyard. They look for any marks in the ground at the graveyard and study them. Depending on the types of marks, they can deduce what animal the dead person is transformed into.[44] The group offers sacrifices to the dead person begging him/her not to harm people in the community.

The other reason for *"kuzonda manda"* is to find out whether the person came back to life and needs to be directed back home. The group would then be able to collect him or her back home and there are stories that indeed some people who had been buried dead would be found on the gravesite alive but usually speechless.[45] This tradition is widespread among Baptist churches in the South. Even though the theology behind this practice is not known, it is syncretistic in nature. This is because it suggests that a person can rise as an animal while the Baptist teaching is that the person either goes to either heaven or hell. One of the argu-

---

[44] For related details see: Matthew Schoffeleers, *Religion and the Dramatization of Life*, pp. 114-138.

[45] A similar scenario was announced over Radio One, Radio Programme Za Maboma, 30.1.2001. It was announced that a certain girl who was dead and buried was found speechless but alive and seated on the veranda of her grandmother's house.

ments the people involved in *kuzonda manda* use is that when Jesus was in the grave, women such as Mary Magdalene went early the morning to his grave. Nevertheless, those women did not go to check on the marks, but went to embalm Jesus' body with spices according to Jewish culture. It was not to check whether Jesus had risen as an animal or to check the graveyard whether he had risen from the dead. The Bible teaches that resurrection of the body does not happen now. It is a future event that will be seen by us all.[46] The reality is that the majority of women are oppressed by this culture. They can only be liberated if they correctly interpret this culture with their Baptist polity and doctrine. As these women claim to believe in the scriptures, they can be liberated if they take scripture seriously and apply it to their own lives.

2.7.9 After burial

After the burial the bereaved *Umodzi* women do have a challenge to live their Christian faith. They are often subjected to cultural elements that can be oppressive to them. If it is the husband of the *Umodzi* woman who has died, the widow may not be allowed to have a bath or to sweep the house, for a few days up to a week. Even after that, she is supposed to put on a black dress and wear it for a period of a year.[47] This custom is oppressive to the women in that it is against their health and also stigmatizes them, especially in the current period where most widows are labelled as victims of HIV/AIDS. This in turn may even reduce their chances to remarry if they wish to do so.

When an *Umodzi* woman looses a child, she is not allowed to eat salted food for some time. She is not allowed to have sexual relations with her husband during the mourning period, and women sleep separately from men.[48] Baptist women, even in a matrilineal culture, loose property in the event that their husband dies. The government has set guidelines for distribution of property but because of lack of civil education, not many women are aware of this.[49] It would be better if Baptist

---

[46] Int. South East regional meeting delegates, 3.5.2000.
[47] Int. Mrs Mauluka, Mauluka Baptist Church, 24.3.2000.
[48] Rev Ntuwe, Chipimimbi Baptist Church, Zomba, 19.5.2000.
[49] *Malamulo Okhudzana ndi Kagawidwe ka Chuma cha Masiye*, supplement to *The Lamp*, March/April 2001, 8 pp. is a Catholic attempt to combat property grabbing. The booklet was produced by Women and Law in Southern Africa Research Trust, Malawi Office, P/Bag 534, Limbe (email: wlsa@sdnp.org.mw).

churches made their own guidelines concerning property distribution. Muslim women are more liberated in this area because distribution of property is regulated by the guidelines in the Quran.[50]

The struggles Baptist women face with funerals show that Baptist women have a long way to go before they can be fully liberated from cultural traits linked to funerals that are oppressive. The church needs to teach how the gospel interacts with such cultural issues, and in my view, all cultural traits that are against the gospel should be discouraged for the sake of the gospel. This is what Evangelicals are meant to teach.

The churches should also know that choosing the gospel at the expense of some cultural demands, such as *kuzonda maliro*, might subject members to adverse consequences. Some who have done that have been accused of witchcraft, which can stigmatize someone in the community. Therefore, it should be important that the church as a community sanctions such decisions instead of leaving it to the individual consciences.

2.8 The *Umodzi* uniform

The *Umodzi* uniform adds colour to funerals but more so it is a means of identity with their church. This is much more important than the meanings because few church members are aware of them.[51] However it is necessary to have an overview of how grassroots women have actualized the tradition of the uniform.

2.8.1 The origin

The perceptions about the origin of the uniform are diverse. Interviews show that some believe that the Baptist Convention Secretariat started the uniform. As a central administrative body, it is just assumed to be responsible for major decisions such as this. This perception is not according to Baptist polity because such decisions are often made by the majority vote of the grassroots people. Others think that the uniform either came from Zimbabwe or the United States of America when Baptist

---

[50] Quran chapter 4:12: In what your wives leave, your share is a half, if they leave no child. But if they leave a child, Ye get a fourth; after payment of legacies and debts. In what ye leave, their share is a fourth, if ye leave a child.

[51] See Rachel Banda, *Umodzi* Uniform and its Implications for Baptist Beliefs, Forum Paper, Post Graduate Colloquium, 1999.

work started in Malawi in 1961. This dating is even documented in the *Umodzi* booklets.[52]

Mrs Malikebu of South East region for example, believes that the uniform originated from America. But the truth is that, the uniform did not come from America because there has been no uniform there.[53] According to Mrs Agnes Maya, the missionary women who were there at the introduction of the uniform did not like the idea, because their Baptist colour (gold) could not be found in Malawi.[54]

Local Malawians started the uniform in 1967, much earlier than the *Umodzi* organisation. There was a national women's general meeting held in Lilongwe in this year, at which the uniform was introduced. At that time, the key local women leaders were Mrs Mary Galatiya, Mrs Elizabeth Phiri and Mrs Mallungo.[55]

The other view about the origin of uniform is that it was started in Jali. This view is held by most women in the South East region such as Mrs Tanganyika of Songani Baptist Church in Zomba.[56] This view is not true, but it is a valid argument, because during this period, Jali was a central point where all women activities in the South East region were coordinated.

2.8.2 The uniform design

2.8.2.1 Composition

Originally the uniform was a white short-sleeved shirt with a short collar, a purple pleated skirt, headdress and belt. The white shoes are a later addition. The current uniform is slightly different in style as it has a round colour blouse. The purple is also deeper than the original one. This was not by design but because it was not available in the early days. In fact around Jali area, *Umodzi* women used a black shirt instead of purple because of the scarcity of materials. This fashion is believed to have been

---

[52] See 1961 *Umodzi wa Amayi a Baptist a ku Malawi*, BCM, p. 1.
[53] Int. Woman volunteer, Oklahoma Partnership, Lilongwe Baptist Seminary. Also see Rachel Banda, *Umodzi* Uniform and its Implications on Baptist Beliefs, 1999.
[54] Int. Agnes Maya, Zomba Baptist Church, 28.10.2000.
[55] Int. Mrs Hilda Mallungo, Mtendere Baptist Church, 14.3.2000.
[56] Int. Mrs Tanganyika, Songani Baptist Church, Zomba 1999.

adopted from the Zion Church uniform.[57] It was a long battle to persuade the woman in Jali area to switch to the right uniform prescribed by the national leadership.[58]

Apart from the dress, the uniform has a pin on which is inscribed the map of the world, a candle, a Bible and the words: *"Umodzi wa Amayi a Baptist a ku Malawi BCM."* This badge is also available in America.[59] The complex design of the badge has raised up the question about who designed it. Some believe it was designed in America, which of course is plausible because it is also found there. Others believe it was created in Zimbabwe and has been adapted to Malawi, Zambia and even to the American context. This thinking is affirmed by the fact that Zimbabwe was a British colony and has had progressive artistic skills as evidenced from their wood carving work.

2.8.2.2 Uniform design and meanings

Others believe that the theological meanings behind the inscriptions on the badge suggest that the badge is an African creation for the following reasons. The symbol of the candle is ideal in the African culture that is pregnant with evil forces and darkness. The women are confronted with a challenge to be a light to these evil spirits and other spiritual beings in their culture. The candle is a testimony to them that Jesus whom they believe in is able to protect them and guide them in their culture infiltrated with dark forces. However, it is too narrow to limit such a theological meaning to the African context alone. This symbol of a candle is appropriate world wide. It can be compared to the lamp symbol in the Bible. In the Bible, God is a lamp and the Bible is also a lamp to God's people's feet (2 Sam 22:29 for example says "You are a lamp, o Lord"). In the New Testament Jesus uses a lamp as a symbol to teach his disciples about the importance of evangelization. He challenges them that no-one puts a lamp under a bushel, but rather puts it on a hill for everyone to

---

[57] Int. Rev Lichapa, Makolije Baptist Church; Int. Mrs Hilda Mallungo, Mtendere Baptist Church, Lilongwe, 14.3.2000.

[58] Int. Rev Malikebu, Thundu Baptist Church, 19.5.1999 Int. Rev Maida, Chayima Baptist Church, Jali, Zomba Rural.

[59] Int. Rev Lichapa, Makolije Baptist Church, 20.3.2000.

see. The symbol of a candle therefore can be used worldwide because it is biblically based.[60]

The white and purple colours in the uniform also have a theological meaning. However, the majority of Baptist Convention members do not know these meanings, which remain a secret even to some *Umodzi* women who have been schooled thoroughly about them. Of six interviewees in Zomba area, only one knew the meaning of the uniform. Four gave wrong meanings (guess work) and one did not know.[61]

Theoretically the purple colour shows that *Umodzi* women, since they know Jesus Christ, belong to a kingly rule (God's rule). In the olden biblical times, the priests of the kingly origin used to put on purple to show that they belonged to this order. The white colour on the other hand shows that the *Umodzi* women are holy. The white colour is part of the uniform in most churchwomen's organization and has this same theological meaning to show holiness and purity.[62]

2.8.3 Rationale for Umodzi uniform

Baptist women had a good reason to have a uniform. It was a common phenomenon among many Christian cultures in Malawi, and it was logical for Baptist women to have a uniform to match the other Christian cultures in which *Umodzi* women were ministering. The uniform played a role during the national meetings. They produce a common identity and are a bridge among women from different regions and social and economic backgrounds.

2.8.4 Regulations for uniform ownership

The regulations to acquire the uniform are as follows:

(a) They must memorize the seven aims of the organisation with the verses that go with them. These are to learn the Bible (Psalm 119:11); to pray (John 14:13); to fellowship with one another (He-

---

[60] Int. Oklahoma volunteer, Lilongwe Baptist Seminary, Lilongwe Baptist Seminary, 1999.

[61] See also Rachel Banda's forum paper presented at the Postgraduate Colloquium 1999, p. 8. The Mvano of Blantyre Synod, Legio Maria in the Catholic Church, Dorcas of Seventh-day Adventists, among others, have this white colour. For more details see Rachel Banda, A Comprehensive Study of Christian Women's Organization in Southern Malawi, Module 3 paper, MA church History, University of Malawi.

brews 10:25); to evangelize others (Acts 1:8); to give (Malachi 3:10), to have a Christian home (Joshua 24:15); to know God's word (Mathews 28:19-20).

(b) To learn the women's' song.

(c) To learn the "steps to salvation" verses as shown above.

(d) Must have received Christ.

(e) Must have a Christian family.

However, in practice, only a few of these conditions are fulfilled before one can have a uniform. Many *Umodzi* women have not memorized the verses and the song. Since they face frequent divorce, women in the Southern region have a big challenge of having a Christian family, one of the prerequisites to have a uniform. In a survey of 44 *Umodzi* women, 26 were already in their second marriage. Out of them only one remarried because her husband had died. Three women were in their third marriage. 15 women on the other hand had their first marriage and were very young. It is likely that many of these 15 in a short while will also move on to another marriage.[63] The reasons for this high divorce rate have been widely speculated upon. Helen van Koevering attributes it to loose ties in matrilineal families in the absence of dowry.[64] Such reasoning is also confirmed by some of the Baptist women in the matrilineal societies of the South East region.[65] One additional factor for the high divorce rate in matrilineal societies of the South East region is probably the influence from Islam predominant among the Yao of this region.[66] Even though Baptists do not encourage divorce, women in Baptist churches who have been divorced even two times have the freedom to own the *Umodzi* uniform. This is not common in the Catholic Church where remarriage after divorce is perceived to be sinful.[67]

2.8.5   Regulations for uniform usage

Except at funerals, the uniform is used at joint women's meetings whether associational, regional or national. It is also used during visita-

---

[64] Helen van Koevering, "Dancing their Dreams", pp. 22-23.

[65] Int. focus group, South East region women's meeting, Zomba, 3.3.2000.

[66] For Muslims, divorce is permitted and chapter 4 of the Quran is dedicated to guidelines for divorce. A wife can seek a divorce under certain circumstances.

[67] Int. South East region women delegates to sewing and evangelism training school, Zomba Baptist Church, 13.10.2000.

tions and while doing charity work. In many congregations the uniform is also worn at weekly meetings and in a few of these, women are fined if they forget to put on the uniform. However women in the South East region enjoy relative freedom in the usage of the uniform.

2.9 Leadership structure

Umodzi groups at every level; congregation, association, region[68] and nation, have an executive committee comprising of chairlady, secretary, treasurer, *mlangizi* and committee members.[69] However, unlike in other women's organisation, where the executive members are decision makers this power in *Umodzi* groups is with the ordinary members. The executive members can formulate proposals to run the organisation but decision-making is in the hands of the grassroots people. This is not to withstand the fact that executive members do have responsibilities to fulfill within such an arrangement.[70]

2.9.1 The chairlady

In the local congregation, she is an ex officio member of the church council.[71] Although the church council does not make all decisions for the running of a congregation, it has power to make some decisions and formulate proposals. The chairperson of *Umodzi* is therefore able to influence the congregation in this way. She fosters communication between women's ministry and the church by presenting reports from the women to the church.[72]

2.9.2 The pastor's wife

The chairperson is in most cases a layperson because the pastor's wife is perceived to have anyhow a leadership role in the church. Pro-

---

[68] Associations are composed of local congregations and regions comprise of associations.

[69] See *Umodzi* wa Amayi a Baptist a ku Malawi, BCM 1961, pp. 24-25.

[70] Each Executive Committee runs the region for a two year term and then new leaders are elected. The current chair, Mrs Lufani, has been chair for two terms from 1996-2000, and she is a pastor's wife.

[71] This is according to Baptist polity.

[72] Such reports may include, women's weekly activities, budgets, which the local church must know and even consider supporting. Zomba Baptist Church for example has often sponsored women to go for meetings outside Zomba.

grammes formulated by *Umodzi* groups have to be communicated to the pastor's wife, before they are implemented. The pastor's wife is seen to be active in all areas of ministry the women undertake. She is also an advisor both to the executive and the grassroots people. The chairperson is not necessarily responsible for either the teaching or preaching of the Bible or the teaching of the *Umodzi* practices. This is usually done by the pastor's wife who has been trained in the organization and the Bible.[73] However in cases where pastors' wives are functionally illiterate, spiritual ministry is usually left to a literate laywoman.[74] Even in urban congregations, where pastors are normally paid a salary, it is only the pastor who is employed by the church, though the perception is that the pastor's wife must also have a spiritual ministry with the women in the church. The problem is that some women are not called to be in such a ministry or are not able leaders and they feel forced, and in many cases that brings frustration on both the pastor's wife and the *Umodzi* women.

Although the pastor's wife is perceived to take such a responsibility alongside her husband, she usually does not receive a salary. She earns some income through business or other employment. But even this is sometimes negatively perceived by the *Umodzi* women especially in congregations that hold weekly meetings on a weekday. The pastors' wives failure to attend such weekly meetings because of business or employment is looked upon lack of as commitment to God's work. In fact, her husband's performance can be negatively rated because of his wife's lack of involvement with the women. Some pastor's have been denied a job with a congregation because of having a working wife.[75]

2.9.3 The chairperson at association and regional level

The chairperson at these levels is not a member of the general association at these levels, however she is often called upon by the general association to give reports concerning *Umodzi* work in her area. Apart from this responsibility, there are usually joint meetings at such levels and the chairperson is supposed to lead the meetings or delegate the responsi-

---

[73] Pastors' wives go for a short training on women's organization and the Bible; during the time their husbands receive theological training.
[74] This is very common in the rural congregations of the Southern region.
[75] Very few congregations such as Zomba Baptist consider an allowance for her, and even in this case, it is more to cut down tax on the husband's salary.

bility to someone. In this role, she mainly is a master of ceremonies, but in certain cases, some chairpersons dominate such meetings by doing most of the activities such as preaching and teaching by themselves.[76] The concept of delegation of responsibilities is not well understood in rural congregations. In cases where certain women play other people's roles, this is easily looked upon with suspicion of usurping someone's power.[77] In most cases delegation is not planned but happens by accident, for example, when the person responsible is absent or has some problem to carry out the responsibility.[78]

The joint meetings always end with a business meeting for general questions and discussions as well as reports whether from congregations, if it is an association meeting, or from associations if it is a regional meeting. At such business meetings, the chairperson is the facilitator. Although a chairperson can be a layperson, the South East region has had a pastor's wife in this capacity for a long time.

2.9.4 The chairperson at the national level

Since 1992, she is constitutionally a member of the BACOMA executive and as such she is expected to attend all BACOMA executive committee meetings. In this way, she is able to represent women's views to the central body of the church. Although power is with the local congregations, this central body is still powerful in that it strategizes programmes to be carried out in a given period. Since through the chairperson, the women's views are represented, they are not easily left out. The chairperson also presents reports of women's work from all the regions of Malawi to the national executive. While there is a concern, that in certain cases, women are elected to such positions as tokens,[79] this woman is not because the women themselves do democratically appoint her. This is important because it is not the presence of a female in the decision making body that counts, but it is how serious her views are taken. Historically it can be proven that the *Umodzi* chairperson's views have been taken seriously and have had an effect on the life of the church in the

---

[76] This is according to Baptist polity.
[77] Refer to a survey of some of the committees for such set-ups in chapter 2.
[78] This was common at the South East regional meeting in 2000.
[79] See Kenneth R. Ross (ed), *God People and Power in Malawi: Democratization in Theological Perspective,* Blantyre: CLAIM-Kachere, 1996, pp. 71-105.

Southern region. The introduction of the training center for women at Balaka farm in 1999 is such an example. It was initiated by the *Umodzi* chairperson to the BACOMA committee, which accepted it.

2.9.5 The treasurer

She keeps money at each level from the congregational level to the national level. The money is used only for the running of *Umodzi* programmes. At local congregations, this money comes from weekly contributions in form of offerings taken at each meeting. In some cases, *Umodzi* groups receive donations from well-wishers. *Umodzi* women also hold income generating activities, for example, cooking doughnuts for sale. This money is used in activities such as visiting the sick in hospital or in their homes. In this case, money is usually used for transport and/or for buying a present for the sick person. Some of the money is to be given to the association and usually each church is requested to give a certain amount.[80]

At the associational and regional level, the treasurer keeps money that is brought to the joint meetings, in form of a registration fee.[81] If it is a regional meeting, in addition to such fees, each association gives a lump sum of money to the joint meeting.[82] This money is used for buying food for the conference.

In most cases, the treasurers for the associations and regions do not have any significant amount of money left. This is because food items are expensive and cannot be covered by registration fees. The regions and associations rarely receive money from central funding for food costs.

One of the rare occasions was when the regions received project money from Hilfe für Brüder in Stuttgart, Germany.[83] In 1996, when Martha Chirwa was the president of *Umodzi* at the national level, she wrote a proposal for a sewing project. It was approved and the result was that

---

[80] Mpinda Baptist Church in Zomba does this once in a while.
[81] In the South East region, this fee is K15.00 per delegate.
[82] In the South East region, each association gives K70.00 to the region. This money is divided by the number of congregations within associations to find out how much each congregation should give. Associations in this area usually have about 8 congregations.
[83] Hilfe für Brüder is an interdenominational Evangelical aid agency, similar to the British TEAR Fund.

Hilfe für Brüder donated two sewing machines for each region and about K5,000 to go with each machine. The money was to be used for purchasing initial materials for the training of women in sewing. This was a rare time when regional treasurers have held such big money.[84]

Very little accountability is shown by some regional and association leaders because of illiteracy. The regional treasurer of the South East region in 2000 for example, has never given financial reports at regional conferences. Although she can read and write, she finds it difficult to work with figures. She was given the post not based on the knowledge of financial accounting but on integrity, which she really has.[85] But is integrity enough qualification for financial accountability?

2.9.6 The national treasurer

She keeps money for projects, donations from elsewhere, and contributions from delegates to the national *Umodzi* conferences. Lay people have for years taken up this post. *Umodzi* women from the Southern region have shared in such positions. Mrs Margaret Nyika, a member of Blantyre Baptist Church, served in this post from 1992 to 1996.[86]

2.9.7 Treasurers and week of prayer programme

All the treasurers at each level also keep money given at a week of prayer. This programme is run internationally and it is mandatory that those who come for such prayers should give a cash contribution at the end of the prayers. The prayers are held at each congregation. The money is received by the treasurers at the congregational level who pass it on to the associational level. The regional treasurer gives the money to the national treasurer. This money is not used locally, it is sent to America, where the WMU headquarters is. The money in used for the running of the office but also to support *Umodzi* projects worldwide.

---

[84] Another such rare cases was when the Oklahoma volunteer women came to the South East region conference and gave K2000 towards the food budget.
[85] Int. Margaret Nyika, Blantyre Baptist Church. I attended both regional conferences in the South East region in 2000.
[86] Int. Martha Chirwa, Blantyre Baptist Church, 14.12.2000.

2.9.8 The secretary

The secretary, at all levels, takes minutes and reads the previous minutes at executive meetings. The secretary also records the money kept by the treasurer. The office of the secretary is defined by the literacy of the person. At associational, regional and national meetings, the secretary reads and writes minutes. She also writes memos to people concerning the decisions made.

2.9.9 Mlangizi

Such position is present at all levels but is more active at regional and associational level. The *mlangizi*, at such joint meetings, provides a forum where women discuss marriage issues and issues relating to their sexuality.[87] At the congregational level, she arranges church initiation for girls. This is only in congregations that practice this tradition.

2.10 Conclusion

Through *Umodzi* groups, women in Convention churches in the Southern region make significant contributions to the life of the church although they cannot enjoy optimum positions in the church. As an organisation, they are conscious of the culture in which they serve and, they seek to present themselves in a way that the communities understand them. Because cultures change, congregations capitalize on their freedom to make decisions that will be relevant to their setting. It is therefore likely that the picture of *Umodzi* women depicted in this chapter will change over time. This should not be seen as a weakness but as an expression of freedom. Further, through the experiences of these women with culture, it is clear that liberation can only be realized if they learn to adapt their gospel to face those elements that are oppressive.

---

[87] For more details see chapter 4.

Chapter 3

A STRUGGLE FOR FREEDOM AND NATIONAL IDENTITY: 1985-2000

Women's work in 1985-2000

By this time, women's work spread to almost all districts of Southern Malawi. The means of propagating the Baptist beliefs included all the methods mentioned in the earlier chapters. Evangelism through development work such as sewing, done during the first period continues to make an impact, with a difference that such development activities have become more specialized. Currently, for example, women learn to sew not only by hand but also by machines. To this, a sewing centre at Balaka farm was opened in 1999, where women selected from all regions in Malawi converge for sewing. Tracts and revival crusades continue to be used in evangelism however with much decline. The Bible Way programme which is perceived to have contributed much to growth in Baptist work has been stopped due to change of policy in the Baptist Mission.

Even though women's work spread to almost all areas, the question as to why some areas embraced this work later than others is a good question. District such as Mangochi only opened in 1988. Mwanza opened to Baptist work in the 1990s. It is clear that some factors contributed to the blockage of women's work in these areas. In Mangochi, the Muslim faith proved to be a big challenge to such growth. In Mwanza, the Seventh-day Adventist faith, which dissuaded Mrs Galatiya and her husband in the earlier period to open Baptist work there seemed to have continued to present a challenge to the spread of women's work there. Thus, although women's work seems to be well organized in some areas, this work is still new and there is still need for teaching women in the work in these areas.

Zomba and Blantyre where women's work started continue to provide leadership in the development and specialization of women's work in this region. However, in other areas, women's work is slowing down for many reasons. Some of them are lack of supervision from the leaders and the fact that there is no longer missionary support for women's activities. But there has been progress in the position of women in the church as will be shown in this chapter.

Baptist women are supposed to be more liberated because of their Baptist doctrine and polity. However, up until now, they are restricted from attaining optimum freedom because of interplay of elements within and outside themselves. Nevertheless, some congregations have been able to realize more freedom compared to women in other church traditions through several factors.

Preaching has been singled out because it demonstrates public leadership over both men and women. The issue of ordination will also be discussed but in lesser detail, because it is a less important issue among Baptists, as these believe in the priesthood of all believers. On the other hand, since men are ordained, the issue of why women are not ordained will be discussed.

A struggle for freedom among these women exists not only in the realm of leadership, but also among common members of congregations. They struggle to find out what roles they play in relation to those played by their male counterparts. The above issues will be discussed in view of restrictive elements such as church tradition, culture, biblical interpretation, political environment, *zeitgeist*, male egoism, and lack of sufficient theological training. Factors that have helped women to attain better freedoms such as theology, external influences and *zeitgeist* will also be discussed. This chapter, therefore, is an answer to one of the key questions facing Baptists today, in relation to their national identity. Is this identity of Baptist women in Malawi, different or similar to that of the early missionaries from America? It accounts for the effects of missionary Christianity on the current freedoms and the national identity that Baptist women in Malawi have or have not.

3.1 Gender roles at grassroots level: a case study of Nsomo Baptist Church

Before we discuss the relative freedoms the women enjoy in relation to women of other Church structures, it is reasonable to discuss such freedoms within their own churches in relation to men. This is depicted in the roles women play in their local congregations but also in levels of leadership in various church structures.

A case study of roles of church members at Nsomo Baptist Church, a leading congregation in Lower Shire (Chikwawa) from 1983 to 1989 showed these results:[1]

Date	Women's responsibilities	Men's responsibilities
19/3/83	-	Bring firewood
4/4/83	Collecting water for a meeting	-
24/4/83	Sweeping at church	Sweeping at church
8/5/83	Women to bring water to church for moulding bricks	Men to dig soil for bricks
19/06/83	Pounding maize in preparation for a meeting. Collecting firewood for the meeting	-
3/7/83	To carry moulded bricks to the kiln	To carry moulded bricks to the kiln
7/8/83	To collect firewood for burning bricks	To collect firewood for burning bricks
15/9/83	-	Burning bricks
18/3/84	Carry bricks for building	Carry bricks for building.
12/8/84	Beating sorghum branches to harvest seeds	Building pit latrines
26/8/84	Beating sorghum branches to harvest seeds Collecting firewood	Building a plot
7/10/84	Visiting the sick Visiting the sick	Visiting the sick[2] Visiting the sick[3]

---

[1]   The information in the table is constructed from the registry of church announcements in these particular years. The dates are not dates at which activities were done, but dates of announcements, which were always on Sundays.

[2]   Among men who went visiting were Mr Samu, Mr Chilokoteni, Mr Kudzala, and Mr Sabe. Among women were Mrs Nsambo, Mrs Chideya, and Mrs Chikaoneka. They went as a group to visit Mr Mmenyede. Nsomo Baptist, Zolengeza [announcements], 7.10.84.

[3]   On the same date, another group of men and women went to visit a woman member of the church, a sister to Mr Malizani who was sick. Those who went were: Mr

14/10/84	Visiting the sick	Visiting the sick[4]
4/11/84	Carrying bricks	Carrying bricks
11/11/84	Carrying bricks	Carrying bricks[5]
18/11/84	Praying in church	Praying in church
25/11/84	Visitation	Visitation[6]
27/11/85	To garden to visit the sick	To garden to visit the sick
24/2/85	Collecting water for a meeting	
5/8/89	Beating sorghum seeds from branches. Visiting the sick	Building toilets and bath rooms. Visiting the sick

3.1.1 The importance of Nsomo Baptist Church

Nsomo Baptist Church is the main supervising congregation in the Lower Shire, and therefore has an influence on the behaviour of other Baptist congregations in this area.[7] Because of the influence Nsomo Baptist Church has over a number of churches in Lower Shire, the table above, showing roles of women and men, is a good illustration concerning what is happening in the Lower Shire. Nsomo Baptist Church was started in 1973 and later in the same year opened by Revs Galatiya and Charles Middlestone. From 1976 to 1990, Nsomo has not only initiated Baptist congregations in Nsanje district,[8] but also within Chikwawa district.[9] Nevertheless, even those congregations that were not initiated by

Chideya, Mr Tomasi, Mr Mpinganjira, Mr Phwafu, Mrs Nora, Mrs Saliyeni, Mrs Zakariya, Mrs Thuchira. Ibid.

[4]   Both men and women went to visit Mr Malizani who was sick. Those who went were Mr Chideya, Mr Tomasi, Mr Mpinganjira, Mr Phwafu, Mrs Salijeni, Mrs Zariya, and Mrs Thuchira. Nsomo Baptist Church, Zolengeza 14.10.84.

[5]   It was emphasized in the announcement that both men and women should participate in the carrying of bricks. Nsomo Baptist Church, Zolengeza, 11.11.84.

[6]   The group visiting chief Nsomo, who was sick, was composed of these members: Mr Chilokoteni, Chief Chamboko, Mr Thonje, Mr Kashoti, Mrs Pompi (pastor's wife). Mrs Makola, Mrs Mpinganjira and Mrs Chideya. Ibid. 25.11.84.

[7]   The registry is named: Nsomo Baptist Church, Zolengeza.

[8]   Int. Rev Jimu Kalenga, Nsomo Baptist Church, 28.9.2000.

[9]   Int. Mrs Christina Kalenga, Nsomo Baptist Church, 28.9.2000. Other congregations have been started by initiatives from the two earlier congregations in Chikwawa districts. These are: Chikwawa Baptist Church in T/A Mlilima at Domasi village in 1969, Nchalo Baptist Church in 1970. Int. Jim Kalenga, Nsomo Baptist Church, 28.9.2000 and Mrs Kalavina, Nchalo Baptist Church, 27.7.2000.

Nsomo look to Nsomo for direction in matters relating to their church.[10] Although, it is only men such as Rev Jim Kalenga, Rev Pompi and Rev Phiffer, Southern Baptist Missionaries who began such adventures, women in Nsomo Baptist gave leadership to women in Nsanje congregations. In any case, Nsanje congregations up until 2000 had no independent association. They always have been part of Ngabu association where Nsomo Baptist Church is the main supervising church. Women such as Mrs Christina Kalenga and Mrs Sagonja from Nsomo Baptist Church have been visiting Nsanje congregations for discipleship.[11]

3.1.2 Factors defining gender roles at Nsomo Baptist Church

The table above have shows certain church roles are divided on sex lines. Collecting water, pounding maize, and beating sorghum branches to harvest seeds was only done by women. Digging soil for moulding bricks, burning bricks, building pit latrines and building a church block was done by men. Such a division is based on cultural attitudes concerning which chores are for women and which are for men. It is not based on the ability to do such chores, since both men and women can do these chores because they are not biological. However, roles assigned to men seem to demand more energy and time. This may seem appropriate because women need to save energy and time for other activities not culturally done by men. It is also seen from the table that 38 jobs were done by women. Men did only 18 jobs. This is also because for two slots women were given a double load as compared to men.

The table also shows that some roles in the church are done by both men and women: according to the case study, such roles were sweeping at church, carrying bricks to the kiln, collecting firewood, praying, gardening and visiting the sick. According to job types, both men and women did six of them; men did four separately and women did three separately. This shows that in Baptist congregations in this area, women have more opportunities to work with men as equals than work by themselves. However, women have a greater challenge because although women did

---

[10] Ibid. Mbang'ombe Baptist Church was started in 1976, Ntondo in T/A Tengani and Kalonga Baptist Church near Makhamba railway station for example were started in p1977. In the same year, Baptist churches were started at Nangalembe and Reno. Other congregations include Bile Baptist Church, near Ngabu Trading Centre, Mangadzi and Makande.
[11] Int. Mrs Christina Kalenga, Nsomo Baptist Church, 28.9.2000.

only three types of jobs, these jobs were more frequent than other types. This means that women tend to be busier than their male counterparts. The challenge is that the church should sensitize men to also participate in such frequent types of jobs. Men's jobs, even though they were four types, are usually rarely done. Moreover, they mainly relate to building and one does not always build, unless it is one's profession.

In the behaviour of *Umodzi* groups as shown in chapter two, it can easily be assumed that *Umodzi* women are the only ones involved in visitations. The table above shows the contrary. Men are also involved in visitations on the church weekly programmes. In fact in other Baptist congregations *Umodzi* women are restrained to make such visits by themselves unless it is visiting women in *chikuta* and their fellow *Umodzi* members. At Zomba Baptist Church, for example, women were stopped to visit the sick without the male members of the congregation. This was done because some male members of the church were suspicious of their wives in that they were not sure whether they were indeed going out for such visitations or other agendas. The other reason was that, if women did visitations by themselves, the male members of the congregation would be looked at as uncompassionate by church members.[12]

The issue of groupings in the table above is also interesting. Although both men and women went for visitation in groups, none of the groups had a couple in the same group.[13] This is unlikely a coincidence because of its repetitive nature. Was it that members felt restricted to fellowship with others as they visited, if in the presence of their spouses? Alternatively, is it that it was necessary for a spouse to remain behind so that he or she can look after the affairs of the home? The other possibility is that this group working sprit is a development that had been carried over from the revival period. This is a possibility because effects of a revival do not necessarily subside in the later period. There is a chance for them to remain in the later period although to a varied degree.[14]

---

[12] Report by Mrs Topesa, deacon, to *Umodzi* weekly meeting, Zomba Baptist Church, 1999.
[13] This was on 19.6.1983 and on 26.8.1984.
[14] See Klaus Fiedler, *Story of the Faith Missions*, pp. 113-114.

3.2 Gender roles at leadership level

3.2.1 Preaching: the situation

The issue of leadership is discussed with reference to roles of preaching apart from women deacons and other leadership roles. Such roles are referred to because they demonstrate public leadership over both men and women. While outside the Sunday services women seem to enjoy relative freedoms in the roles they play, this must also be viewed in respect of what roles they play, in spiritual ministry, for example, on a regular Sunday. Therefore this section discusses women preaching on a Sunday. The following table shows a representative picture of the freedoms Baptist women enjoy in their congregations in preaching.

Name of congregation, location and year when it started	Women preaching	Occasion	Who started and when	Reasons
1. Ntokota in Thyolo, 1976	Yes	Women's Sunday	Mrs Kwalira (layperson) 1987	-Men capitalize on the verse that says that women should be silent in church[15] -Since then, those who are willing preach. The change came with influences from Blantyre women preachers who visited the area.
2 Mpando in Thyolo, 1975	Yes	Regular Sunday & Women's Sunday. Women's Sunday Women's Sunday (there was preaching only once in 1994 and then no one ever preached till 1999	Mrs Kantunda (pastor's wife) 1977 1994 Mrs Chrissie Chikwakwa (60 yrs) Mrs Martha Kholomana, Mrs Maclaudi	-preached because husband, pastor fell ill. -No women preached till 1994 because women were not allowed to preach.[16]

---

[15] See chapter 1.
[16] Int. Mrs Martha Kholomana, Mpando Baptist Church, Thyolo 26.7.2000.

			(35 yrs)	
3. Mambo in Thyolo, 1985[17]	Yes	Women's Sunday	1987 Visiting women from Blantyre.[18]	In Blantyre, women were already preaching on a Women's Sunday then.
4 Ndirande in Chikwawa, 1998.	No	-	-	They are not free to preach.[19]
5 Nchalo Baptist Church in Chikwawa, 1970	Yes	Women's Sunday	1994 Mrs Kalavina (pastor's wife) 1999 Mrs Falaminga	They haven't been preaching till 1990s because the Bible says women should not preach.[20]
6 Nsomo Baptist Church in Chikwawa, 1973	No	-	-	They do not have a Women's Sunday. Women preach only to fellow women during weekly meetings and Sunday school classes.[21]
7 Most congregations in the South East like Gomeya/Balaka	Yes	Women's Sunday	-	Because of monthly period.
8 Zomba Baptist Church	Yes	Women's Sunday & Sunday regular	1993 Teresa Day (missionary) English service Mrs Chauluka (Chichewa service) Now women preach regularly in English	Because of monthly period. – Influenced by Dr Klaus Fiedler, member of congregation, lecturer in Chancellor College (English service). Influence from Women Aglow (Chichewa service).[22]

---

[17] Mambo Baptist Church was occasionally being visited by women from Blantyre such as Mrs Kawamba, Mrs Kayiya and Mrs Chitseko. One of these must have given this sermon. Int. Mrs Martha Kholomana, Mpando Baptist Church, 26.7.2000.

[18] Int. focus group (4 women), Mpando Baptist Church, 26.7.2000.

[19] Int. Mrs Bonwell Kachere, Mrs Marina Chinangwa, and Bertha Joseph, members, Ndirande Baptist Church, 27.7.2000.

[20] Int. Mrs Kalavina, Nchalo Baptist Church, 27.7.2000.

[21] Int. focus group, Nsomo Baptist Church, 27.7.2000.

[22] Women Aglow is an interdenominational women's organization with a Charismatic touch.

			and Chichewa	
9. Mpheta Baptist Church	Yes	Regular Sunday and Women's Sunday	The founder Mrs Agnes Lufani, a pastor's wife	Every home crusade in Chikwawa since 1980.[23]
10. Makolije Baptist in Zomba rural 1962.	Yes	Women's Sunday	1999	Women must be quiet because of the Bible. Some feel they are not gifted.[24]
11. Ntokota Baptist, Jali, Zomba 1961	No.[25]	-	-	-
12 Thabwani Baptist, Jali Zomba	No.[26]	-	-	-
13 Chayima Baptist Church, 1960	yes	Women's Sunday	Mrs Thunga Mrs Kamunde, Mrs Kashoni	They do not believe that women should be silent in church.[27]
14 Mwanafumu Baptist 25/5/1975	yes	Regular Sunday	Mrs Mellia Makina 1988	She became the pastor of the church, after Nicholas Mlenga left the church because of polygamy.[28]
15 Chiliko Baptist in Mphyuphyu association	yes	Women's Sunday	-	-
16. Mpinda Baptist Church, Mikuyu association, Zomba	yes	Women's Sunday	Mrs Samu	Women are afraid to preach, tradition makes them not to preach. The perception is that even though they are Christians they are still blind to cer-

---

[23] Int. focus group of executive committee members in South East region, Zomba, 3.3.2000. Int. Mrs Agnes Lufani, Mpheta Baptist 3.3.2000. This was also confirmed by members of the executive of South East region that met the same day.
[24] Int. Rev Davidson Lichapa, Makolije Baptist Church, 8.3.2000, Jali, Zomba.
[25] Int. Elizabeth Lichapa (pastor's wife), Makolije Baptist Church, 8.3.2000, Jali, Zomba. Also int. focus group, Makolije Baptist Church, 22.3.2000.
[26] Int. focus group, Ntokota Baptist Church, 19.3.1999. At this time, Thabwani Baptist members also came for the service.
[27] Ibid.
[28] Int. Pastor Maida with two women members of the congregation, Chayima Baptist, 20.3.2000.
[29] Int. Mwanafumu focus group, Mwanafumu Baptist Church, rural Jali, Zomba, 21.3.2000.

				tain biblical truths.[29]
17 Chilambe Baptist Thyolo.	No	-	-	Women are not allowed to preach in the presence of men.[30]
18 Mitumbira Baptist Blantyre rural	No	-	-	-
19 Ndala Baptist Blantyre rural	No	-	-	-
20 Misesa Baptist Blantyre rural	Yes	Women's Sunday.[31]	-	-
21 Jerusalem Baptist, Blantyre	Yes	Women's Sunday[32]	-	-
22 Blantyre Baptist, near Chichiri Stadium	Yes	Women's Sunday	-	Tradition and Bible, missionary influence.[33]
23 Living Stones Baptist, in Soche Suburb, Blantyre	No	-	-	Women refuse, maybe it has to do with the way the church started, probably women's leadership was discouraged[34]
24 Thundu, Jali, Zomba	Yes	Women's Sunday	Mrs Malikebu 1999	They had heard that women could preach.
25 Nasongole Baptist, Liwonde, Machinga	Yes	Regular Sunday	Mrs Agnes Lufani 1986	She was pastor of the church.
26 Mpheta Baptist, Liwonde, Machinga	Yes	Regular Sunday	Mrs Agnes Lufani 1991	She has been preaching since 1986 when in the previous church.
27 Chinyung'unya Bap-	Yes	Regular Sunday	Mrs Sellina Nasimango	She was pastor of the Church.

---

[30] Int. Rev Medson Kathumba, Chirima Baptist Church, Mphyuphyu, rural Zomba, 31.7.2000.

[31] Mauluka Baptist started the following churches: Chirima in 1989, Kango in T/A Mwambo in 1991, Chimwayi Baptist in T/A Kuntumanje in 1992, Khumba Baptist near Lake Chirwa in 1994, Tala Baptist in 1996, Nanchengwa Baptist in 1998, both in Mphyuphyu association. All these churches are supervised by Mauluka Baptist Church and in all of them women preach only on Women's Sunday.

[32] Int. Rev Tambula Mwanakhu, Mpinda Baptist Church, Mikuyu association, rural Zomba. 13.7.2000.

[33] Int. Mrs Kample, treasurer for *Umodzi*, Chilambe Baptist Church, Thyolo rural.

[34] Int. pastor's wife, Misesa Baptist Church, at Lilongwe Baptist Seminary, 13.3.2000.

tist, Liwonde			1970	
28 Mwanafumu Baptists, Jali, Zomba	yes	Regular Sunday	Mrs Mellia Makina 1988	She was pastor of the church.

Although there are about 300 congregations in the Southern region, the above sample is an illustration of the views these congregations have towards preaching, firstly because it is a random sample from various districts of the region where major Baptist work is. These congregations are from Chikwawa, Thyolo, Blantyre, Zomba and Balaka. Secondly, both rural and urban churches are represented. Thirdly, some of the congregations such as Mpinda, Makolije and Nsomo are supervising churches and represent the views of a cluster of congregations.

3.2.2 Factors relating to women preaching

The illustration shows that generally, Baptist women began to preach either on Women's Sunday or regular Sundays, mostly at the turn of this century, even though some women started preaching much earlier.

The first women preachers were a result of external influences brought in by Rev Galatiya in New Jerusalem Church. These first local women preachers only existed in New Jerusalem Church in the late 1960s to the early 1970s; there was a marked decline in women preaching in the South South region even at New Jerusalem till the 1980s. During this period of decline, women did not preach on either a Women's Sunday or a regular Sunday except by accident.[35] Women preached only to fellow women, typical for this missionary period. After the decline, not all congregations have allowed women to preach, even though there has been an increase in women preaching in the 1990s. This is a move from the negative missionary view on women's preaching to national identity. In the South South region, the initiative for women's preaching fortunately started with the old congregations that also had a supervisory role over a cluster of congregations. However, such initiatives came only in 1994, the year of Malawi's democratic elections. This is also enough proof that political transitions do not necessarily influence significantly

---

[35] Mrs Kantunda, a pastor's wife, preached in 1977 in Mpando Baptist Church because her husband got very ill and could not preach in that particular service. Int. focus group (4 women), Mpando Baptist Church, 26.7.2000.

the history of the church.[36] In the South East region, women were more progressive even before the democratic elections.

3.2.3 Women pastors

The earliest occurrence of women preaching was in the rural areas as early as in the 1970s, but only in congregations where women were pastors. It is Baptist doctrine and polity that allowed local women to assume such roles that were contrary to the views of their missionary counterparts. Such occurrences of early preaching were in congregations such as Mwanafumu Baptist,[37] where Mrs Mellia Makina was pastor of the church, Chinyung'unya Baptist[38] where Mrs Sellina Nasimango was pastor, and Nasongole Baptist where Mrs Agnes Lufani was pastor. This identity was local, and not influenced by Southern Baptist missionaries.

3.2.3.1 Mrs Mellia Makina

Mrs Mellia Makina was not the first pastor of Mwanafumu Baptist Church. She became a pastor when her uncle Nicholas Mulenga, who had been founder and pastor of the church since 1975, fell out of fellowship with the church when he married a second wife in 1988 and the church did not feel that it was right for the pastor to be polygamous. The church dismissed him as their pastor in the same year 1988. Mellia Makina, who was among the founding members of the church, was voted in as the pastor. By then, she was a widow.[39] The church found no reason to reject her abilities because of her singlehood. Instead they affirmed the position that women with no husbands are also full human beings and suitable for any service in the church, even the holy ministry of being a pastor. This was regardless of the fact that she was one of the young widows whom Paul in his letter to Timothy advised to get married.[40] In her capacity as pastor, she had to preach all Sundays except when Rev

---

[36] This stand is also shared by Mrs Martha Chirwa. Int. Mrs Martha Chirwa, Zomba Theological College, 9.1.2001.

[37] Int. Mellia Makina, Mwanafumu Baptist focus group, Mwanafumu Baptist, 21.3.2000.

[38] Int. Sellina Nasimango, Zomba Baptist Church, 28.10.2000.

[39] Int. Mellia Makina and focus group, Jali, 21.3.2000. Mwanafumu was a branch from Makolije.

[40] 1 Tim 5:14.

Davidson Lichapa from Makolije Baptist Church visited.[41] Mrs Mellia Makina was pastor of the church for two years, until 1990, when she remarried an evangelist (mlaliki) Makina.

Even though Mellia Makina was more competent than her husband to pastor the church, leaders from the supervising Makolije Baptist Church appointed him as pastor.[42] However, Mellia is still respected and referred to as pastor in her church and in the region.[43] This shows that if the local congregation was given an option to decide on who should be pastor of their church, they were likely to reelect Mellia as their pastor.

Even though there was this change, in practice, Mellia still remains the pastor of the church in her own right. She has continued to exercise her pastoral role even after her husband was elected pastor. She leads songs at the gravesite; she visits and preaches at daughter churches such as Namatope and Chinangwa Baptist in Jali area, and this she does with the cooperation of her husband.[44] Through her, women in this Jali area have caught the vision to preach. She is currently serving as the Umodzi chairperson for Jali association. The decision to replace Mellia Makina as pastor with her husband is a testimony as to how autonomy of the church in Baptist churches gives relative freedoms to women. This decision to rob Mellia Makina of her pastoral duties was only possible when the local congregation decided to consult other powers, from its supervising congregation, leaning more towards methods churches of centralized governments utilize.[45] Centralized church structures have tended to oppress women in churches by denying them freedom to engage themselves in spiritual ministries they feel called to.[46]

---

[41] Rev Davidson Lichapa's church, Makolije was the supervising church of Mwanafumu. Int. Davidson Lichapa, Makolije Baptist Church, 8.3.2000.
[42] Mwanafumu originated from Makolije but supervises Namatope and Chinangwa. Int. focus group, Mwanafumu Baptist Church, 21.3.2000.
[43] At women's regional meetings, she is addressed as a woman pastor, for example at a regional conference on 3.3.2000, Zomba Baptist Church.
[44] Int. Sellina Nasimango, Zomba Baptist Church, 28.10.2000.
[45] Although PIM is also Baptist, allocation of pastors to congregations is done by their central government - the board. Int. Patrick Makondesa, Kachere Research Institute, Chancellor College, 21.1.2001.
[46] Even though some women in Livingstonia felt called to be ministers, they had to wait till their Synod approved that women could be ordained.

3.2.3.2 Mrs Sellina Nasimango

Mrs Sellina Nasimango was born in Kuntumanje village in Zomba. She was born a Catholic and was baptized in the Catholic Church. However she, together with her family, abandoned the Catholic Church when the church refused to give a church funeral to one of her sisters.[47] In 1970, she became a Baptist when a deacon known as Madzi Nkutenga in Liwonde preached to her about his Baptist faith. By then she was staying in Chinyung'unya where there was no Baptist church nor any other church, since the area was predominantly Muslim. She however decided to start holding prayers in her house together with her husband who had left Islam to follow her. Her husband did not experience any alienation from family members because of leaving his Islamic faith.

Sellina Nasimango, Liwonde: 2000

Other people joined these home prayers. She preached on Sundays and led the congregation in singing.[48] However, Holy Communion was administered by a visiting pastor known as Mr. Jera who belonged to a Baptist church near Lake Chirwa. Sellina's restriction to administer Holy Communion was not imposed by the church; she argues that she did not feel called to administer the sacraments. The fact that the church respected her individual conscience was liberating to her because she could feel free to be a pastor while at the same time define her role ac-

---

[47] Int. Mrs Nasimango, Zomba Baptist Church, 28.10.2000.
[48] Ibid.

cording to her convictions. This is strange in other church cultures. If one becomes a pastor, it means you agree to do all that an ordained pastor should do.

Sellina Nasimango does not have any theological training. Her theology is traced from her involvement in the Catholic Church. During her Catholic days, her mother was in the leadership of Legio Maria. She was a teacher and because of her age, she would sometimes ask Sellina to help her teach the women. Her father was an *agrupa*[49] and through him, she learnt a lot about Christian religion. This experience became very useful in her pastoral responsibilities. Further, she was a friend of a CCAP woman Emma Katungwe who used to preach in her church.[50] Emma was fond of the Bible and they would once in a while spend time together reading the Bible.[51] Sellina has been pastor of this church until 1996. Even now, she is refereed to as a woman pastor.[52] The current pastor of Chinyung'unya is Rev Kazembe. Sellina still preaches regularly. Sellina feels that God called her to start the church, and that anyone can come in and be pastor of this church that she founded. The fact that a male pastor replaces her is not a sign that she failed in her responsibility.[53]

3.2.3.3 Mrs Agnes Lufani

Mrs Agnes Lufani started Nasongole Baptist Church in 1986.[54] At that time, her husband had gone to Bible School in Lilongwe and there was no Baptist Church in the area where she lived. During this time, she used to organize open-air meetings at a market in this area. She had learnt this strategy through her involvement with Every Home Crusade[55] while she was in Chikwawa.[56] Through such meetings, some were converted

---

[49] *Agrupa* are leaders of the Catholics in a certain location.
[50] Int. Sellina Nasimango, Chinyung'unya Baptist, 28.10.2000.
[51] Ibid.
[52] Int. Agnes Lufani, Liwonde Baptist Church 3.3.2000; int. focus group. South East regional conference, Zomba Baptist Church, 3.3.2000. The South East region conference addressed her as a woman pastor (*mbusa wa chizimayi*) just as in the case of Mellia Makina.
[53] Int. Sellina Nasimango, Chinyung'unya Baptist Church, 28.10.2000.
[54] Ibid.
[55] Every Home Crusade is an international interdenominational organization that tries to reach every household with the gospel.
[56] Int. Agnes Lufani, Mpheta Baptist Church, 3.3.2000.

to become Baptists. Since there was no Baptist congregation in that area, she organized them into a church. By the time her husband came, he found this church active. Her husband would assist to pastor the church during holidays but when he was in Bible School, pastoral responsibilities were left in her hands of Agnes.[57] Agnes would preach on Sundays and also held funeral services in the absence of her husband. After the husband finished theological training, they moved to Mpheta where they founded Mpheta Baptist Church in 1991.[58] Just as at Nasongole, Mrs Agnes Lufani did some preaching on a Sunday. By this time, she had also gone through theological training as pastor's wife. However, she attributes her zeal to preach to her involvement with Every Home Crusade while she was in Chikwawa.[59]

3.2.4 Perceptions on women pastors

3.2.4.1 Male pastors interviewed

It is evident that these women's pastoral responsibilities earned them the right to preach. However there are various views from the church about their pastoral role. While most women look at these women pastors with pride as evidenced in their regional meetings, some male members of BACOMA remain skeptical about these women pastors.

A survey conducted among key pastors in the region shows perceptions concerning women pastors. One argument given was that Mrs Nasimango and Mrs Makina have never been pastors, because they were not ordained. But there are many pastors that are not ordained in Baptist congregations, and Baptists do not demand that a pastor must be ordained, but some pastors demand this of women. For those that are ordained it is not the governing body, the Convention, which ordains them, nor the seminary at the end of their training, but ordination is an issue decided by the local congregation. It is usually done after one has served

---

[57] Ibid.
[58] Int. Agnes Lufani, Mpheta Baptist Church, 3.3.2000.
[59] Int. Rev Malikebu, Thundu Baptist Church, 19.5.2000. Every Home Crusade played a major role in the revival of that period.

as pastor for sometime, sometimes as an affirmation that they like his services.[60]

The theology at grassroots concerning the procedure of ordination to pastoral ministry is interesting. One pastor described it as buying a Bible and presenting it to the pastor to be ordained in a church service and instructing the pastor into issues of stewardship after which there is a party. When presenting the Bible, the pastor candidate is told to hold the Bible while the pastor that ordains him or her stretches his hand on him and makes this pronouncement: *Mtendere ukhale ndi inu* (peace be with you). Some men use such procedure to prove whether there have been women pastors or not. The argument is that these women have not gone through such procedures, therefore, they are not pastors.[61]

Another view about women pastors is that these women who are called pastors by some, are just in church leadership. They distinguish being leader of the church from being pastor of the church, a true distinction because not all leaders are pastors. And in Baptist churches we have leaders such as members of the council that include the deacons and others which may be involved in social and development work or other spiritual ministries such as prayer. But not all are called pastors. Therefore the fact that these women were called pastors means they are pastors. This view is also represented by the views of a pastor who argued that Mrs Makina was just a leader of the church, not a pastor. He went on to say that Rev Davidson Lichapa was the pastor of Mwanafumu Baptist Church. It is interesting that even though these do not recognize these women as pastors, they frequently met them at the pastors' meeting.[62] This goes to say that the decisions made at a congregational level are more important than views from other congregations. The congregation at Mwanafumu decided that Mellia Makina was pastor and this is what made her a pastor, irrespective of the fact that others did not see it this way.

Along the same views, one pastor said that Mrs Nasimango was not a pastor. He argued that the fact that she started a church did not make her pastor. Sometimes a woman can start a church, but there must be a

---

[60] In Zomba Baptist Church for example Rev Oscar Matupi buried people, baptized and administered Holy Communion even before he got ordained.
[61] Int. Agnes Lufani, Zomba Baptist Church, 3.3.2000.
[62] Int. Rev Davidson Lichapa, Makolije Baptist Church, 8.3.2000 and Int. Rev Mwanakhu, Mpinda Baptist Church, 3.3.2000.

pastor to do the pastoral work. This attitude was also expressed in actions by the Westers in the early period when instead of making Andisambula who started Mandawala Baptist Church a pastor, they installed a male deacon to be such. To such people, Mrs Nasimango just started the church but was never pastor of Chinyung'unya Baptist Church, just a supervisor of the place.[63] Some however admit that she is pastor but argue that she has usurped the pastoral role from her husband. The assumption is that she was very bossy over her husband. Some attribute the role of a caretaker to her. She is famous for being pastor because she is bossy over her husband, but it is the husband who is the pastor of the church.[64]

The other view against women is administrative. These argue that there are no women pastors in Southern Malawi, because in the registry of pastors in Malawi there is no mention of any woman pastor.[65] However not all pastors in the region are in the registry. As such there is nothing irregular if these women pastors are not in the registry. On the other hand, it is unlikely that such records would show names of women pastors because it is men who have always compiled the list as such it is just a testimony of male negative views against women pastors. It is very rare that women have started churches; as such these women are an exception. Similarly, among all church founders, it is rare that they have been refused to be pastors.

Yet another view against women pastors is traditional, that a woman cannot be a pastor. But if a woman can be a chief, there is no reason why she cannot be a pastor. Those holding such a view do not have an explanation as to why a woman cannot be pastor. It is likely that this view is conditioned by the fact that in Malawi churches people are unaware of the presence of women pastors, because even churches that have them are urban and therefore such developments may still be unfamiliar to the rural majority.[66]

The negative views against women pastors are complemented by some of the practices in BACOMA. In the case of Sellina Nasimango, she used to be invited to attend pastors meeting when Galatiya was the

[63]   Int. Rev Malikebu, Thundu Baptist Church, 19.5.2000.
[64]   Int. Rev Macfarry Kamwendo, Mtengo wa Moyo Baptist Church, 13.8.2000.
[65]   Int. Rev Davidson Lichipa, Makolije Baptist Church, 8.3.2000.
[66]   Int. Rev Davidson Lichapa, Makolije Baptist Church, 8.3.2000.

chairperson of the Convention.[67] After Galatiya's time, she has never received such invitations.

He was responsible for encouraging women to preach in New Jerusalem Church in Blantyre in the late 1960s. After he left, there was a decline in women's preaching in that church. Mrs Mellia Makina on the other hand was being invited, not through the Convention but by Rev Lichapa, the supervising pastor. However Rev Lichapa always emphasized that he invited her just as a representative of her church, which did not have a pastor yet.[68]

Although these women pastors perform a significant amount of roles relating to their pastoral role, they are denied opportunity to do some. They preach on Sundays, care for their flock in everyday life, do administrative duties of the church but they are not allowed to administer sacraments: Baptism and Holy Communion. While administration of sacraments is pegged to ordination in some churches, the issue in Baptist churches is rather of gender, because men who are not ordained do administer sacraments on the strength of the priesthood of all believers. In the event that their congregations need such sacraments, male pastors or other male leaders would be invited to administer them.

Some favours in BACOMA are restricted to male pastors. Mrs Sellina Nasimango recalls that one time she had been invited by Jimmy Hodges Ministries to attend their meetings.[69] At the end of the meetings, every pastor was given a bicycle except her. When Rev Galatiya learnt of this act, he registered his discontent with Jimmy Hodges leaders.[70] The actions of Rev Galatiya towards women pastors show that not all Convention pastors deny the fact that there are women pastors.

Against negative views from some of the male members of the church, the majority of women have affirmed the pastoral role of their fellow women. At both regional women's meetings I attended in 2000, these women were addressed as pastors (not pastors' wives [amayi mbusa] but abusa achizimayi [women pastors]). They were also given the special privilege of receiving officially new congregations such as Holy Mount Baptist Church in Jali. I cannot guarantee that all women are

---

[67]   Int. Sellina Nasimango, Zomba Baptist Church, 28.10.2000.
[68]   Int. Mellia Makina, Mwanafumu Baptist Church, 21.3.2000.
[69]   Jimmy Hodges is an interdenominational ministry started by a Baptist, with the aim of starting churches. Int. Rev Chisi, Ufulu Baptist Church, Lilongwe, 23.6.2000.
[70]   Int. Sellina Nasimango, Zomba Baptist Church, 28.10.2000.

positive about women pastors, but if there are who are negative, I have not come across any. For those I have asked as to why they believe that women can be pastors, they argue that *azimayi ndi adindo amphamvu* (women are strong leaders). Their stand is supported by what women have been able to accomplish in history. For example, it were women who went to the grave and saw Jesus risen from the dead while Peter and his fellow male disciples were in hiding, afraid.[71] Some women say that even at a funeral, it is the women that sit near the coffin while the men sit outside the house. Again others argue that it is women that have brought humanity into existence through delivery. Thus they see no reason why women cannot be pastors, in fact they add, if women can preach, why can they not be pastors?[72]

3.2.5 Restrictive factors to women preaching

It is evident that Baptist women do not always enjoy optimum freedom in the area of preaching, which are a high-ranking form of leadership in a Baptist church. Out of the 25 churches above, eight churches do not allow women to preach. This in no way should be understood statistically to represent about half of the congregations in the region. The problem is not the frequency of the problem, rather that women are not able to preach in some congregations. Several reasons have been given for not allowing women to preach and some of them are represented below.

3.2.5.1 Tradition

From the above table, women do not preach, because traditionally they are not to preach in the presence of men. But do women not speak in public? In both patrilineal and matrilineal societies women do speak in public for example at a traditional court to give witness or to defend themselves. At political meetings even during the autocratic rule, women gave public speeches. And in matrilineal societies women have been leaders such as spirit mediums and chiefs.[73] It would be wrong therefore to suggest that women couldn't preach because traditionally they cannot speak in public.

---

[71] Int. focus group, Mwanafumu Baptist Church, 21.3.2000.
[72] Int. focus group, Zomba, 3.3.2000. Regional women's meeting.
[73] Isabel Phiri emphasises that. See Isabel Phiri, *Women, Presbyterianism and Patriarchy*, pp. 32-34.

Maybe the word tradition needs to be well defined because it is likely not referring to the *traditional* tradition. However there are other aspects of tradition that are used as a scapegoat against women preaching such as menstruation. In some congregations women do not preach because of the traditional belief that a women's menstrual blood makes her unclean, and therefore unfit to preach.[74] This relates to the Jewish belief expressed in Leviticus.[75] It is however not clear whether Baptist women get this stand from the Bible or from their culture, although there may be a possibility that some may use the Levitical passage to cement the view.[76]

The word tradition could well be the *zeitgeist* of today, which was more pronounced in the earlier years than now. The Baptist Christian tradition may well also be implied here. Traditionally early Baptist women missionaries were not involved in preaching. This has meant that local Baptist women would have no role models for preaching.

3.2.5.2 Biblical interpretation

The other reason why women do not preach has been based on the Bible. Some interpretations of the Bible have influenced congregations to deny women their freedom to preach. Since Baptist women do not live in a vacuum, such interpretations do influence negatively their belief in the priesthood of all believers. Women that are liberated in the area of preaching, base their stand on the historical evidence in the Bible. To a question which I asked women in the South East region "why do you preach if the Bible says you should keep quiet?" women answered either that they ignore the verses or do not believe them because they see women preaching in the Bible.[77]

Those that subject women in the church to silence, base their stand mainly on the verse that says that women should be silent in the

[74] See also: Felix Chingota, "A Historical Account of the Attitude of Blantyre Synod of the Church of Central Africa Presbyterian towards Initiation Rites," in *Religion in Malawi*, no 5, 1995, pp. 8-15.
[75] Ibid.
[76] In 1990, we had to deal with the problem in rural Jali area where women could not participate in Holy Communion when they were having their period.
[77] See Rachel Banda, Baptist Women of the Book and Culture, paper presented at Postgraduate Colloquium, Department of Theology and Religious Studies, University of Malawi, 2000.

church.[78] Those that believe that women ought to preach, argue that such a statement is not in resonance with Paul's historical stand on women in the church. He involved women in ministry and freely writes about them, such as Priscilla and Phoebe, whom he addresses as ministers of the gospel.[79]

Some men do not believe that God would use women in such spiritual ministry, and they also refer to the Bible for this stand. Some, for example, believe that women are blind to certain truths, even though they are Christians, or they say that they are not as gifted as men. However, if women are blind to certain truths, what kind of Holy Spirit do women receive if the role of the Holy Spirit is to lead Christians into all truth?[80] Is the Holy Spirit men receive different from the one women receive? Then which Holy Spirit do women receive?

Again, if women are not gifted, do they have the Holy Spirit that is said to give gifts as he determines?[81] This is true. However if women are not gifted then at least they have a gift of prophecy as predicted by the prophet Joel:

> In the last days, God says, I will pour out my spirit on all people and your sons and daughters will prophecy.[82]

3.2.5.3 Unwillingness

Some women in Baptist churches do not preach because they are afraid to preach or unwilling to do so. Such restrictions are based on cultural beliefs and biblical interpretation or a lack of self-confidence. Women at Living Stones Baptist Church in Blantyre for example are allowed to preach on a regular Sunday but have so far refused to take up this role.[83] These women are usually influenced by other church traditions, which refuse women to preach.

---

[78] 1 Corinthians 14:33-34: "As in all the congregations of the saints, women should remain silent in the churches. They are not allowed to speak, but must be in submission, as the Law says.".

[79] See also Janet Kholowa and Klaus Fiedler, *Mtumwi Paulo ndi Udindo wa Amayi Mumpingo*, Blantyre: CLAIM-Mvunguti, 2001.

[80] John 16:13. "But when the spirit of truth comes, he will guide you into all truth.".

[81] 1 Cor 12: All these (gifts) are the work of one and the same spirit, and gives them to teach one, just as he determines.

[82] See Acts 2:17ff.

[83] Int. Pastor Amos Phiri, Livingstone Baptist Church, Blantyre, 26.5.2000.

3.2.5.4 Lack of external influences

The table above shows that a greater number of congregations in rural areas compared to urban ones do not allow women to preach. This is probably because rural congregations lack outside influences, from urban areas, where women are able to preach within their churches or at interdenominational meetings. Rural churches tend to be slow at getting information about programmes of their churches. Baptist Convention churches have four Sundays in a year, which are allocated to women. At such Sundays, women are given opportunity to lead the whole Sunday Service, including preaching. If these rural churches knew about this Sunday, they would have women preach in churches where women are willing to do so.

3.2.5.5 Lack of theological training

In most rural churches, women do not preach because they have insufficient theological training. Theological training has been restricted to pastors' wives except in the recent period. But even for pastors' wives, they would become better preachers if they received more theological training and their courses in seminary were more diverse. On the contrary pastors' wives spend more time on learning theology related to their women's organisation. This, therefore, has restricted even pastors' wives to preaching to fellow women alone.

3.2.6 Lack of acceptance

Even though there are oppressive elements dissuading women from preaching, an increasing number of congregations allow women to preach. However, there are two levels of preaching as shown by the table above. Of the thirteen churches that allow women to preach, eleven of them allow women only to preach on Women's Sunday. Only three congregations allow women to preach on a regular Sunday. To preach on Women's Sunday is an expression of freedom for Baptist women but it is optimum freedom if they can also preach on any regular Sunday. Churches that allow women to preach on Women's Sunday alone may be suffering from lack of acceptance that women should preach in church. They only have agreed to involve women in this way to be obedient to church programmes or to appease the women members of the congregation. To allow women to preach on a regular Sunday on the other hand shows complete acceptance by the congregation that women, just as men, are equally called to be leaders in the church. Only when a church reaches this point they can consider ordaining a woman as pastor of a church, as being a pastor of a church always involves preaching.

3.2.6.1 External influences

The table above shows that only a minority of congregations enjoys this privilege of women preaching. According to the table, a common reason for this is tied to the presence of an external influence. Zomba Baptist Church for example started involving women in preaching firstly in the English service. This was through the encouragement of Dr Klaus Fiedler. His sermons encouraged women to preach. Since 1993, women started to preach in this service on a regular Sunday. Among them were Mrs Grace Matupi, Mrs Theresa Day, Mrs Martha Chirwa and Mrs Rachel Banda.

In the Chichewa service, women started preaching because of some women who were involved in Women Aglow, an interdenominational women's organisation.[84] As such the first women who preached in this service were members of the organisation, like Mrs Linly Chauluka and Mrs Mlenga. These were later followed by the likes of Mrs Topesa, Mrs Mangwele, and Mrs Banda. This church is liberated in the area of women preaching to an extent that during the time they were looking for a pastor in 2000, the name of a woman was suggested as a candidate for being pastor.[85]

However external influences do not always determine the move towards women preaching. Even such influences have to be assessed by the local congregation, and it is up to a local congregation to either accept or reject the influence. When Dr Klaus Fiedler for example preached a sermon in Blantyre Baptist Church in June 1998, implying that women could preach, a missionary, Jerkins left the congregation in protest against that implied message. His wife also followed. Jerkins summoned

---

[84] See Rachel Banda, A Comprehensive Study of Women's Organisations in Southern Malawi, MA Module Paper, Department of Theology and Religious Studies, Chancellor College.
[85] Pastor's search committee at Zomba Baptist Church suggested the name of a woman in 2000.

the leadership of Blantyre Baptist Church to express his discontent at Dr Fiedler's message. The church however supported his stand as in accordance to their Baptist doctrine that women just as men can preach. Akim Chirwa, General Secretary of BACOMA, also affirmed this view. He wrote a memorandum to Jerkins that the Convention supports Dr Fiedler's stand.[86]

3.3 Other leadership roles

There are three levels of leadership women take up in a congregation. Firstly, women lead fellow women. This is in the confines of their women's organisation especially during their weekly meetings. Secondly, women lead children, this can be either in a youth group or teaching a Sunday school class. The third role is to lead both men and women and it is here where women struggle to have optimum freedom. The early missionary women—by example—taught local women to lead fellow women. For the same reason, missionary women organized periodic training sessions and even funded them fully up to the late 1970s. During this period women were trained in the distinctives of their organisation and Baptist beliefs. Although there were exceptions such as in the area of women pastors in the South East region and women preaching in New Jerusalem church, women were basically restricted to leading fellow women. During a Sunday morning, if women led, it was in support ministries such as singing in a choir.

This was well demonstrated by missionary women except that missionary women could also do a drama. Doing a drama was relevant to local needs because local women were already aware of such vehicles of instruction through culture, for example in *chinamwali*.[87] However it is interesting that locals have not taken up the use of drama (except during church *chinamwali*) has not been taken up by locals.

3.3.1. Positions women in urban congregations currently enjoy

The number of women in the urban congregations continued to increase. The English congregation started at Cliccord House is currently called Blantyre Baptist Church. One of the new members in this period was Mrs

[86] Int. Akim Chirwa, June 1998, BACOMA office; Int. Raynor Kawamba and Margaret Nyika, 17.11.1999. BACOMA offices Blantyre.
[87] See *Chinamwali* document in R. Banda, Coming of Age, Zomba: Kachere, 2005.

Sutcliff. She was a South African married to a British. Her husband was a medical doctor in Malawi for several years, and served mostly at Kamuzu Central Hospital in Lilongwe. Unlike his wife, he was not a Christian. Mrs Sutcliff had been one of the early women in Capital City Baptist Church in Lilongwe who came to Blantyre in the late 1980s upon retirement of her husband who chose to live in Malawi, New Lands in Blantyre for the rest of his life. His wife is fondly remembered for her hospitality and financial support to women's work, and when she died, her clothing and other things were sold to help with women's work as she had stated in her will.[88]

In the current period, the majority of women in urban churches are still restricted to support roles. In a programme of leaders made by Soche Baptist Church in Blantyre in 1999, most of the song leaders in the month of May were women.[89] A programme by Living Stones Baptist Church in 1997 is another illustration of women taking support roles. From March to July, all eleven worship leaders were women; no woman was a preacher, no woman was on the church council except the chairperson of *Umodzi*. No woman was on the team that served the Lord's Supper and Baptism.[90] In Blantyre Baptist Church, three of the nine deacons were women in 1999. All members of the kindergarten committee were women. No woman was on the preaching programme.[91] Some women were in the youth committee. However for Blantyre Baptist Church to entrust the responsibility of church administrator to Mrs Margaret Nyika, demonstrates their faithfulness to the Baptist doctrine of the priesthood of all believers. During her time as an administrator, Mrs Nyika achieved much for the church. She was able to oversee the construction of the magnificent church building as well as scheduling different speakers for the Sunday services. This was because at this time the church did not have a pastor. Their former pastor had left and the assistant pastor, Rev Vincent Chirwa, was in South Africa pursuing further studies in theology. Margaret Nyika was therefore key in running the day-

---

[88] Int. Mrs Margaret Nyika, Blantyre Baptist Church, 26.5.1999; Int. Mrs Fanny Kwelakwela (nee Malabwanya), Bangwe Baptist Church, Blantyre, 30.4.2000.
[89] Only one out of four was a man. Int. Rev Gunya and Mr Ng'oma, Soche Baptist Church, Blantyre, 25.5.1999.
[90] Int. Rev Amos Phiri, Livingstone Baptist Church, Blantyre, 26.5.1999.
[91] Int. Mrs Margaret Nyika, Blantyre Baptist Church, 26.5.1999.

to-day activities of the church. She left this role when the church engaged an interim pastor from America, Rev Covington.

In Zomba Baptist Church, in the South East region, women have tremendous amount of freedom to preach. This was not the case in the earlier years. But since 1999, a woman preaches in this church at least once a month. Women's freedom is not restricted to preaching, they can also serve in other leadership roles. In 1990, the church secretary was a woman, Mrs Rachel Banda. She served in this position until 1993, with a brief break in between when she was dismissed from the church because of a conflict surrounding the dismissal of Rev Kachasu Gama junior. When the issue was settled, Mrs Banda was reinstated but did not serve the church much longer because she went to Lilongwe where her husband had found another job.

In 1999, Mrs Sichinga was the church secretary. Her role as a secretary was more pronounced than that of a chairperson. This is true for all church secretaries in Zomba Baptist Church, because it is the secretary that makes announcements in every Sunday service, it is the secretary that writes minutes and reads them at every council meeting. In the absence of the pastor at church, she is the one who organizes programmes relating to the church. Mrs Sichinga left her post as secretary because she had to follow her husband in Mzuzu where he got employed. Thus, while the chairperson is more involved in the council meetings, it is the secretary that is seen to be engaged in the day-to-day activities of the church.

Mrs Mulenga was church secretary in 1996 to 1998; she was replaced by Mr Mojoo who is currently (2001) the church secretary. Since Zomba Baptist Church has two services, English and Chichewa, it has been advantageous that all the secretaries were literate in both languages.

Zomba Baptist Church has had no struggles about involving women as deacons since the church started. Currently there are two women deacons out of six.

In Nchalo Baptist Church in Lower Shire there were no women deacons by 2000. The only time this church had women deacons was in 1985, when Rev Kalavina was pastor. These women were Mrs Gonkho and Mrs Ambress who at that time were widows.[92] The reasons given for choosing these widows suggest that singlehood did matter in patrilineal

---

[92]   Int. Mrs Kalavina, Rev Kalavina, Nchalo Baptist Church, 26.7.2000.

societies unlike in the matrilineal societies of Zomba. These women had been chosen as deacons because they were elderly and beyond the age of marriage. This alludes to Paul's passage about young widows to get married, which seems to be influenced by patrilineal as well as matrilineal cultures. In matrilineal culture, Mrs Makina, still within marrying age, was given the highest leadership position, that of a pastor. After the deaths of Mrs Ambress and Mrs Gonkho, no other woman has been elected to the office of a deacon.[93]

As regards the role of preaching, even in this century, women do not preach in the church. Mrs Kalavina preached only by accident, once in 1994, when her husband was sick. The reasons given for women not preaching have been stated before, centering on tradition and interpretation of Pauline passages. Women are so restricted in this church that even a role that has been widely accepted in the Baptist tradition, that of a woman deacon, is not a reality in this church. As such, no women are in the church council except the *Umodzi* chairlady.[94]

The examples above show that not all urban congregations have given optimum freedom to women to serve in leadership. Women mostly serve in support roles. Few congregations involve women in the office of a church secretary of which Zomba Baptist Church and Blantyre Baptist Church are comparatively more liberated in this area. Nchalo Baptist, Living Stones Baptist and Soche Baptist still fall short in this area. Even in this century, women are not in the church council. This implies that there are no women who are deacons, because deacons, in Baptist congregations, are members of the council.

3.3.2 Positions of women in rural congregations

3.3.2.1 Women deacons

Unlike in the urban congregations, the issue of women in the Church Council even apart from being deacons has not been a struggle for rural women in the South East region. Since 1967, almost all rural congregations in this region, such as Mpinda, Ntokota, Makolije, Chayima have had women as deacons and women serving in other positions in the

---

[93] Ibid.
[94] Ibid.

church council.[95] In Ntokota Baptist Church in Jali, women assumed positions of treasurer and secretary in 1967.[96] Such roles may seem insig-
nificant but at that time, many other Christian churches with a few exceptions such as PIM had no women deacons.[97] Certainly the engagement
of women in such roles is a proof that local Baptists in this region were
more liberated.

At Nsomo Baptist Church in Lower Shire, the first women deacons
were elected in 1990 even though the church was started in 1973. These
first women were Mrs Kantefa and Mrs L. Samu and have been such till
2000. This situation is different from the realities of the matrilineal cultures of Zomba area where women have been deacons since the early
1960s.

There are other women leaders in Nsomo Baptist Church but their
roles do not make them members of the church council, which guides the
local congregation in decision making. This means that women's views
are not well represented, apart from those presented by the *Umodzi*
chairlady who is mainly concerned with *Umodzi* activities in the church.
Some of the women in other roles in the church are Sunday school
teachers such as Mrs Pitison, Mrs Dombe and Mrs Christina Kalenga.
The majority of women were in support roles such as being members of
a choir.[98]

At Ndirande Baptist Church in Lower Shire, there is no woman deacon even though 30 out of 38 members of the congregation are women.
This seems to be due to an influence from Nchalo Baptist Church, which
is the supervising church, where there are no women deacons. Just as in
the supervising congregation, no woman preaches during a Sunday service and the church does not have a Woman's Sunday, which is a common practice even among mainline churches that are restrictive to
women preaching.[99] This condition is unlikely due to patrilineal tendencies alone, because in other patrilineal societies, such as the Northern
region of Malawi, women do preach, for example in Livingstonia Synod.

---

[95] Int. Rev Tambala Mwanakhu, Mpinda Baptist Church, Zomba, 13.7.2000.
[96] See Gazamiyala diary.
[97] Int. Patrick Makondesa, Kachere Institute, Chancellor College, Zomba.
[98] Int. focus group, Nsomo Baptist Church, 27.7.2000. In 2000, 2 out of 12 deacons
were women.
[99] Int. Mr Bonwell Kachere, Mrs Maria Chinangwa, Bertha Joseph, Chikwawa,
26.7.2000.

However it is true that there seems to be less freedom among rural churches in the South South region concerning women serving as deacons, preachers and church council members as opposed to rural churches in the South East region. This difference may be linked to cultural differences between matrilineal and patrilineal societies, in which case the involvement of women in preaching in Livingstonia Synod may be due to theology. However since Baptist theology attests to the priesthood of all believers, one would expect that if it were a matter of theology, then Baptist women would have enjoyed relative freedoms as well in patrilineal societies. Could it be possible that the patrilineal societies of Southern Malawi are different and more oppressive than those of Northern Malawi? The difference is possible because the two societies do have different origins and are separate entities separated by the Chewa of the Central region.

It is however clear that patrilineal elements in the South South may have been suppressive to women leadership, while matrilineal elements in the South East region may have been more liberating to the women in these societies. This is probably because matrilineal societies traditionally have been more sympathetic to women leadership. However it is also true that among the patrilineal societies of the South South region, women leadership is also well accepted.[100] Therefore the oppression of rural women in the South South region is likely due to the kind of evangelicalism that missionaries in the South South held. Baptists are of varying evangelicalism and if those with conservative leanings worked with women in this region, then there is a high chance that this oppression was due to missionary influence.

At Ntokota Baptist Church in Thyolo the first woman preached in 1987, not as a member of this church but visiting from Blantyre. She had come to the church for a weekend to train women, but since she planned to attend the Sunday service before she returned to Blantyre, the church asked her to preach. The second woman to preach was Mrs Kwalira. She was an immigrant into the area. She and her husband had come to Thyolo from Salima because Mr Kwalira was employed in the tea planta-

---

[100] See Matthew Schoffeleers, "An Outline History of Territorial Mediumship in Nsanje" in: *Religion and Dramatization of Life*, Blantyre: CLAIM-Kachere 1996, and Isabel Apawo Phiri, *Women, Presbyterianism and Patriarchy: Religious Experiences of Chewa Women in Central Malawi*, pp. 21-47.

tions in Thyolo. On the other hand, there have been women deacons in this church since it was started.[101]

At Mpando Baptist Church, no woman has been a deacon since it was founded in 1975.[102] Women just sing in the choir and preach on Women's Sunday, which is usually twice a year.[103] The women who preached were Mrs Chiseko, who used to come from Blantyre and Mrs Kwalira, who was a member of this church before transferring membership to Ntokota. Mrs Kwalira used to transfer membership within Thyolo from one congregation to the other deliberately in order to strengthen women's work in the congregations.[104]

This trend of women serving increasingly in leadership positions continues even to the present times. There are more women serving in leadership positions in rural congregations in the South East than in urban congregations. However it is interesting that local Baptist women have enjoyed such freedoms in these other roles as opposed to preaching. It seems women are largely tolerated in this kind of leadership. This may be because such offices are more of support roles. They are linked to administration, visitation and hospitality work, which keep women in the background of the church. Such roles were even typical among the early missionary women. Mary Chandler, for example, was the mission treasurer from 1970 to 1987, the time she left Malawi.[105]

3.3.3 Women at associational level

While the struggle for freedom continues at the local congregation levels, women have yet another challenge, that of being represented at general committees of the Convention. It is evident that the local culture of women leading fellow women only, and patronizing support roles is carried forward to this level.

At the associational level in the South South region, no woman had ever been on the committee for Blantyre association. Mrs Ng'oma is the

---

[101] Int. Mr and Mrs Filemon Kambalame, Mrs Agnes Kambalame, Ntokota Baptist, Thyolo, 26.7.2000.
[102] Int. Mrs Martha Kholomana, Mpando Baptist Church, Thyolo, 26.7.2000.
[103] The church started in 2000.
[104] Int. Mrs Martha Kholomana, Mpando Baptist Church, Thyolo, 26.7.2000.
[105] Int. Rev Hany Longwe, Lilongwe Baptist Seminary, 13.3.2000.

first woman to be in this committee beginning 2000.[106] Since Rev Galatiya's time, Mrs Ng'oma has continued to exhibit liberative tendencies to go against the flow of women leading fellow women only. She was the first woman to preach in the South South region in New Jerusalem Church, and became the first woman to serve on the general committee (*association ya azibambo*)[107] of the Convention at the associational level. Mrs Ng'oma is however a migrant to the South. She is married to an Nkhata-Bay resident but is a Zimbabwean by birth.

Up until 2000, Thyolo and Mwanza belonged to Blantyre association.[108] In Chikwawa district no woman is represented on the general association committee. However, the leadership of *Umodzi* such as treasurer, chairperson and secretary are always invited to attend the general association committee meetings.[109] The general association of Chikwawa started in 1974 much earlier than the youth association and women's association that only started during the current period.[110] Nsanje has been part of Chikwawa association up to 2000.[111]

In the South East region, since 1967, all Baptist congregations in the area were coordinated informally from Jali. Mulanje and Balaka congregations were also coordinated from Jali.[112] Jali association was formally established in 1974 together with the women's association (*association ya azimayi*), and youth association (*association ya achinyamata*).[113] In the South East region, the general association is often referred to as the men's association (*association ya abambo*). The committee of the general association has been exclusively male for a long time. Changes to this state have started during this period. The first woman to appear on the general association in the region was Agnes Lufani. She is also one

---

[106] Int. Mr V.W. Chitsukwa, Chisomo Baptist Church, 28.3.2000. She was chairperson in 2000. There are three types of associations: Youth, Women and General association (for all members of the BACOMA in that association).

[107] The perception that the general association is such came because attendance at the meetings was dominated by men. This was not deliberate but because it was customary that leaders of local congregation attended such meetings, mostly men.

[108] Ibid.

[109] Int. Rev Jimu Kalenga, Nsomo Baptist Church, 28.9.2000.

[110] Youth Association started in 1993, while Women's Association started in 1981. Ibid.

[111] Ibid.

[112] Int. Rev Davidson Lichapa, Makolije Baptist Church, 8.3.2000.

[113] Int. focus group, Zomba Baptist Church, 3.2.2000.

of the first women preachers and pastors in the early period, and continues to exhibit her liberative tendencies over male domination.[114] She is
also a migrant, a Sena from Nsanje district.[115]

Against the common negative perceptions about women leading in
public, especially in the area of preaching and pastorship, the appointment of these women preachers to the *association ya azibambo* shows
that men have affirmed the fact that indeed these women are leaders in
their own right. This behaviour is local and different from the American
Southern Baptist missionary world.[116]

The wave of having women in the general Convention committees at
association level in this region continues to spread. In Mphyuphyu association, comprising churches near Lake Chirwa, Mrs Vuta became a
committee member succeeding Agnes Lufani in 1987.[117] Even in 2000,
although the majority in this committee are men, secretary and treasurer
are women. The secretary is Mrs Linje and the treasurer is Mrs Nanthambwe. In Mikuyu association, Mrs Manyungwe became the first
woman to be on the general committee in 2000.[118]

Although Jali association was the first to be established, women have
not been well represented at the general committee until 1990. Even
then, they have only served in the capacity of treasurer and committee
member. They are elected treasurers, because women are perceived to
be more reliable in matters of money than men.[119] In 2000, Mrs Mzeka
and Mrs Mapesi were committee members and Liness Makupe was
treasurer.[120] The disparities in the leadership freedoms of women from
one association to the other are characteristic of Baptist distinctives.
Each association and ultimately each congregation is autonomous and is
not obliged to follow decisions made by other associations. Dictates is-

---

[114] Ibid.

[115] Int. Mrs Agnes Lufani, Liwonde Baptist Church, 11.2000.

[116] While in many denominations in the west the trend is that women's rights are increasing, the Southern Baptist Convention is moving in the opposite direction. In
2000, the church issued a statement against ordination of women. Their stand is
based on the Ephesians 5 passage, and specifically on the verse that a man is head
and a wife should submit to her husband. Int. Oklahoma volunteers, Zomba,
25.9.2000.

[117] Int. Focus group, Zomba Baptist Church, 3.2.2000.

[118] Ibid.

[119] Int. Mrs Margaret Tepula, Makolije Baptist Church, Jali, 8.3.2000.

[120] Int. focus group, Zomba Baptist Church, 3.3.2000.

sued at the central office are not always followed by the grassroots for the same reasons.

From the observations above, it seems there is a relationship between women leadership in local congregations and in the associations. There is low women leadership development in local congregations in the Lower Shire and Thyolo as compared to local congregations in the South East region. Women in the South East region are more represented at general committees of associations than in the South South region. This shows that the progression in women leadership starts at the grassroots level and not at the central structures, even though the central structure may imagine having control over the grassroots.

3.4 Leadership at regional level

Women are less represented at regional level as compared to associational level. If changes came from the central structure, then there should have been change at the regional level as it is a bridge to the grassroots. In the South South and South East regions, no woman has been a member of the general Convention committee at regional level. All positions are taken by men.

While changes have been taking place at the bottom and at the top, the regions are still male dominated. The region is not only struggling to change but also to impact changes on the grassroots women. As a bridge of communication between the national office and the grassroots, it conveys decisions from the central office to the grassroots. This is because, by constitution, the chairlady of the region is a member of the central executive. She is the link between the national office and the grassroots people.

However, national decisions are usually not taken as a whole by the region. In 1999, the central executive, for example, sent Mrs Lufani (the regional coordinator for *Umodzi* in the South East) to inform associations about the items each region should bring to the 4-6 May 2000 Annual General Meeting, which was held at Lumbadzi Baptist Church in Lilongwe. Each region was to contribute K300 to the conference and in addition, each association was to bring K200 and each delegate K100 for food. When this decision was announced to the associations in the region on 2.2.2000, the associations rejected the decision and made alterations. They decided to bring items such as beans, tomatoes, chickens and maize flour to the meeting. They also decided to pay K100.[121] When delegates from the associations in the South East arrived in Lilongwe, the central office demanded their K300 from each association. However, the delegates gave their K100 contributions arguing that they could not afford any extra, since they had spent money on transport and did not have any paid employment. The central committee complained but had no powers to exclude the South East from the conference.

The region has also limited capacity to influence the grassroots people. Up to 2000, for example, the regional executive would set dates to visit different associations in the region. The region would then communicate such dates to the grassroots people through association leaders. However, often the regional committee would find no women at the meetings on those set dates. When this problem was presented to the regional meeting, the association delegates told the regional executive that such dates should be decided by the grassroots people and be sent to the regional committee members and that their visits to associations should be requested by associations as need arose and not be forced on them. The association delegates also felt that there was less need these days for women from the region to teach in the associations, as there are qualified women within associations or in neighbouring associations who would teach the local people. Examples of such a situation are Balaka and Zomba associations. The women from these associations are quite able to train their own people and can be invited to train other associations; as such they see no reason to invite women from other regions to train them.[122]

The central office also fails to communicate to the grassroots people in order to enforce change. At the South East women regional meeting of 2.2.2000 held in Zomba Baptist Church, for example, a letter from the central office, signed by the *Umodzi* national president, Mrs Raynor Kawamba was read to the associations present and was written in English. This was offensive to the people, because most of them do not understand English. The regional coordinator, Mrs Agnes Lufani also complained to fellow local women that even her felt mistreated during the central executive meetings when at these meetings English was used

---

121 Ibid.
122 Ibid.

even though the fellow executive members knew that her English was bad.[123]

The central executive sometimes has ideas that are foreign to the locals. In the machine-sewing project, assisted by the German Evangelical foundation, Hilfe für Brüder, and Oklahoma Baptists in the USA, the national office asked the region through an English letter to invite only women with at least a primary school certificate to come for training. This was unwelcome to the grassroots people in the South East region because the majority of women in this region are functionally illiterate. However, according to them, it is the illiterate that need sewing skills because those that are literate may not desperately need such skills. As such, local women in the South East have decided to patronize the local sewing projects, by hand, which is offered to all including the illiterates.[124]

The freedom not to follow the dictates of the national office presents a struggle to the national *Umodzi* executive. Even though, since the inception of *Umodzi*, the national office has worked hard to reinforce the distinctives of the organisation relating to uniforms and regulations of the organisation, the grassroots people have often reinterpreted these locally, and with much variety. As such regulations of the organization that the South East region follows are not identical to those followed by the South South region, and in fact whatever each region follows is not necessarily what is prescribed by the national office.

For example, the national office requires that the *Umodzi* uniform be worn only at the funeral of a deacon, a pastor or *Umodzi* woman, but in the South South and South East, *Umodzi* uniform is worn at the funeral of every member of the congregation including children who have undergone "*kutengedwa*."[125]

In the South East region no uniform is worn at a funeral of an *nthayo* (still-born), while in the South South region, a headdress (*duku*), which is part of the uniform, is worn at such a funeral.

The national office demands that only women who have memorized the prescribed verses should have the *Umodzi* uniform, but in the South East, many congregations commission women to have uniforms without

---

[123] Ibid.
[124] Ibid.
[125] Int. focus group, regional women's meeting, Zomba, 3.3.2000.

memorizing verses. This is also prevalent in the South South, but it is more serious in the South East region where illiteracy is very high.[126]

The national office demands that *Umodzi* uniforms should have round collar blouses, but the majority at the grassroots level does not follow this. A good number of women in the region still use the shirt collar blouses.

The above disparities give Baptist women their local identity and freedoms. They affirm the Baptist polity that power to make decisions is with the majority at the grassroots and not at the top. Local Baptist women freely choose to adjust national office dictates to be relevant to their local setting in which they serve.[127]

3.5 Leadership at national level

Until 1992, women were never part of the executive committee (EC) of BACOMA.[128] The first woman to break this tradition was Mrs Martha Chirwa, a migrant from Dedza living in the South South, married to Rev Akim Chirwa from Nkhata-Bay district. For several years Martha and her husband had worked in Blantyre till God called them to pastoral work in the Convention. Martha was a primary school teacher, but resigned to become pastor's wife on a full-time pastoral basis. She was in Blantyre in 1992, because at that time her husband Akim became pastor of Soche Baptist Church.[129] Martha was voted into the National *Umodzi* Executive in 1992 as the chairperson (President). Beginning the same year, the Convention had decided through the constitution that the national *Umodzi* chairperson should become an automatic member of the BA-COMA Executive Committee. This move was necessary because the Convention leadership felt that the *Umodzi* movement was running as a separate entity from the Convention. It was time that the organisation was seen to be included in the Convention. It is possible that the men perceived the organization's growth and expansion as a threat, and this was one way of controlling women. If their leader could be included in the EC, then the men would be able to check the developments within

---

[126] Neither regional nor national *Umodzi* tried to develop a method for oral learning.
[127] Baptist women in the centre may also be different from those in the South and the North. Each region is free to have its local identity.
[128] Rev Kaiya reported this at the Annual General meeting of 1999-2000 of the Baptist Convention.
[129] Int. Martha and Akim Chirwa, Blantyre Baptist Church, 14.12.2000.

the organisation and contain them.[130] Even though the motive may have been wrong, this provision of having a woman member in the EC was liberating to women. She became a voice of the women to the church. Through her, women's issues were known and discussed. Since 1992, the Convention has freely deliberated on women's issues.

It also became apparent that there were more women in BACOMA than men, and that it was absurd to leave out the majority in the EC. Martha Chirwa's era brought in changes not only on Convention level but within Umodzi as well. Women who were not pastors' wives in the Umodzi started to be elected as leaders in the National Executive, which was previously an option for pastors' wives only, as in Nkhoma Synod.[131] The first laywoman to enjoy this privileged position was Mrs Margaret Nyika, who was voted as treasurer of Umodzi at national level.[132]

While lay involvement at national Umodzi executive committees was scarce, it was not an issue at the grassroots level, as from the local congregation to the associational level; laywomen had taken leadership roles.

3.6 Leadership at international level

There are other women who have been leaders at an international level. From 1961 to 1964, Baptist Convention work in Zimbabwe, Zambia and Malawi was under one umbrella. In 1964, Baptist work in these countries became independent. This was not done to follow the political developments that occurred during this period but it had been the missionaries' intention from the beginning. But even with that independence, Baptist Convention, Providence Industrial Mission (PIM), Evangelical Baptist and Seventh Day Baptists, have continued to fellowship under one umbrella, Baptist Women Union of Southern Africa (BWUSA) and Baptist World Alliance. Baptist Convention women have not been leaders in the Baptist World Alliance, although they have attended conferences, which are usually held every 5 years. Martha Chirwa attended such a meeting in 1995 in Buenos Aires, Argentina, and Mrs Raynor Kawamba attended such a

---

[130] Isabel Phiri also shows how Chigwirizano in Nkhoma Synod was perceived as a "church within the church". See Isabel Apawo Phiri, Women, Presbyterianism and Patriarchy, pp. 71-90.

[131] See Isabel Phiri, Women, Presbyterianism and Patriarchy, pp. 80-102.

[132] I use "lay" to distinguish women that are not pastors' wives, to pastors' wives who are counted as clergy by the people.

meeting in 2000 in Melbourne, Australia. Both went to such meetings as chairpersons of the national Umodzi.133 However, at the African level, women from the South have been leaders.

3.6.1 Elizabeth Njolomole

Elizabeth Njolomole became the first to be elected to the BWUSA committee in 1972 as the chairperson,[134] and remained in this position till 1977. During this time she was able to interact with Mama Cecilia Kadzamira, the Official Hostess of the Nation and other Government officials especially organizing the BWUSA meetings. It is customary that at such meetings government officials be invited to attend. In 1977 she was reelected as the vice chairperson of BWUSA. Elizabeth Njolomole comes from the central region but became a historical figure in the Southern region because she was an influential national leader. Further she also served in Blantyre as a pastor's wife briefly before she went to Lilongwe where her husband was director of the Bible School.

Elizabeth Njolomole greeting Mama C. Kadzamira in 1972 at Zomba State House

---

[133] Int. Martha Chirwa, Blantyre Baptist Church, 14.12.2000.
[134] Int. Hilda Mallungo, Mtendere Baptist Church, Lilongwe, 14.3.2000.

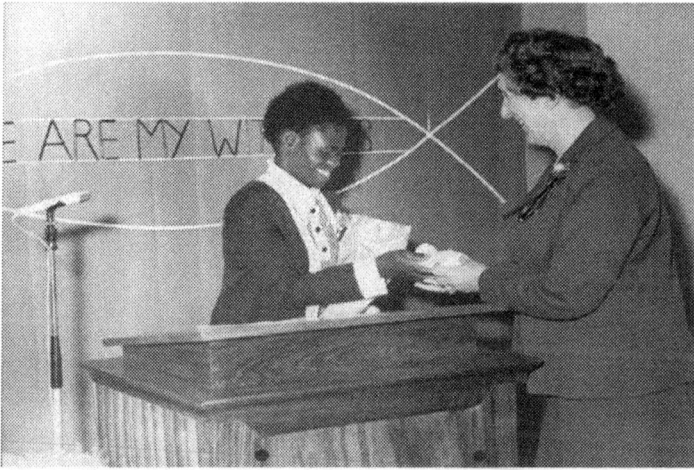

Elizabeth Njolomole taking up her second term of office in 1977

3.6.2 Lillian Jonga

The only Baptist women from the Southern region, that became a member of the executive committee of the Baptist World Alliance on the African level was Mrs Lillian Jonga.[135] She was voted as chairperson at a Baptist World Union of Africa meeting held in Kenya in 1982. She served in this office for one term, which lasted till 1987. The circumstances surrounding Lillian Jonga at the time she was in this leadership position were not easy. Even the fact that she was elected to this post remained a wonder to some as some Malawian women were disappointed that she was voted into this post.[136] They felt that Lillian Jonga was voted into this prestigious post without proving her worth on the national level. This was because she was never in the executive committee in Malawi. So why should she serve at a higher level? Her marriage was also beginning to crumble. According to the Malawi team that went to Kenya at that time, another woman would have deserved the post.[137]

---

[135] Ibid.; Int. William Jonga, Lunzu Baptist Church, 26.5.1999.
[136] Int. Hilda Mallungo, Mtendere Baptist Church, Lilongwe, 14.3.2000.
[137] Int. Raynor Kawamba, Blantyre Baptist, 26.5.1999.

Lillian Jonga at a BWUSA meeting held in 1977 sitting besides the speaker

However it is clear that the local perceptions about Lillian Jonga did not match the reality of her leadership experience. In the picture above in 1977 she was already influential among women and was a master of ceremonies even at this important occasion where Bakili Muluzi, the government representative of Malawi Congress Party to the meeting was a guest of honour. Further there are traits in Lillian Jonga's life at this time, which might have contributed to her appointment to the post. Firstly, she was a close friend of Mary Chandler, a missionary.[138] In fact, even though local Baptist women in Malawi did not vote Lillian into any national executive post within *Umodzi*, she was well known to the grass-roots women of the Lower Shire.[139] She had consistently gone there with Mary Chandler as her translator. Secondly, Lillian was most suited to this work because she was fluent in both English and Chichewa. Her knowledge of English was better because she grew up in Zimbabwe.[140] In this

---

[138] Ibid.
[139] Int. William Jonga, South Lunzu Baptist Church, 26.5.1999.
[140] Ibid.

way she was able to communicate with missionaries and transmit their message to the local women.

Her marriage situation was indeed a shortfall, but isn't it true that there are many Baptist women with broken marriages, who are leaders of the organisation and or the church at different levels? In fact Lillian Jonga was the second wife to be married to William Jonga, who had divorced his first wife Cecilia Phoya, a daughter of a CCAP minister, in 1950 due to disagreements. His later divorce from Lillian Jonga also centres on disagreements.[141] Is it likely that William Jonga met with difficult wives twice or that he was the one who was difficult to live with? Culturally, it is very easy to blame divorce on a wife, but it is better not to pass such judgements without concrete facts. William Jonga is now married to the third wife[142] while Lillian is still single and a minister in the United States of America.[143]

Lillian Jonga joined Blantyre Baptist Church in late 1969. She and her husband were attracted to the church because of the friendship they had with the Westers. Blantyre Baptist also was ideal for the Jongas because it had an English Sunday School for their children, who could not speak fluent Chichewa because they were born and lived in Zimbabwe for a long time. Lillian was in the Church of Christ before she became a Baptist. However, when Lillian was going through marriage difficulties with William, she decided to move her membership from Blantyre Baptist Church to Providence Industrial Mission. She was well accepted by PIM women because she was also their leader in the Baptist World Union of African (BWUA).[144] She received all the respect of a leader among PIM women. Lillian finally divorced William just before concluding her term, so that at the following BWUA meeting in 1987, held in Kenya, delegates from Malawi were embarrassed with her.[145]

---

[141] Ibid.
[142] Ibid.
[143] Int. Mrs Martha Chirwa, Zomba Theological College, 12.1.2001.
[144] Ibid.
[145] Int. Raynor Kawamba, Baptist Convention Offices, Blantyre, 26.5.1999.

3.6.3 Mrs Agnes Maya

Another international leader in the Southern region was Mrs Agnes Maya. She is one of the few women who have been missionaries in more than one country doing Baptist work. She was born in 1936 in Kimberley in South Africa. She was a Roman Catholic before she became a Baptist through marriage.[146]

Agnes Maya, second from right, standing at the back

Although she had been married in a Roman Catholic church, her husband left the Catholic Church when he heard a Baptist message preached by Rev Bowlin in Zimbabwe. By then, they were in Zambia. In 1960, Agnes, together with her husband went to Gweru Seminary for theological training. Being good at English, she passed the English proficiency test that was administered at the seminary and attended the same classes as her husband.[147]

Upon finishing their theological training, Agnes and her husband served Torwood Baptist Church in Harare. After four months, a mission-

---

[146] Int. Mrs Agnes Maya, Chilomoni Baptist Church, Zomba Baptist Church, 28.10.2000.
[147] Ibid.

ary from Zambia came to Zimbabwe, looking for a person to help him start a Baptist Church at Broken Hill (Kabwe) in Zambia (Northern Rhodesia at that time).[148] It was during the time of the political struggle for Independence. At this time, the Mayas were not well received by some of the Zambians. Some of them thought the Mayas were collaborators with the Europeans. One day, some of the United Freedom Party (UFP) of Zambia functionaries attacked Agnes Maya's husband, but a certain man who knew Rev Maya as a church minister rescued him. They served in Zambia for 15 years and in 1978 came back to Malawi to serve churches in Blantyre. They started pastoring Chilomoni Baptist Church, which had been started by V.W. Chitsukwa. Because of internal conflicts, Agnes and her husband left Chilomoni Baptist Church and went to start a Baptist church at Che Mussa in 1986. During this time, it was easy to establish a church because of the revival of the 1970s and early 1980s.

Many received Christ during this time. However, women did not preach. Even Mrs Ng'oma, who used to preach in Blantyre in the early years, did not preach then.[149] Apart from getting busy with pastors' wives' duties at church, Mrs Agnes Maya worked as a teacher at a crèche at the Baptist Convention offices in Blantyre, which had been started in the early 1970s by Mrs Patsy Davidson.[150] Mrs Agnes Maya was the second Baptist woman to carry this responsibility, the first being Mary Galatiya. The supervisor at the crèche was however Patsy Davidson till 1975 when she left Blantyre for a new assignment in Gaborone in Botswana.[151]

Mrs Agnes Maya was very much involved in the establishment of the Baptist church at Che Mussa. Just like her husband, she used to be involved in door to door evangelism. They used to run evangelistic crusades under titles like *"Ndichitenji kuti Ndipulumuke"* or *"Ndilibe nthawi yopemphera"*.[152] Apart from these evangelistic campaigns, some women became Baptist through Bible Way Bible studies. The Baptist Church at Che Mussa was one of the churches that gained members from this enterprise.

---

[148] Ibid.
[149] Ibid.
[150] Int. Mrs Marylyn Upton, Area 36 Baptist Church, Lilongwe, 5.1.2001.
[151] Ibid.
[152] "What must I do to be saved?" or "I have no time to pray".

The Bible Way programme is a Bible correspondence programme. Those that complete these courses are encouraged to join a Church that would encourage them in their walk with God. There is a big claim that several Baptist churches have been started in this way because Baptist Publications produced the materials.[153] This claim needs to be substantiated with further research. From the research I made, Bible way programme indeed had enrolment by candidates throughout Malawi. However neither all were Baptists nor did all become Baptist after completing the programme. The programme did not discriminate against women although a smaller number of them enrolled in the programme. In a national sample of 352 only 73 were women. In Jali area, out of 103 only five were women. In Mayaka, out of 66 enrolled, one was a woman.[154] Fewer women as opposed to men enrolled in the Bible way programme likely because of the problem of illiteracy that was much more pronounced among women.

Mrs Maya's role was to teach these women converts the Bible and homecraft skills. She used to buy rejects from David Whitehead Clothing factory and helped women to sew patchwork products. In 1985, Agnes and her husband Sabudu Joly Maya decided to leave Blantyre and settle in Liwonde. They felt they needed to settle somewhere because of age. Chief Chilongo gave them land and now they grow maize and groundnuts for food and for sale. In Liwonde, Agnes has continued to serve as a pastor's wife at their newly established church – Mombe Baptist.[155] Agnes Maya is remembered for being a woman who has helped to spread Baptist Convention work in three different countries, Zambia, Zimbabwe and Malawi.

3.7 Women in theology

In the area of theological training Baptist women no longer go for theological training only if they are pastors' wives or aspiring to be one. Baptist women can now study theology independently of their husbands.[156] The wave of change is a more plausible explanation for this because

---

[153] Int. Rev A.C. Chisi, Ufulu Baptist Church, 14.10.2001.
[154] This information was collected by studying records in the Baptist Publications Unit in Lilongwe, 13.3.2001.
[155] Ibid.
[156] Mrs Liddah Kalako was the first woman to graduate from Lilongwe Baptist Seminary. She was a native of Ntcheu and died in 2000.

even in other churches such as Blantyre and Livingstonia Synods, where such did not happen, women are now studying theology independently of their husbands.[157]

3.7.1 Mrs Molly Longwe

The first woman to go into theological training on her own account in the Baptist Convention was Mrs Molly Longwe. Even though she was already a minister's wife by then, she did not go to Zambia Theological Seminary in Lusaka on account of following her husband Hany Longwe. She was sent there in 1994 together with her husband to get theological training that would equip them both to teach at the Baptist Theological Seminary in Lilongwe. She completed her BTh (Bachelor of Theology) in 1995.[158] Together with her husband she is now a lecturer at Lilongwe Baptist Seminary. Molly Longwe is the first Malawian woman to teach pastors at the Baptist Theological Seminary. She even teaches them New Testament, a key subject in theological training. However her role as a lecturer met with some resistance from men in the beginning.

Some pastors could not easily accept to be taught by a woman because women were to be silent. However, with time, Molly has earned support as a lecturer even by such students. She has studied in South Africa and Ghana for her Master programme.[159] Molly becomes important to the history of women in Southern Malawi because as lecturer she influences pastors in the Southern region and their wives.

3.7.2 Mrs Martha Chirwa

Martha Chirwa also began to study theology on her own in 1994. She decided that her training as pastor's wife in Gweru, Zimbabwe was not enough. She therefore started her theological training through part time studies, but then decided to study full time at Zomba Theological College in 1999, and received a Bachelor of Divinity Degree in 2001.

---

[157] But though women are welcome to study at ZTC, they cannot do so if the husband is studying there.

[158] Int. Rev Hany Longwe, Lilongwe Baptist Seminary, 13.3.2000.

[159] MTh in African Christianity with University of Natal and Akrofi Christaller Centre, Akropong, Ghana.

3.7.3 Mrs Rachel Banda

Whereas Martha Chirwa and Molly Longwe were pastors' wives, Rachel Banda was the first laywoman to undertake theological training in her own right. She had been married to Jande Banda who was a lecturer in Public Administration in Chancellor College when she started studying theology. She was previously involved with an international organisations, Campus Crusade for Christ, and had the desire to do more theological training. In 1994, through the encouragement of Dr Klaus Fiedler, lecturer at Chancellor College, she decided to study theology.

She was at Zomba Theological College for two years till 1996. In 1996, her husband got a scholarship to study at the Australian National University in Canberra, Australia. She decided not to live apart from him and applied for a place in Australia to continue her theology. She was admitted to Canberra College of Theology in Australia where she finished her Bachelor of Theology in 1998. She received her MA in theology from the University of Malawi, in 2001, and then registered for PhD.

3.7.4 Mrs Grace Matupi

The other Baptist woman in the Southern region to study theology in her own right is Mrs Grace Matupi. She was also a trained pastor's wife but decided to do more theological training. In 1995, she was accepted to study theology at the African Bible College in Lilongwe where she graduated in 1999 with a BA degree. She is currently teaching (2002) at Zomba Baptist Primary School.

With this change of women taking up initiative to study theology on their own, women have liberty to choose what subjects they want to study including ethics and preaching as was the case with Martha Chirwa in Zomba Theological College. Again theological training is not only aimed at pastoring a church but it is to equip a person for spiritual growth and any other ministry, as one is called.

3.7.5 Issues relating to women studying theology independently of their husbands

3.7.5.1 Effect on family

While pastors are blamed for not taking their wives for training, women have left husbands at home to do theology and are not blamed. Mrs Molly Longwe was in South Africa and Ghana in 2000, while her husband was in Lilongwe, lecturing. Mrs Grace Matupi was away in Lilongwe for much of four years while her husband pastored Zomba Baptist Church. Also Martha Chirwa was studying in Zomba while Akim Chirwa, her husband, was the General Secretary of the Convention and living in Blantyre. Why it is that there seems to be acceptance of this move that women are able to leave their husbands at home while missionaries are blamed for not letting pastors bring their wives to Lilongwe Theological School? Is this a lesser evil than the original arrangement where husbands left their wives when they went to Bible School in Lilongwe?

3.7.5.2 Sponsorship

In the earlier period Southern Baptist missionaries sponsored theological training for pastors and their wives, but in this new dispensation, theological training for women has been highly supported by the German church. Molly Longwe is the only one among these women who was sponsored by Southern Baptist Missionaries (while studying for her BTh), and for her MTh she was largely sponsored by an Africa Theological Initiative scholarship.

3.8 Conclusion

This chapter shows that Baptist women are still struggling to attain optimum freedoms, especially in areas of leadership such as preaching and pastoral ministries. However they are a step ahead in their struggle at a time when there is less Southern Baptist missionary influence. Their struggle is related to how Baptist polity and doctrine that is liberating to women is applied in these women's lives and their church. It is evident that in the event that their Baptist distinctives, a summary of Baptist doctrine and polity, are sacrificed due to factors such as culture, missionary influence, biblical interpretations, *zeitgeist* among others, these women enjoy less freedoms.

During the period the character of *Umodzi* has changed. While there was an intense attempt to use home management training in the period of the 1960s and 1970s, by the missionary women and their local disciples, this strategy diminished in the 1970s and mid 1980s probably because of external influences brought by revival.

However, in the current period, *Umodzi* has regained the use of homecraft management training as a means of proclaiming Baptist beliefs. This development is again tied to missionary influence just as in the earlier period, although that, short term missionaries are also involved as opposed to long term missionary endeavors by Southern Baptist missionary women. The first sewing project was funded by German Christians through the donation of machines and money to start sewing. Thereafter, there has been an influx of other missionary donations. Churches in America have sent sewing kits to Malawi, the Oklahoma partnership has not only funded the establishment of Balaka sewing training school but has even provided a missionary women to facilitate sewing among women, Hughes Baptist Church in Canberra, Australia, Bethsaida Evangelical Church in USA, and other churches in Canada have sent donations to revive the use of homecraft training in proclaiming Baptist beliefs. Is the claim that such donations are responsible for creating a spirit of poor giving among Baptists valid? If it is, why are the local Baptist women succumbing again to the same trap?

Chapter 4

BAPTIST WOMEN AND MARRIAGE

In the conversion document, marriage is seen to play a role in women's lives in deciding to join the Baptist church. Twenty-five women from churches such as Zambezi Evangelical Church, CCAP, Church of Christ, Roman Catholic, Masiye, Nakhule and African International Church and also from Islam joined Baptist Churches because they followed their husbands.

In some cases, women followed their husbands without being forced because they also liked the Baptist Church. Mrs Magoli of Balaka Baptist for example left CCAP because it was dull to her, and was already deciding to leave the church when her husband invited her to join the Baptist Church.[1] The Baptist church was more relaxed and Mrs Magoli liked the freedom to sing choruses. Mrs Magombo who was formally a Roman Catholic also enjoyed the freedom to sing choruses in the Baptist church.[2]

However, women were sometimes forced to follow their husbands. Mrs Rev Lutepo for example left CCAP and followed her husband because her husband forced her.[3] Some men use culture or the Bible to back up their position that wives ought to follow their husbands. Women who were formerly members of Church of Christ at Mandawala left the church for the Baptist Church at the command of their husbands arguing that culturally that was the right thing to do. This was even emphasized in the conversion story of Mrs Rosebay Botoman Nkhoma.[4] Efraim, her husband challenged Rosebay with a proverb *"sindinaone mphuno imodzi kulowa zala ziwiri"* (I have never seen a nose which can accommodate two fingers). This proverb was meant to emphasize that if Rosebay was married to Efraim, she was one with him and needed to leave CCAP and

---

[1]   See appendix 1.
[2]   Ibid.
[3]   Ibid.
[4]   Ibid.

join his new church. This explanation was even complemented with a threat from Efraim "if you do not come with me to the Baptist church, you will find me gone back to my home". This threat was enough to force Rosebay out of CCAP to join the Baptist Church.[5] Her husband left CCAP and joined the Baptists because the CCAP demanded that he should marry Rosebay in church wedding to be fully accepted. When one day Rosebay's husband met Rev Mukhola of the Baptist church, the pastor told Efraim that if he joined the Baptist church, there was no need for a church wedding for them to be accepted as full members of the church.[6]

Although, in this sample, no woman gave the Bible as a reason for following her husband, the verse that says man is the head of woman is sometimes used as a backing in other conversion stories not recorded in this document.

On the other hand, some women follow their husband's churches as a habit. They just feel it is right to do so. Some of them do it even at the expense of their faith. A good example is Mrs Malesi Salifu of Jali. She had been married and divorced three times by the age of 35. Each time she married, she followed her husband's faith. As such she even became a Muslim when she married a Muslim husband. She is currently a Baptist where her last husband left her.

It is intriguing that in this matrilineal society, either women follow their husbands in joining the church or husbands follow their wives to join the Baptist church.[7] This shows that even in this society where a husband often follows a wife at marriage, there are changes to this rule. In this analysis of how marriage affects conversion, it is evident that the demand of a church wedding becomes a restriction to membership in some churches. As such, Baptist women enjoy relative freedoms in that they are not forced to have a church wedding for them to become full members of the church. Further, this analysis also shows that the freedom to sing choruses attracts women from churches such as CCAP and Roman Catholic where such is rarely done.

---

[5] Ibid.
[6] Ibid.
[7] In the conversion document three husbands followed their wives and twenty five women followed their husbands. The numbers are not significant in comparing frequencies of numbers of women and men in this behaviour, because one needs an equal sample of both men and women to be able to do this.

However Baptist women do not always enjoy freedom. This analysis shows that culture has forced some to make decisions that will not be in line with their conscience, an ingredient that Baptist polity claims to have.

4.1 Other factors for conversion apart from marriage

There is a general perception that most women join churches following their husbands. This is not always true. Apart from issues relating to marriage, there are other factors that influence women to join the Baptist church. In the conversion survey fifteen women claimed their conversion to the Baptist church because of believing in the Baptist message. This is also an important point of conversion. Marriage issues seem to mainly affect the conversion of changing from one church to another. But there is also conversion of the heart, which sometimes is followed by joining another church but not always.

The conversion stories of women that joined the church because of believing the Baptist message show some of the traits that are distinct to the Baptist heritage and may be appealing to some. In the case of Mrs Khuzu, the doctrine of salvation attracted her to the Baptist church.[8]

Mrs Walasi was converted to Baptist Convention when Rev Lichapa challenged her on the essence of keeping the Law.[9] This was liberating to her and she decided to join the Baptist Convention. Mrs Bakiri left the Roman Catholic Church because of being attracted to the Baptist teaching on baptism by immersion. Further she was also convinced that this was the right baptism because it is done when one is able to know what is wrong and what is right.

However, most of the conversion stories that hinge on believing in the Baptist message are general and do not reflect what exactly attracts people to the Baptist message. Some of these are probably just interested in the church,[10] for one reason or the other including the fact that it comes from America[11] and conducts leaderships training.[12]

Some conversions of women are due to the social services women receive from those preaching the Baptist message. One of the key areas

---

[8] See conversion document.
[9] Ibid.
[10] Like in the case of Mrs Chidzambuyo, Ibid.
[11] See conversion document.
[12] See the conversion of others to Chayima Baptist Church.

is the ability to sing at a funeral of a non-member of their church. Such is not possible in for example Roman Catholic and CCAP. In the conversion document, members joined Malirano Baptist Church in 1998, when their Four Square Gospel Church denied them a decent funeral.[13] Some joined because of receiving material help. Some members joined Thundu Baptist Church because of free distribution of *kaunjika* (second hand clothes). Some of these were formerly Muslims.[14]

Some joined the Baptist Church because of political reasons. Mrs Kanichi for example joined Makolije Baptist church in 1978, when the Ngwazi banned Jehovah's Witness in Malawi.[15] She left with her children and joined the Baptist church because of the torture Jehovah's Witness went through at that time.[16]

Distance is another influence in joining the Baptist church. Mrs Agnes Chikadula for example left the Church of Christ to join the Baptists, which was closer to her than her former church.[17]

The above factors that encourage women to join a Baptist church may show that Baptist churches are not restrictive to women. They sometimes are. This is seen in the reverse conversion stories in section B of the conversion document. A member at Chilambe Baptist Church for example, left the Baptist Church on her own because of sexual promiscuity, someone also left the Baptist Church because she brewed *kachasu* and was drinking the beer.[18]

4.2 Types of weddings acceptable in Baptist churches

Baptist women enjoy all the three types of weddings present in a matrilineal society: the *chinkhoswe* wedding, the blessed wedding (*ukwati wodalitsa*) and the church wedding. *Chinkhoswe* wedding is a wedding done traditionally outside the church. The uncles of a girl and a boy agree to marry the two. The agreement is called *unkhoswe* and the

---

[13]   Conversion document.
[14]   Ibid.
[15]   For other details on the persecution of Jehovah Witnesses see Klaus Fiedler, "Power at the Receiving End: The Jehovah's Witnesses' Experience in One Party Malawi", in Kenneth R. Ross, *God, People and Power in Malawi: Democratization in Theological Perspective*, CLAIM-Kachere: Blantyre, 1996, pp. 149-176.
[16]   Conversion documents.
[17]   Ibid.
[18]   Ibid.

ceremony is known as *chinkhoswe*. Even though the maternal uncles make the agreement, the ceremony is attended by many, especially close relatives. At such an occasion, even though the uncles may have been aware of the intentions of the boy and the girl marrying, they pretend to have no knowledge of such schemes. This pretence is dramatized at the occasion by the uncles in this way: The uncle of the boy pretends to have come to the uncle of the girl's home and in a riddle questions the uncle of the girl as to whether he had seen his cock (his boy) in his surroundings. The uncle of the boy also pretends at least more than once, as time might allow, not to have seen the cock. In such a pretence, he requests his family members to go and look for the cock in the surrounding, but for at least more than once, they pretend not to have seen the cock. As the uncle of the boy continues to insist, the uncle of the girl agrees to have seen the cock. The uncle of the boy shows relief on his face and tells the uncle of the boy that his cock was spending time with his hen (girl) there. The uncle of the girl pretends not to know the hen he is referring to. At this time the boy who is about to marry avails himself to the group. The uncle of the girl sends someone to bring all the hens (the girls) he had for the cock (the boy) to choose which one he was spending time with. All the girls are covered in cloth from head to toe and usually the right girl is not out in front. The boy makes guesses and eventually picks the right one. There is ululation from the crowd. The girl sits next to the boy and the uncles seal the marriage by the exchange of a cock and other items. The boy's uncle produces the axe and hoes to signify his support for the girl. The girl's uncle produces some kitchen items such as a broom, a pot, a plate, cup, spoon and so on, to signify that the girl will cook for the boy.

At such traditional wedding, no bride price is paid. The only expenditure is in form of the gifts for exchange and food for the celebration. In rural areas, food is usually contributed by family members and well-wishers. But in urban areas, this tradition is getting more and more expensive because of urban influence. In this kind of marriage, a woman either goes to the husband's home and this tradition is called *kuulowoka* or *chitengwa*, or the more common way is where a man goes to stay in the woman's home, called *chikamwini*.

A survey of Baptist women has shown that women do opt for *chitengwa* or *chikamwini*. In certain cases, one option is followed but others follow both options, however, the most common option even among Baptist women is *chikamwini*. In this arrangement, the man stays in the home of the wife as long as the marriage lasts. In case of divorce, the husband leaves the home, and if he has children, the children remain with his wife. However, this arrangement varies with the economic status of the husband. If the husband is richer, he might attract his children to his home. But in most cases, even in this situation, the husband sends support for his children to the wife's family.

Even though the husband stays in the wife's home, this does not mean that the woman is leader of the family. The husband usually controls the affairs of the family. This is seen even in decisions concerning the use of money.

An examples of this is shown in the experiences of two women in the South East region. In both cases, the husbands denied them access to the money they earned after selling their produce. In one case about K60,000 was realized from tobacco. After getting this much money, the husband ran off to Lake Chirwa, without consulting the wife on how to spend the money. He only came back to his wife after all the money had gone, claiming that he had been robbed. In the other case, the woman who is also a pastor's wife, worked so hard in the maize garden. For several years she had grown maize together with her husband and did not get any money from the sales. This year she decided that she would have her own garden so that she could have sales of her own. After harvest, she had gone somewhere and when she came back, all her maize was sold, and worse still, the husband did not show her the money.

The tradition of men living in the woman's home is slowly changing. There is a new trend emerging, where a man offers to stay in the wife's home for one year or so, to prove his worth of behaviour and support and subsequently, the man requests to take his wife to his family. Some attribute this change to mere choice and agreement between the husband and his wife, other women claim that they run away from interference in the affairs of their family from the uncles who usually dominate families in this culture. Others move to the husband's home for more land for farming and other social amenities. However, in this arrangement the wife is not bound because there is no bride price. In case of any marital problems, she is free to go back to her home. And sometimes, the husband may even follow her.

The other trend in the region is that although men often stay in the wife's home, practically they are never in these homes. A few spend most of the time away from these homes and occupy themselves in business. This has an effect on church growth and membership. In Mwanafumu Baptist Church, Thundu Baptist in Zomba and Ndirande Baptist in Chikwawa, for example, the majority of members are women. Many men from Zomba rural live most of the times along Lake Chirwa fishing for income.

At Ndirande Baptist Church, husbands are busy working in a cane factory and rarely attend church. Some men have moved to other regions such as Central and Northern region to work as tenants on estates, leaving their wives at home.

Apart from agricultural businesses, men in this region venture in other small businesses in urban areas, and this, too, takes them away from home. On the other hand, such movements have been key in the spreading of the Baptist faith out of the southern region to other places.

4.3 Chinkhoswe wedding

A survey of Baptist women in the Southern region has shown that the majority of women marry by *chinkhoswe*. In a sample of pastors' wives and church leaders, 15 women of 24 were married under *chinkhoswe*. 6 women were married under blessed marriage *(ukwati wodalitsa)* and only three were married through a church wedding (*ukwati woyera*). In essence blessed marriages are all firstly *chinkhoswe* weddings and for this reasons, we can say that 21 out of 24 were married under *chinkhoswe*. If this is the extent to which *chinkhoswe* weddings are common among Baptist women leaders, how much more are they common among the common grassroots people?

The key question regarding this stand is why is the church accommodating such kinds of weddings that are seen to be unchristian in other church cultures? The reasons are both practical and theological. Theologically, Baptist churches have not condemned such weddings, as they accept them as valid marriages. It is also possible that they have searched the scriptures, as people of the Bible, and have not found any instance where *chinkhoswe* weddings are condemned. Neither have they found the Bible teaching about a boy and a girl walking the church isle, the girl dressed in white dress and a veil and a boy in an expensive suit (including matching shoes) to receive a blessing from a pastor. However, they have read how Isaac found his wife Rebecca, traditionally. They

have looked at the commandments, and have not found church weddings to be one of them.

Practically, the church has seen that church weddings are unattain-
able for the rural majority. They cost a lot. The wedding dress and the
suit are expensive. Of course one may argue that one cannot run away
from a church wedding because of the high cost of a reception because
even at *chinkhoswe* weddings, one has to have a reception.

The difference is that even those who have a church wedding still
hold a *chinkhoswe* reception before the wedding. Is it not less costly to
have only one reception rather than two? Because of the high costs of
church weddings, others are barred from having a Christian wedding and
to this Klaus Fiedler rightly argues, for the sake of Christian marriage,
abolish church weddings.[19] Practically *chinkhoswe* weddings are sufficient for the exchanging of marriage vows. The uncles, the bride and
bridegroom, the relatives are present and the agreement is made there
and then. Why not just call for the pastor of the church to bless the marriage after the exchange of the cock and the gifts? Moreover, even at
such an occasion, church members and friends would surely be welcome to witness such an important event. The practical implication of
allowing such a *chinkhoswe* marriage is giving freedom to church members including women.

Churches that have emphasized church weddings oppress women.
This is seen in the way this has influenced some of their sheep to run
away to Baptist churches where they find a home.

4.4 Blessed marriages

Even though Baptist Convention women enjoy freedom with *chinkhoswe*
weddings, there is a slow move towards having blessed marriages (*ukwati wodalitsa*). There is no theological backing for this, but it seems
there is a general recommendation that church leaders such as deacons
should have such weddings. At one urban church even though this alarm
has been raised, only one of all the deacons who enjoy *chinkhoswe*
weddings has taken heed of such a call. The main drive to this move
seems to centre on power. The pastors, who can only "bless" a blessed
marriage, find an opportunity to exercise power over church members.

---
[19] Klaus Fiedler, "For the Sake of Christian Marriage, Abolish Church Weddings",
Religion in Malawi no. 5, pp. 22-28.

For many couples, *chinkhoswe* weddings are enough, because there is an agreement, their only challenge is to *live* a Christian marriage. For many, a blessed marriage is just to show off to the public and is a waste of resources.

4.5 Baptist Convention and women of difficult marriages

Baptist women in the Convention enjoy relative freedoms in the area of marriage as opposed to women of other Christian cultures. This is seen in the way Baptist Convention churches accept women of difficult marriages. Unlike in some other Christian cultures, women who have faced divorce or gone through remarriage, are easily accepted in the Baptist Convention. This is because of factors related to Baptist polity and doctrine. Baptists for example, do not have the church wedding as a prerequisite to receiving Holy Communion, and in this they differ from churches such as Roman Catholic, CCAP and Churches of Christ where church weddings seem to be taken as an eleventh commandment. The lax attitude Baptist women enjoy in the area of marriage has given them considerable freedoms and in many cases has been a reason for conversion from other churches.

This trend of acceptance can be traced as far back as the beginning of Baptist work in Malawi. Southern Baptist missionaries have been blamed for it and accused to have done it out of desperation to get members into their church. But the fact that this trend has continued even to this day shows that Baptist tradition, even on the local scene, does not see problems with such a stand. In this the Baptist faith has been relevant to the matrilineal societies of the southern region where divorce is common. Early missionaries, as well, easily adjusted to this reality probably because even in their home country, at the time they came to Malawi, the divorce rate was already on the increase.[20] This argument is fully supported by a survey of conversion stories I made.[21]

In a survey of more than 104 conversion stories,[22] there is evidence of factors that force women out of their churches, whereas such factors do

---

[20] Currently in the United States about half of all marriages end in divorce.

[21] See conversion document in appendix no. 1.

[22] 11 members in this document come from the central region. I speak of more than 104 because some group conversions were counted as one individual instead of a total number in that group because their conversion experience was at the same time and related to the same factors.

not bar women from being accepted members of Baptist Convention churches.

In the sample fourteen members (of which three were originally Roman Catholic, six CCAP, three Church of Christ and two Muslims), left their previous faith communities because of divorce. On the other hand, none of the members from other church traditions such as African International Church, Zambezi Evangelical Church, Assemblies of God, Church of God, Evangelical Baptist, Salvation Army, Masiye Church, Four Square Gospel, Atopia Church, Nakhule Church, Jehovah's Witnesses, Seventh Day Baptist, and Providence Industrial Mission left their churches on account of divorce. Although this evidence does not claim that none leave such churches on account of divorce, from this survey it can be argued that divorce is less a basis for leaving these churches compared to the faith communities listed earlier (CCAP, Church of Christ, Roman Catholic and Muslim).

The disparities as to why some faith communities are restrictive or liberative to women who are divorced, seems to lie in their teachings and the roles accorded by them to these women. Such teachings are highlighted by the stories of the women in the document as follows:

4.6 Former CCAP members and divorce

Three former CCAP women became leaders in the Baptist Church in the South East region who left their churches because they fell out of grace when they divorced their husbands, or were divorced.[23] The reasons why they left are highlighted by some of the demands CCAP placed on them. One woman said that after her divorce even though she wanted to continue being a CCAP member, she was disciplined by her church and the church demanded that she attend some classes before she could be re-accepted as a full member of the church.[24] When she found out that the Baptist Church did not demand classes or even discipline before she could become a full member, she joined. Divorce was not only restrictive to women but also to men.[25] The CCAP teaching is that the divorcee

---

[23] See conversion document in appendix no. 1.
[24] Ibid.
[25] M.R. Jonga, Rev David Malikebu faced the same, see conversion document in appendix no. 1.

should present a divorce certificate to the leadership of the church, for that divorcee to be accepted as full member of CCAP.[26]

4.7 Former Roman Catholic members and divorce

In this survey only three women joined the Baptist Church from the Roman Catholic Church. Divorce is a sin in this church. The only option for divorce among Catholics offered in Catholic Canon Law is annulment. Such annulment can be granted (by Rome alone) for example if there is an incidence of incest, a partner killed a previous partner, or if the marriage can be proved to have been forced on the couple or the husband never wanted children.

When a member is divorced, she is excommunicated from full membership in the church. One woman in the conversion stories left the Catholic Church because, when she divorced her husband, the church wanted her to wait for a long time before she could become a full member of the church.[27] The other woman could not fit in a Catholic Church because, apart from being divorced, she also remarried. The Catholic teaching is that marriage is permanent and even after one is divorced, she still remains the wife of that man until he dies. It is only after the death of the man (husband) that she can remarry. On the other hand, Baptist churches accept such members who have been divorced and even those that remarry afterwards.

4.8 Former Churches of Christ members and divorce

Divorce in this church is also taken seriously. Mary Taiby for example left Churches of Christ because she divorced a man she had had a church wedding with.[28] In the other case, the woman even remarried.[29] These women left Churches of Christ because they could not enjoy the status of full membership with divorce. In this church divorce is only allowed if a spouse is unfaithful. If one divorces for other reasons, one is excommunicated from full membership. She can only be admitted if she reconciles

---

[26] Int. Rev Dr Felix Chingota, Department of Theology, Chancellor College, 20.1.2001.
[27] Conversion document in appendix no. 1.
[28] Ibid.
[29] Ibid.

herself to her husband. She can also remarry if the spouse dies or marries another woman.[30]

4.9 Former Muslim women

Unlike in the faith communities above, divorce among Muslim women does not affect full membership in their faith community. In the Quran chapter four is dedicated to teaching on divorce. In Surah 4:34, second section, it is written: "As to those women, on whose part you fear disloyalty and ill conduct, admonish them first, next, refuse to share their beds, and last beat them lightly, but if they return to obedience, seek not against them means of annoyance." In this section, it is clear that divorce is taken an option if the woman does not conform to discipline by her husband. In chapter 4:35, it is written: "If you fear a breach between them, then appoint two arbiters [ankhoswe], one from his family and the other from hers and if they wish for peace, God will cause their reconciliation".

Divorce among Muslim women is not only a possibility but women are actually empowered to seek self repudiation (dissolution of marriage). In this the money the husband paid to the wife at the wedding is paid back.[31] Since divorce does not bar women from remaining within the Muslim faith community, women who left this community to join the Baptist Church were mainly influenced by their actions after divorce. In the case of Mellia Thombozi, she divorced a Muslim man and chose on her own to join the Baptist Church.[32] Reasons could be that she believed the Christian message, and could not join other churches because it would take her time to be accepted as a full member. Baptist congregations would not require her to go through classes before she can became a member.

4.10 Reasons for divorce among Baptist women of Southern Malawi

Divorce is a common occurrence among women of the Southern region. The reasons for divorce are many, but it is not always the husband leav-

---

[30] Pastor, Churches of Christ, Zomba Theological College, 23.3.2001.
[31] The Quran verses were kindly supplied by Dr Shareef Mohammad, Department of Theology and Religious Studies, University of Malawi.
[32] Conversion document in appendix no. 1.

ing the woman, the opposite also frequently happens. This section discusses a few of the reasons for divorce and how the church has reacted to them.

Mistrust: Mistrust has caused women to divorce or be divorced. Some husbands do not trust their wives when they go for church meetings away from their village. Such meetings are either association meetings, regional or national meetings, or even other special meetings such as *Pasca* meetings. When women go for such meetings, some husbands take the opportunity to bring another woman into the home, and when the wife comes back, she finds stories of her husband having an affair. This can cause the wife to divorce her husband, especially in view of the HIV/AIDS epidemic. Some husbands are also suspicious about the behaviour of their wives when they leave their home and go to such meetings. Some men perceive their wives to have love affairs with other men. Such fears are sometimes genuine but in many cases they are not. In 2000, one woman told her husband that she was going for leadership training in Zomba, however, instead of going to the meeting, she went to visit a lover. This confirms the view of a Baptist woman in Mayaka Association who reported that the issue of mistrust is on both husband and wife, because love affairs are being undertaken by wives as well. In certain cases, women engage themselves in love affairs for economic reasons. They go for well to do men to support themselves financially.

Mistrust surrounding the *Pasca* tradition is widespread among Baptists in the South East region. This tradition is practiced by a few congregations only, and it is rumored that there is high probability of wife exchange during such times. A group of women are selected from a congregation to go and cook for visitors at another church. The visitors are normally pastors. It is then rumored that it is generally understood that part of the responsibility of these women is to be everything to the pastors they cook for. This is backed up from Romans 16:1-2 where Paul says: "I commend to you our sister Phoebe, a servant of the church in Cenchrea. I ask you to receive her in the Lord in a way worthy of the saints and to give her any help she may need from you. For she has been a great help to many people, including me". For these women to be of everything to the pastors, they must also satisfy their sexual passions, since they are away from their wives. Because of the use of Romans 16:1, this is also known as "Phoebe" tradition. During *Pasca* of 2000, I had a two-day leadership training with one of the rural congregations.

When I asked where the Pastor was, I was told that for the rest of that week the pastor would be away to minister in different Baptist congregations, since it was *Pasca*. The pastor's wife was at home. The following day, I saw a group of pastors that passed by this church going to another church. I later learnt that indeed the pastors go to different congregations unaccompanied by their wives and that they do not stay in one place for that week. They visit different congregations, and at each congregation, they find different women to cook for them.[33]

One pastor's wife tells a story of how the first marriage of her husband ended in divorce because of *Pasca*. Her husband as usual went to *Pasca* meetings together with a group of other pastors. While there, one pastor in the group excused himself from the programme under the pretence that he had received a message that his child was ill at home. Meanwhile, there was rumour that this particular pastor was having an affair with his wife. He then decided to also go back home just to check whether this man was not going to his wife. Indeed his intuition was right. He found the particular pastor committing adultery with his wife. The pastor divorced his wife and married the current wife.

Mistrust is sometimes based on mere speculations, but in certain cases, immorality is indeed involved. Immorality of either husband or wife sometimes results in divorce, though not always. Those who deny divorce even with unfaithfulness of their husband base their argument on their understanding of the Bible. The following passages are frequently used to back up their position.

4.10.1   1 Ephesians 5:22,23

"Wives, submit to your husbands as to the Lord. For the husband is the head of the wife as Christ is the head of the church, his body, of which he is the saviour." Even though most of the Baptist women in the South region are rural, the biblical verse that says that women must submit to their husbands because he is the head of his family is well known, even when most of the women do not even know where the verse is found.

This means that where a wife is faced with a difficult husband such as an immoral one, the wife feels duty bound to remain in the family be-

---

[33] From the limited evidence available, it seems to be that immorality is not officially part of the Pasca tradition, but may be sometimes connected with it, with Biblical excuses.

cause she feels obliged to do what God wants, so she is to submit to her husband against all odds. This claim is even applied in cases of a husband that beats his wife or denies her rights in the family. While this is enslaving among Baptist women in urban areas, it is much more enslaving to those in the rural areas. This is because most of those in the rural areas largely rely on their husbands for survival, while those in urban areas may have opportunities to support themselves through employment.

The crucial question for Baptist women who opt for divorce in such circumstances is whether this passage of submission is intended for all families or only for those families where the husband fears God and loves his wife. Their argument is that God intends them not to be abused but to be happy, and therefore God would not want them to remain married to an abusive husband. The fact that the church accepts divorced women into full membership is a testimony that such views are also adhered to by the church.

4.10.2 Passages that teach forgiveness

Baptist women who remain married to unfaithful or abusive husbands also base their argument on the biblical theme of forgiveness that runs through the Bible. These women know that Jesus taught to forgive one another 77 times.[34] However, many Baptist women have problems with this. One such isolated case is a woman whose husband was working in Blantyre. One day he went to work and never returned till the early hours of the morning. When he knocked at the door, his wife went to open for him. She was shocked to see that her husband was in his birthday suit, yet coming from work. All his nice clothes, including his underwear that she had bought for him, were gone. He had lost all to the woman where he spent part of that night. The wife divorced him on that account and is now remarried to another Baptist man. However, not all women were supportive of her action, some confronted her as to why she could not forgive him and take him as her husband. Her reply was simple. She couldn't just have resumed marriage relations with that picture of him having slept with another woman.[35]

---

[34] Matthew 18:22: "Jesus answered, I tell you not seven times, but seventy-seven times."
[35] Marriage seminar, South East region, Zomba Baptist Church, 3.3.2000.

In the case of unfaithfulness, those who opt for divorce, do it because they have lost trust in their spouse or because of the possible consequences of unfaithfulness, especially HIV/AIDS. Even though there is education to use condoms to protect against HIV/AIDS, most husbands object to use them because they claim that no one would enjoy a sweet in a wrapper. Some women fear that condoms might break. Other women have doubts as to whether condoms are really useful in the control of HIV/AIDS since they are a less effective means of child spacing. For these reasons, some Baptist women prefer to have a divorce.

Apart from biblical reasons some women opt for divorce for other reasons like lack of sexual fulfillment. Even though it is very rare to find husbands who are impotent, some women experience difficulties in getting fulfilled in their sexual life. While women are taught to satisfy their husbands sexually even through a vigorous sexual dance, as taught in *chinamwali,* men seem to have difficulty in fulfilling their wives who take longer to reach an orgasm. Women require their husbands to be patient and to take this need seriously. Unfortunately, some husbands are only concerned about their own sexual fulfillment rather than about their wives'.

Because of perpetual lack of fulfilment, the wife may be tempted to look for "greener pastures" elsewhere and in this way be immoral. However even though immorality of a husband is offensive to women, culturally men are more agitated by the unfaithfulness of a wife. And even though many women have been willing to forgive their husbands, a few men have been able to forgive their wives who are caught in immorality. This leads to divorce.

Baptist women, including those that are divorced, passionately feel that God desires that families should be permanent. For this reason, they have taken steps to strengthen marriage ties. Among Baptist women in the south, this is actively done through *ulangizi* seminars and church *chinamwali.*

4.11 Ulangizi Seminars

Ulangizi seminars are a highlight of every joint meeting women have. These could be associational, regional and national meetings. It is customary that at each of such meetings an evening is set aside where women are given a chance to learn more about how to keep their marriages strong. As seen from the history within women's organisation leadership structure, at each level, a woman is appointed as *mlangizi*. During such joint meetings, she is the one responsible to run the *Ulangizi* seminar. The procedure of the seminar is very informal. It is more of a question and answer format than a lecture. In this way, there is a lot of participation and enthusiasm from the participants. Women are very free to share their struggles in marriage or in their former marriage. Others give wisdom on such issues. Although the *mlangizi* starts the ball rolling in many cases, with time, her role is mainly restricted to that of making sure that questions from the crowd are thoroughly addressed and women are given freedom to air their views and share their experiences.

These seminars, just as *chinamwali,* are exclusively attended by women and in seclusion normally in a church building. Attempts are made as much as possible to shield their discussions from men. This is because they talk about things that may be offensive to men. To give a general picture of what the seminars are like, see some of the questions that have been asked by the women and their answers at such meetings. The main aim of such seminars is to strengthen marriages by increasing knowledge concerning marriage issues that may encourage divorce.

Q1   The Bible teaches us to be submissive and to forgive others but I have a problem. I have been with my husband for 10 years but throughout those years, we have not always been together. At least four times, our marriage has been interrupted by him running off with other women. He usually does this after harvest time, when we have sold our produce. He usually comes back during rainy season and tells me to forgive him and accept him in marriage. Now he is coming from a fourth woman, seeking me to accept him as my husband. What should I do? Should I continue to forgive him?

Answer: Yes, forgive him, God says we must forgive; forgive him, but do not accept him as husband; he will bring you AIDS. Just tell your a*nkhoswe* and the church that you do not want him as a husband any more.

Q2   My husband is very rich but he hides his money, and does not give me enough to run my family. One day, when he was away, I discovered that he keeps the money in a mattress cover. There was lots of money. I was shocked to see this because that day I had just inquired from him about some money, and he told me that he did not have any. Now that I know where the money is, it is very difficult to accept his empty excuses. Should I tear the mattress and get the money or should I tell him about this?

Answer: Do not tear the mattress because God says we should not steal. If you tell him about the money in the mattress, he might be angry with you and punish you for that. Just pray for him: One day he will realize his mistake. The other view was to tell the husband of the money and to discuss with him why he was doing that. No matter which view the woman took, she was cautioned to approach the matter with diligence, to keep the marriage.

Q3   My husband and I have not been having sex for ten years. I still desire sex but each night I ask him to have sex with me he declines. When I ask him about problems he has about sex, he says he is not interested anymore because of age. What should I do, I tried to do all I can to be inviting to him and encourage him to have sex with me, but this is not happening. He is a pastor and I am a pastor's wife. I do not want a divorce. What can I do?

Answer: At this juncture the *mlangizi* told this 70 years old woman to meet with her privately. The group was very concerned about this. I had an opportunity to go with the *mlangizi* just to find out what her advice would be. The *mlangizi* told her just to pray for her husband and to continue to be inviting him.

Q4   I have passed the age of bearing children and my husband still asks me to sleep with him. I refuse because I feel I am now too old to do such things. My husband is a very understanding man, we still go together to church and he is a leader in our church. He does not have affairs with other women.

Answer: At this point one lady stood up, she was also well above child bearing age and told the group that she had consulted a doctor on whether she can continue to have sex with her husband after menopause or not. The doctor assured her that this was even a better time to have sex because she doesn't have to worry about getting pregnant. The woman continued to say that she enjoys sex with her husband even now.

Even though women divorcees are accepted in the church, this does not mean that Baptist do not care about divorce. The church takes an opportunity to counsel the family so that marriage is saved. In certain cases, women have been disciplined for leaving their husbands. This for example happened in a certain urban congregation in the South. A woman was a member of the congregation since 1989. She was married to a Baptist. For some times she was a full time housewife but later found a job in a non-governmental organisation. The man was not working. The wife started an affair with a certain man, and still continued to go to the church. Her husband was aware of the wife's love affair but in exchange also did the same and drank beer even. The wife then left the husband and went to live with her lover. The Church approached the couple and disciplined both of them for the divorce. The wife was unrepentant and left the congregation for another church. The husband on the other hand stuck with the same local congregation. After some time the church restored the man to fellowship with the church. He has since remarried.

4.12 Widowhood

A woman in the event of the death of her husband is not treated differently in the church in terms of membership and positions in the church. In certain cases, widowhood is a blessing in that such women are easily accepted as leaders within the church especially if they are widowed at an advanced age. In Nchalo Baptist Church, the first and the only deacons ever were widows: Mrs Gonkho and Mrs Ambress.

The church, which traditionally did not include women in such a role, chose these women because they were single and were elderly and well beyond the age of marriage. Leadership of widows is not restricted to the local congregation, but even found on higher levels. Mrs Margaret Nyika was the fist administrator at Blantyre Baptist Church and the first woman to act as BACOMA general secretary. Mrs Margaret Nyika was married to a Methodist, Lovemore Tamburanwa Nyika from Zimbabwe in 1968. She was married by a civil wedding, however Margaret maintained her CCAP membership. Margaret Nyika lost her membership with CCAP because of forgetting to get a disjunction certificate from a Presbyterian Church she fellowshipped with in Austria during her studies. When she went to a Baptist Church in 1970, she found a home there and has been Baptist since then. Her husband died in 1988 of heart problems. During her time of widowhood, she has served as treasurer in the National Committee of the Convention Executive Committee from 1996 to 2000. From 1998 to 1999, she was appointed by the church to be the administrator of Blantyre Baptist Church. This was at a time when the church did not have a pastor, and she was responsible for the everyday running of the church including arranging speakers for the Sunday services. In 1999, the General Secretary of the Convention then, Rev Akim Chirwa was leaving for a Baptist World Alliance meeting in Australia. During this time, the Convention executive committee appointed Mrs Margaret Nyika, who was a member of their committee, to act as General Secretary.

Widows in the Convection are confronted with cultural constraints that go with widowhood, and these constraints can limit their opportunities of leadership in church. When the husband dies, a woman is not supposed to put on oil or have a bath until the husband is buried. This is to symbolize that she is mourning. In certain cases, a widow does not put on oil for at least six months after the death of the husband. Traditionally a woman mourns for her husband for at least a year. During this period, she is not supposed to cut her hair and sometimes even has to put on a black dress. During this period, it is unlikely that such a woman would be free to take up leadership roles in a church.

In certain cases, this hair can only be cut after the widow has sex with one of the relatives of the husband. This tradition is called *kuchotsa fumbi*, literally meaning removing dirt. This ritual is sometimes performed much earlier, as soon as the burial of the husband. Again, this custom is a challenge to women's belief of sexual purity, even as singles. The church is partly responsible for such women's oppression.

Baptist Convention churches leave such traditional rituals to the family members. But in a way, because they do not openly condemn this ritual, it sounds as if the convention approves *kuchotsa fumbi*. It is not enough to let Baptist women under these circumstances follow their individual consciences. The church should make a statement about this oppressing ritual. Further, even though the church is mostly seen at the burying of the husband, giving condolences and comforting the widow, the Baptist Convention does not have special programmes for widows, but once in a while through sermons, they are encouraged to remarry. At a church wedding in Zomba one pastor preached a sermon to this effect. He pointed out that widows join the group of singles and according to Genesis 2:18, it is not good for them to be alone. They must go out and find another husband. Such admonitions to single women are oppressive if they are not complemented with the teaching that women can enjoy full humanity even without marriage.

4.13 Challenges of singlehood

Widowhood and divorce are the only causes of singlehood I have found. I have never come across Baptist women who have been single from birth.[36] This is probably because culturally girls are expected to marry at a tender age. Baptist women who are single are faced with the challenge to live their faith. Culturally, single women are perceived to have casual sex, even though they do not. It is unfortunate that this view is also shared by Baptist women. The man this woman has for casual sex is referred to as *kachiwala* (grasshopper). When I inquired about why the name *kachiwala* is given to such a man, this response was given: "He is *kachiwala* because he is someone whom a single woman would invite at

---

[36] This does not apply to expatriate members of the Baptist Convention.

night and before daybreak she would make sure the man leaves before the deacons or leaders of the church see him."

The role of *kachiwala* or casual sex was rated very important at one of the *Ulangizi* seminars. One woman gave a scenario of how one woman in Lilongwe, a renowned leader in *Umodzi*, died because of lack of vitamin K [supplied by a *kachiwala*]. According to her, vitamin K is essential for the normal development of a woman. This vitamin K is only given through sperms that can only be received through sexual intercourse. One woman also stood up to tell the group that even though she was about 50 years, she was advised to marry because she needed this vitamin K for her health.

This suggests that most women who are single and healthy are perceived to be immoral to get vitamin K. However this does not imply that all single women buy this myth. There are some, although few, who still live morally clean lives.

The other challenge for singlehood is remarriage. Baptist churches allow woman to remarry after divorce and widowhood. However in the face of HIV/AIDS, remarriage is a problem. It is difficult to find spouses who are free from this disease and among widows, a number of them are infected with AIDS often by their former husbands. For this reason Baptist women who may desire to remarry have to remain single.

Culturally, marriage is not just for the sake of it. It has to produce children. Baptist women who are HIV positive do not want to endanger themselves and risk to bear children who may also be HIV positive. Some single women remain single because of such realities. However some women ignore such risks because of seeking economic support from a new husband.

4.14 Conclusion

Marriage freedom in the Baptist Convention contributes to its church growth and therefore the church should maintain its stand as regards traditional weddings, divorcees and widows. However traditional weddings can be enriched by including the exchanging of church vows. This may contribute to stability in marriages in this area as the couple will not only be responsible to the *ankhoswe* but also to the church.

Ulangizi seminars make a significant contribution to liberating Baptist women in their families. They give opportunities to critically look at the

lessons they learned through *chinamwali* and come up with better solu-
tions to the building of a marriage. These *Ulangizi* seminars provide an
outlet to the women's hurts in families, which are rarely shared by their
spouses. In this way they become liberated as they gain knowledge of
how to handle them.

These seminars are enriched by marriage perspectives from other
cultures including the Chewa of the central region and tribes of the
northern region who have migrated to the South. At such seminars
women benefit from each other and gain knowledge to build their families. During such times, as women are enlightened about what happens
in other tribes, they feel confident to run their families. However not all
women are able to attend these seminars. These depend on knowledge
gained during church initiation.

Chapter 5

WOMEN OF THE BIBLE AND CULTURE

The history of Baptist women in southern Malawi shows that the freedoms these women enjoy within their church, because of factors relating to their Baptist polity and doctrine, are affected both by the culture in which they live and by their understanding of the Bible. This answers the dilemma as to why Baptist women have not realized their optimum freedoms which their Baptist polity and doctrine would make possible. Baptist women in this region are born in a particular traditional culture, and live among other existing Christian cultures, which also have biblical interpretations regarding the position of women in the church, which are not always the same as their own. Further they are constantly confronted with outside influences, which sometimes press them to change their understanding of their polity and doctrine. It is with this background that the experiences of women in Southern Malawi should be viewed.

Hence, it is clear that this book does not claim total liberation of these women, even though their Baptist polity and doctrine would allow such a claim. It is however true that the freedoms these women enjoy have progressed over time, in tune with their increased understanding of their polity and doctrine which is also influenced by the local and global changes as regards the position of women in church and society.

In chapter 1 we have seen how Baptist women were mainly involved in support roles, but that this was not without an exception. Mrs Ng'oma of New Jerusalem Church in Blantyre and an expatriate woman, Mrs Effie Cameroon in Cliccord House, assumed leadership roles. The claim that revival gives more room for equal opportunities seems to be true in that there was a slight move towards more women liberation during the period of revival. This shows that even though missionary Christianity had oppressive elements, outside influences gave more freedom to some women.

This can be contrasted with the experiences of Jali Baptist women, who lacked relative freedoms because of low literacy and being in a

closed society that lacked outside influences.[1] Even though this freedom
was enjoyed only by a few, it was a significant achievement within the
church, and also if compared to experiences of women in other Christian
cultures. In CCAP of Blantyre Synod, for example, no woman was able
to preach in those days on a normal Sunday except during Women's
Sunday.

On another level, traditional matrilineal culture has been applauded by
many scholars for elevating women's engagement in society, and this
has raised the concern that these women do not always have such freedoms in their church. Others have blamed missionary Christianity for being responsible for killing this liberating spirit. But this study shows that
Southern Baptist missionary Christianity, even though it encouraged
women to assume support roles in church, did not always rise above the
influence of traditional culture. Thus Baptist women in matrilineal societies show relative freedoms in their engagement in church and society,
as opposed to women in the patrilineal societies of Lower Shire.[2] Women
in matrilineal societies of the South East region enjoyed positions of a
deacon as early as the late 1960s and some even became women pastors.

This can be contrasted with patrilineal societies of Lower Shire where
women only became deacons in the 1980s, much later than in the matrilineal societies. In fact, there has been no woman pastor in these patrilineal societies. This shows that missionary Christianity did not always
change culture, as it was not supposed to. The other reason why missionary culture failed to change these women's culture is that these
women were born in this culture and are well conditioned to it.

The negative cultural attitude towards women's engagement in church
in the patrilineal society has continued to excel in BACOMA. But with
time, as we observe in chapter 3, women are beginning to take positions
of leadership in church and society. Women are deacons and some
preach. This change came partly because of external influences. Because of such influences local change was most likely because the
women began to understand what the gospel was. This was weighed
against their culture and the culture of their missionaries, and for the

---

[1]   Helen van Koevering states that Mozambique women suffered because of closed
system. See Van Koevering, *Dancing their Dreams*, pp. 22-23.
[2]   Chikwawa is three quarters Sena, and Nsanje is predominantly Sena. Int. Olive
Goba, St Charles Luangwa Parish, Zomba, 22.12.200.

sake of the gospel, they chose to be liberated in this area of leadership. The change is slow among patrilineal women, likely because the low position of women in the church was cemented not only by missionary Christianity, but also by their traditional culture.

However this history answers one of the key questions: To what extent can a church structure that evolved in a particular historical, sociopolitical and cultural context be adapted to another historical sociocultural context like Malawi where hierarchical structures are the norm. This history shows that there is bound to be a difference and this is shown for example in the tendencies towards centralization. The training of women in *Umodzi* for example is still more dependent on centralized committees whether at regional or associational levels. In fact up to now, there is a national executive that supervises women's work. It is also evident that supervision from centralized groups is a key in making the work excel. In the case of Lower Shire women's work, its excellence is very much dependent on the supervisory role of Nsomo Baptist Church. This move towards centralization will have an impact on the liberation of women in congregations depending on the position the centralized structure holds concerning women's roles in the church.

6.1 Baptist women reading, hearing the Bible

The position women have enjoyed in this history is related to how these women read and hear the Bible. Two main hermeneutics have influenced this history, although not without influences from culture and outside influences.

6.1.1 Missionary hermeneutics

Southern Baptist women missionaries read the Bible as teaching that women should be in support ministries.[3] They have lived this truth since the beginning of Baptist Convention work in Malawi. Since they came,

---

[3]   This view was persistent even in mission societies in America between 1792 and 1799, when the role of the women was only restricted to encouraging their husbands. It is because of this that they started women's mission organisations, to have a voice in the church. See R. Pierce Beaver, *American Protestant Women in World Mission: A History of the First Feminist Movement in North America*, Grand Rapids: Eerdmans, 1980.

they have not been involved in preaching during a normal Sunday service. Because of this inclination to support ministries, right from the beginning, they encouraged the women's organisation, which was already organized in their mother church in America (Women Missionary Union). Even in America, women had already realized that being in support ministries was not enough; therefore through women's organisation they would have their voices heard in the church. This is why we see missionary women being actively involved in teaching local women to be leaders in *Umodzi.*

In chapter 3, it is clear that, although in the beginning, the church felt comfortable with women being leaders over fellow women in the context of their organisation, the growth and effectiveness of *Umodzi* seems to have presented a threat to the church.[4] Therefore the Convention decided to include the national chairperson of *Umodzi* in the executive of BACOMA. This arrangement was done to ensure that the church monitors the ever growing developments within *Umodzi.* However, even if they had this wrong motive, the arrangement has proven to be of mutual benefit to the church and the women, as the women have a channel to make their views known to the Convention.

6.1.2 Local hermeneutics: We see women leaders in the Bible

The progression of women's leadership seen in chapter three seems to be the result of local Baptist hermeneutics. Although local women have enjoyed and appreciated leadership over fellow women, they are not satisfied with such a role. They read the Bible differently from their missionary counterparts. When several women in the Southern region were asked as to why some women are no longer obeying the Bible verse that "women should be silent in the Church", the common response was either, "we do not believe this" or "we ignore it because we see women leaders in the Bible", and they gave examples. Such views were given by both women who are leaders in the church and those who are not. Of those who are not and are of this view, some are not leaders because

---

4   May be *Umodzi* also, just as *Chigwirizano* of Nkhoma Synod, was viewed as a "Church within a church" See Isabel Phiri, *Women, Presbyterianism and Patriarchy*, p. 71.

their churches forbid them to,[5] others, because they do not have the ability or the call to lead. These wish their fellow women who are leaders to continue and that more women, who are capable, will be leaders in the church.

The common biblical example of a woman who inspires women to lead is that of Mary Magdalene who was traditionally called "Apostle to the Apostles". Mary was the one to see the risen Jesus. And Jesus, respecting the role of women, did not hesitate to send Mary to preach the good news of his resurrection to even Peter, key leader of the apostles. Mary brought this good news to all the eleven apostles "I have seen the Lord". Baptist women also quote other examples of women in the Bible in both Old and New Testament who took up leadership positions. As such, the missionary hermeneutic of restricting women to support roles is denied in view of this historical evidence of women leaders in the Bible.

The greater freedoms Baptist women enjoy cannot be appreciated by the public if they lag behind in the most contested position of women in the church, that of ordination. Baptist Convention churches should grace the freedom of these women by beginning to ordain women that feel called to such a ministry. Further it is clear from the experiences of these women with initiation that their liberation will increase liberation of girl children in the church and society. This is possible because Baptist women will be able to define and redefine the liberation of girl children as regards initiation by looking at such from the Biblical and cultural perspective. This would be an important ingredient in the development of Church initiation programmes for these girl children.

The challenge for the Baptist Convention women of Malawi, to ensure greater freedoms of these women lies in their teaching and correct interpretation of Baptist polity and doctrine. It is therefore necessary to further investigate how much the teaching of Baptist doctrine and polity is taken seriously in the congregations, and what kind of interpretations the churches teach. This investigation could involve, for example, a study of sermons preached on a Sunday or contextual Bible studies on some

---

[5] Int. Mrs Gowelo, Mandawala Baptist Church, 9.3.2000. In this church, no women preaches because the church leadership objects to this. This church was started by Andisambula in 1964, who was diverted from being pastor of the church because the missionaries then felt that such a role was for men. An attempt was made in 1999, to include a woman on the preaching roster but the pastor got into trouble with that and has since then opted to comply with the view of the church leadership.

passages regarding Baptist polity and doctrine as they relate to the position of women among others. This study, therefore, shows that it is not just the Baptist polity and doctrine that liberates, but rather their correct interpretation.

APPENDICES

Appendix no. 1

Why People Leave or Join a Baptist Church

Section A: People Joining

This study of randomly picked women's conversion stories was done in 1999 and 2000. The basic question that was asked was "Why did you join BACOMA?" The following were the sampled responses.

1. Lumbadzi Baptist Church (Lilongwe) (Semi urban)

Members	Former Church	Reasons
a. Mrs Roy Banda	CCAP (Nkhoma Synod)	Was excommunicated because she claimed to be born again and attended fellowship groups[1]
b. Mr Roy Banda	CCAP (Nkhoma Synod)	Followed his wife[2]

2. Capital City Baptist Church (Lilongwe)

Members	Former Church	Reasons
a. Francis Mkandawire	Roman Catholic	Was frustrated by his church when he was banned from conducting Bible studies in his church.[3]

---

[1] Int. Mrs Roy Banda, Lumbadzi Baptist Church, Lilongwe, 13.6.2000. - Fellowships refer to meetings of such interdenominational groups as New Life for All, Life Ministry, Women Aglow and so on. Nkhoma Synod did not allow her members to go to such meetings.

[2] Since Mrs Roy Banda was excommunicated and joined BACOMA, Roy Banda decided to join his wife, because he felt Nkhoma Synod was unjust in the decision against his wife. Int. Francis Mkandawire, Capital City Baptist Church, Lilongwe 24.6.2000.

[3] Francis Mkandawire used to conduct Bible studies in the Catholic Church, but this was seen as not in line with this church, and out of frustration he sought for a church that gave him freedom to service. Capital City Baptist not only welcomed him but

3. Ufulu Baptist Church (Lilongwe Rural)

Members	Former Church	Reason
a. Rev A.C. Chisi	ATR[4]	Followed his preacher's church and Mtakula Banda[5]
b. Mrs Nellie Chisi	CCAP	Followed husband.
c. Mrs Regina Mussa	CCAP	Followed her preacher's church[6]

4. Chigwirizano Baptist Church

Members	Former Church	Reason
a. Mr Mchenga Carpenter	African Int. Church	Followed preacher's church
b. Member	African Int. Church	Followed preacher's church[7]

5. Capital City Baptist Church (CCBC) (1983)

Members	Former Church	Reasons
a. Francis Mkandawire	Roman Catholic	Wanting an English service church[8]

---

allowed him to conduct Bible studies, which eventually resulted in the planting of another church - Lumbadzi Baptist Church.

[4] ATR is African Traditional Religion. Because he did not belong to any church, this kind of religion best describes his background before he became a Baptist.

[5] Chisi heard the message of Christ for the first time through his uncle Mtakula Banda, who was already a Baptist in Ntchisi (centre rural) by 1958. Even though he did not become a Baptist then, the seed was planted. When he left Ntchisi, his home area, for Lilongwe, looking for employment, he met Rev Baduya of BACOMA who preached to him about Christ. Chisi followed Baduya to his church (Falls Baptist Church) and has since then been a Baptist. Int. Rev A.C. Chisi, Ufulu Baptist Church, Lilongwe, 24.6.2000.

[6] Regina Mussa joined BACOMA when she went to attend an evangelistic crusade organized by Rev Kumatundu in Chinsapo rural in Lilongwe. Kumatonda was a pastor of Lilongwe Baptist Church. Regina Mussa attended the crusade on 4th May 1997 where Rev Kumatundu preached a message entitled *"Kuwona Kuwala"* (Seeing the Light). She was converted to the message and followed Kumatundu's church which was being planted at Chinsapo in Lilongwe. She is part of Ufulu Church because he and her husband left Chinsapo town to area 23, where Ufulu Baptist is. Int. Regina Mussa, Ufulu Baptist Church, Area 23 Lilongwe rural, 14.6.2000.

[7] Mr Mchenga and Member x became Baptists when Annie Mkandawire, who was Baptist then, shared Christ to these people. At the time Annie Mkandawire witnessed to them, they were half drunk, but since their conversion in 1988, they have been Baptists and have become pillars of Chigwirizano Baptist Church. Int. Annie Mkandawire, Capital City Baptist Church, Lilongwe 24.6.2000.

b. Others   Wanted an English service church.

6. Blantyre Baptist Church (Cliccord building 1961)

Members	Former Church	Reasons
a. Mrs Mary Galatiya and Rev Stephen Galatiya	??	Wanted an English Service[9]
b. Mr J M Ng'oma	??	Wanted an English Service[10]

7. Ntcheu Baptist Church (1971)[11]

Members	Former Church	Reasons
a. Mrs Mary Makhaya	Zambezi Evangelical Church (ZEC)	Followed her husband in 1977[12]
b. Mrs Kayipa	Baptist	Boma Baptist[13]
c. Mrs Chafuya	Zambezi Evangelical church (ZEC)	Followed her husband in 1973[14]
d. Mr Kayipa	??	Followed wife.[15]

---

[8] According to Francis Mkandawire, Capital City Baptist Church (thereafter CCBC) first core group, began to care for expatriates in Lilongwe who were not well versed in Chichewa. It was also for upper class Malawians who desired to mingle with the expatriates. A Southern Baptist Missionary, Jerry Daudy, organized this English Congregation in 1983 in area 43. Some of the first members were Neill Weston and his wife Brenda, Jim Parish and his wife, Andrew and Rosebay Kingston. Int. Francis Mkandawire, CCBC, 24.6.2000.

[9] Int. Rev A.C. Chisi, Ufulu Baptist Church, 23.6.2000.

[10] CCBC took the pattern of the Blantyre Baptist group at Cliccord House in Limbe which started in 1961. The vision of the Southern Baptist missionaries then, was that an English speaking church should be started to cater for the non-Chichewa speaking community in town and also high class Malawians like Aleke Banda. Some of the expatriate members were Mr and Mrs Klova, Mr and Mrs Shide, Mr and Mrs Bright. Int. Mary Galatiya, Stephen Galatiya, Likudzi Estate, Chipiliro Baptist Church, Balaka (rural) 15.5.2000, also Int. J.M. Ng'oma, Soche Baptist Church, 25.8.1999.

[11] Ntcheu Baptist Church started in 1971. Ntcheu is predominantly Zambezi Evangelical Church. Int. Mrs Chipojola, 4.5.2000, Ntcheu Baptist Church, Ntcheu.

[12] This is the daughter in-law to Mary Makhaya. Int. Mrs Makhaya, 4 May 2000, Ntcheu Baptist Church, Ntcheu. The husband was already Baptist because his parents were Baptist.

[13] Int. Mrs Kayipa, Ntcheu Baptist Church, Ntcheu, 4.5.2000.

[14] Int. Mrs Chafunya, Ntcheu Baptist Church, Ntcheu, 4.5.2000.

[15] Mr Kayipa followed his wife who was already a Baptist. Int. Mrs Kayipa, Ntcheu Baptist Church, Ntcheu, 4.5.2000.

8. Balaka Baptist Church (Semi Urban)

Members	Former Church	Reasons
a. Mrs Ngozi	Assemblies of God	Told in a dream to join Baptist Church in 1983
b. Mr Ngozi	Assemblies of God	Followed his wife in 1983[16]
c. Mrs Magombo	Roman Catholic	She was divorced to her husband and came to Baptist in 1988, because she did not have to wait for long to be a full member. She was free to sing choruses[17]
d. Mrs Magoli	CCAP Livingstonia synod	Following her husband joined in 1992. Freedom to sing choruses[18]
e. Mrs Nkolola	CCAP	Following her husband joined Baptist in 1984[19]
Mrs Chidzambuyo	??	Was interested in the church

9. Soche Baptist Church (Semi Urban)

Members	Former Church	Reason for Joining
a. Mrs Annie Kawanda	CCAP Nkhoma Synod	She found the teaching on the word of God being applied and followed
b. Mrs Mpumula	??	She found the teaching on the word of God being applied and followed.[20]
c. Mr J Ng'oma	CCAP	Was convicted of the Baptist doctrine of

---

[16] Int. Mrs Ngozo, Balaka Baptist Church, Balaka, May 2000.

[17] Int. Mrs Magombo, Balaka Baptist Church, Balaka, May 2000. According to the Catholic canon law, marriage cannot be annulled except if it can be proven that the church wedding was not valid for example because of forced marriage. Divorce therefore, is against being a full member of Catholic church and hence you have no access to the church sacraments. Int. Dr Martin Ott, Department of Theology and Religious Studies, Zomba, 14.6.2000. The Baptist Church on the other hand accepts divorcees as full members, and very quickly indeed.

[18] Int. Mrs Magoli, Balaka Baptist Church, May 2000. She also pointed out that even without her husband, she was on the verge of leaving CCAP because it was dull for her.

[19] She is now a widow but is the Vice Secretary of Umodzi, the Women's Missionary Union. She felt not free in her CCAP church and was happy in the Baptist Church. Int. Mrs Nkolola, Balaka Baptist Church, May 2000.

[20] Int. Anne Kawamba, Soche Baptist Church, Blantyre May 2000.

baptism by immersion.[21]

| d. Mrs Ng'oma | CCAP | Followed husband[22] |

10. New Jerusalem Baptist Church (1965)

Members	Former Church	Reasons for Joining
a. Mrs Lazarus Malabwanya	Zambezi Evangelical Church	Became Baptist through material support in 1965.[23]
b. Mrs Fanny Kwelakwela (nee Malabwanya)	Zambezi Evangelical Church	Material support provided by Effie Cameroon and the Kingsleys[24]
c. Mr Gawaza	Baptist	Followed his Baptist uncle[25]
d. Mrs Janet Malabwanya	Baptist	Born a Baptist[26]

11. Bangwe Baptist Church (1967)[27]

12. Living Stones Baptist Church (Semi urban)

Members	Former Church	Reasons for joining

---

[21] Int. Mr J Ng'oma, Soche Baptist Church, Blantyre, 25.5.1999.

[22] Ibid, also Int. Mary Galatiya, Likudzi Estate, Chipiliro Baptist Church, Balaka 15.5.2000.

[23] Mrs Lazarus Malabwanya was blind and was a beggar in the town of Blantyre. Mrs Cameroon, a Baptist herself, offered her quarters as lodging, and the Southern Baptist missionaries, especially Rev Beverly Kingsley and the wife, helped to educate her children by offering financial support. Mrs Malabwanya died in 1995. Int. J M Ng'oma Soche Baptist Church, 25.5.1999. Her son Samuel Malabwanya, educated in this way, became an influential Baptist pastor of Jerusalem Baptist Church from 1994 to 1996 when he left to start Good Hope Church. Int. Mr Gawaza, Bangwe Baptist Church, Blantyre 30.4.2000.

[24] Int. Fanny Kwelakwela, Bangwe Baptist Church, Blantyre, 30.4.2000. Fanny Kwelakwela is the daughter of Lazarus Malabwanya.

[25] Mr Gawaza is the nephew of Rev Maseko who was a Baptist pastor before he died. Gawaza stayed with Maseko for a long time and Maseko influenced him to join the Baptist church. Int. Mr Gawaza, Bangwe Baptist Church, Blantyre, 30.4.2000.

[26] Mrs Janet Malabwanya is the wife of Pastor Samuel Malabwanya, and the daughter of Rev Stephen and Mary Galatiya, who were among the first local Convention Baptists in Malawi. Her mother and father have been Baptists since 1958. Int. Mary Galatiya, Likudzi Estate, Chipiliro Baptist Church, Balaka, 15.5.2000.

[27] Although individual conversion experience were different, the first members of this church were attracted to the church because of distance. There were fewer churches in this locality in 1967.

| a. Pastor A C Phiri | Muslim | Became Baptist in 1978. Following his preacher's church.[28] |
| b. Violet Phiri | Muslim | Followed husband in 1983.[29] |

13. Blantyre Baptist at Chichiri Stadium

Members	Former church	Reasons for joining
a. Mrs Margaret Nyika	CCAP	Was disciplined because she did not bring her disjunction Certificate from Austria[30]
b. Mr Jonga	CCAP	Was divorced and remarried.[31] He was well welcomed in the Baptist Church with his second wife
Mrs Lillian Jonga	Churches of Christ	Followed husband

14. Zomba Rural, (Jali) (Leaders of South East Region)[32]

Members	Former Church	Reasons for joining a Church
a. Member x	CCAP	Divorce and remarriage
b. Member x	Church of Christ	Divorce and remarriage
c. Members x	CCAP	Divorced
d. Members x	CCAP	Divorced
e. Member x	Mpingo wa Ak-	Divorced

---

[28] Amos Samuel Phiri was won to Christ by Pastor A.C. Chisi while in Lilongwe. He joined the Baptist church where Chisi was a member. Int. Rev A.C. Phiri, Livingstone Baptist Church, 26.5.1999.

[29] Violet followed her husband. Int. Violet Phiri, Livingstone Baptist Church, 26.5.1999.

[30] Margaret Nyika went to Austria for studies from 1963 to 1967. During this time, she faithfully attended church but unfortunately when she came home to Malawi, she did not bring a disjunction certificate letter form Austria. Because of this she was on discipline, so that she was not to partake in the Lord's Supper. One time, as she walked past the Henry Henderson Institute at Blantyre Mission, she saw Blantyre Baptist Church and she went into the church and liked the way she was received. She has since then been a Baptist.

[31] Such behaviour deserves discipline in CCAP.

[32] 6 women out of 24 leaders of South East were sampled out for their conversion histories. Theses women came form Mandawala Baptist Church, Mwanafumu Baptist Church, Kachulu Baptist Church, Mpheta Baptist Church, Lomoni Baptist Church and Ntaja Baptist Church. The results were as above. The major reason why they left their church was that they fell out of grace with their former church by divorcing their husbands or being divorced. Int. Leaders of South East Region, Zomba Baptist Church, 3.3.2000.

	hristu	
f. Member x	Catholic	Divorced

15. Makolije Baptist Church - Jali (1962)

Members	Former church	Reasons for joining
a. Davidson Lichapa	Church of God	Baptist Church taught leadership training,[33] Baptist church is more liberated. Baptist comes from America.[34]
b. Deliya Jackson Lichapa	Church of Christ	Followed husband[35]
c. Bambo B P Khuzu and wife, Mr Mankhwala and wife, Mr Nasiyaya and wife		Doctrine of Baptist teaching of salvation and Christ

16. Chayima Baptist Church

Members	Former church	Reasons for joining
a. First core group in 1961 such as Mrs Mayombo and husband, Mrs Chipolopolo and her husband, Mayi Anganeje Tsegula	"Severe" Church (Church of Christ)	Internal leadership disputes[36]
b. Others	??	Were confronted with Baptist beliefs at big and small meetings[37]

---

[33] The leader of Church of Christ under Mr Severe was involved in immorality within the congregation. Even though the problem was with the personality it had an impact on church life in that all the members rejected him as their leader and sought another church to pastor them. They approached Southern Missionaries in Zomba town- Rev Leroy Wester and Blanche Wester who agreed that they should join the Baptist church after fulfilling some conditions that all Baptists have to adhere to. Int. Rev Maida, Chayima Baptist Church, Jali, 20.3.2000.

[34] Small meetings were meetings which lasted for one day. Big meetings lasted for at least 3 days. Ibid. and int. Efraim Botoman, Chisomo Baptist Church, Blantyre, 28.3.2000.

[35] Makolije Baptist Church was started by Davidson Lichapa in 1962 in his home village Makolije.

[36] Int. Davidson Lichapa, Makolije Baptist Church, Jali, Zomba, 8.3.2000.

[37] Ibid.

17. Ntokota Baptist Church Rural (Jali)[38]

Members	Former church	Reasons
Member x	Roman Catholic	Following husband
Member x	CCAP	Following husband because man is head of family
Member x	CCAP	She did not receive pastoral care
Member x	CCAP	She was divorced and in CCAP they disciplined her and wanted her to do classes before she could be full member
Members x	Roman Catholic	Followed her mother, who became Baptist after following her new husband
Member x	Church of Christ	The pastor was not fit to be pastor
Member x	Church of Christ	The polygamist
Member x	Church of Christ	There were disagreements in church.
Member x	Roman Catholic	She could not manage to do classes (4 years) to qualify as full member
Member x	Roman Catholic	She was divorced and remarried
Member x	Evangelical Baptist	There was no Evangelical Baptist Church nearby
Member x	Salvation Army	There was no Salvation Army Church nearby
Member x	Masiye	Followed husband
Member x	Baptist	Born Baptist
Member x	Islam (1999)	Could not understand the teaching. She dreamt that Muslim faith was

---

[38] 17 women out of 20 were interviewed. The results were as above. Int. Ntokota Baptist Church members, Jali, Zomba 19.3.2000. The Muslim woman who became Baptist had an interesting story. She is Baptist on her own right and her husband did not follow her. She had been a Muslim for 20 years but one day, as she was going to the mosque for prayers, she felt as if she could not breathe properly and was also practically blind because she couldn't see the way. She found herself going into the bush. She returned home. One Saturday, she dreamt that she was in a mosque and saw her late son holding a Bible. The son told her that she must go to church. When she woke up on Sunday morning, she went to the Baptist church and has become a full member of this church. - Ntokota Baptist Church was started in 1962. See Gazamiyala's Diary. He wrote this note in 1985: "24 years kufika kwa Mpingo wa Baptist from 1962 to 1985.".

		wrong
Member x	Ulere church	Followed her elder son, who was a Baptist

18. Chisomo Baptist Church (Blantyre rural)

Member	Former Church	Reasons for joining the church
a. Mr Efraim Boto-man Nkhoma	CCAP	The elders in this church asked him to have a church wedding to be a full member in the church.[39]
b. Mrs Rosebay Botoman Nkhoma	CCAP	Followed her husband under coercion.[40]

19. Malirano Baptist Church Mozambique Border (1998)

Member	Former Church	Reasons for joining church
Rev Mtuwe and the wife	CCAP	There was a disagreement about responsibility in the church.[41]
Mrs Martha Chi-waya	Four Square Gospel	Four Square Gospel Church denied her child a decent church burial[42]
Other members of the church	??	Rejection by their former church at funerals. There were churches in the

---

[39] Efraim one day met Rev Mukhora of the Baptist Church. He told him that there was no need to have a church wedding for membership in the Baptist Church. Efraim joined the Baptist Church and was accepted as full member without any delay.

[40] Even though Efraim became a Baptist, his wife Rosebay wanted to remain in CCAP at any cost. Efraim challenged her with a proverb "sindinaone mphuno imodzi kulowa zala ziwiri". (I have never seen a nose which can accommodate two fingers), implying that if Rosebay was married to Efraim, she was one with her husband and needed to do one thing with her husband. This proverb did not convince Rosebay until one day Efraim threatened her with these words: "If you do not come with me to church, you will find me gone back to my home." Rosebay followed her husband to the Baptist Church. Int. Rosebay Botoman, Chisomo Baptist Church, Blantyre rural, 28.3.2000.

[41] Rev Mtuwe and others in CCAP contacted Rev Sabola who was a Baptist pastor at Malirano Baptist to bring his church to Ntchivirivi village. He agreed and Nachanji Baptist Church was started there. Int. Rev Mtuwe, Malirano Baptist Church, Mozambique border, 19.5.2000.

[42] Mrs Chiwaya had lost a child and when she approached her church for help, the church ignored her request and the child was buried mwachikunja, in a non-Christian way. She therefore went to the Baptist Church.

area.[43]

20. Mwaleko Baptist Church in 1973.

Members	Former church	Reasons
a. Rev Paulo Sabola	Roman catholic	His parents were excommunicated in the church while he was a child because the parents married without church wedding. They had to wait for two years to be full members of the church.[44]
b. Mrs Sabola	??	Followed husband[45]
c. Others	??	They came to the church by hearing a church bell that was tied in a tree under which Mwaleko Baptist church met[46]

21. Chipimbi Baptist Church - Mozambique Border (1985)

Member	Former Church	Reasons
a. Rev John Mosses	Utopia Church	Was not happy with the church[47]

22. Thundu Baptist Church (Zomba rural) in 1963.

Members	Former church	Reasons
a. Rev David Malikebu	CCAP Blantyre Synod	Divorced by the wife. Then met a Baptist who told him about his pastor Rev Mbona along Lake Chirwa. When Rev Mbona told David about the Baptist faith

---

[43] Lack of care at funerals of people's relatives became one way why people fled their former churches to join the Baptist Church. Int. Rev Mtuwe, Malirano Baptist Church, Mozambique Border, 19.5.2000.

[44] This was around 1973 and this seemed to have been a procedure in the RC. Because of how his parents were treated, he left the Catholic Church for the Baptist Church. Int. Rev Paulo Sabola, Mwaleko Baptist Church, Mozambique border, 19.5.2000.

[45] There were few churches in the area and a church bell was enough to call people to this church. Ibid.

[46] Int. Rev John Moses, Chipimbi Baptist Church, Mozambique Border, 19.5.2000.

[47] Int. Rev David Malikebu, Thundu Baptist Church, Jali, Zomba 19.5.2000. Rev Mbona used a tract called "Yesu Ndani" in telling him about the faith. He was converted to his message and followed his preacher.

		he was converted.[48] Followed his preacher.
b. Mrs Malikebu	Muslim	Followed husband who told her about Jesus and the Baptist Church[49]
c. Other members	??	"Kaunjika" – Free clothes distributed at the Malikebu's home[50]
d. Other members	??	Attracted to leadership training cinema on biblical characters[51]

23. Mwanafumu Baptist Church (Zomba, rural) 25 May 1975

Members	Former church	Reasons
a. Nichola Mlenga	Nakhule church	Followed Jesus and followed Mr Lichapa's church, who told him about spiritual things[52]
b. Mrs Akuchiwona Mlenga	Nakhule	Followed husband
c. Mrs Mellia Makina	Jehovah's witnesses	Was afraid of persecution.[53]
d. Mrs Mary Taibu	Church of Christ	Was divorced in Church of Christ from a man she had a church wedding with[54]
e. Mrs Malesi Salifu	CCAP	Divorced and remarried to a Baptist and followed him to his Baptist Church[55]
f. Mrs Sumayili	Muslim	Followed his Uncle Rev Mlenga.[56]
g. Mellia Tho-	Muslim	Divorced a Muslim and choose to be-

---

[48] Int. Mrs Malikebu, Thundu Baptist Church, 28.10.2000.
[49] Leroy and Blanche Wester used to distribute *kaunjika* from Malikebu's home. This attracted others to the Baptist faith. Ibid.
[50] Ibid.
[51] Rev Mrs Mellia Makina, Mwanafumu Baptist Church, Zomba rural, 21.3.2000.
[52] Ibid. The Jehovah's Witnesses fell out of grace with Ngwazi's autocratic rule because they could not buy party membership cards. Even though Mellia Makina became a Baptist, she did not buy a card.
[53] Int. Mary Taibu, Mwanafumu Baptist Church, Zomba rural, 21.3.2000.
[54] Mrs Malesi Salifu has been divorced three times at the age of 35. Each time she remarried she followed the husband to his church. At one time she even became a Muslim because she married a Muslim man. This happened just before she became a Baptist. Int. Mrs Malesi Salifu, Mwanafumu Baptist Church, Zomba rural 21.3.2000.
[55] The husband remained a Muslim even when she joined the Baptist faith. Int. Mrs Sumayili, Mwanafumu Baptist Church, Zomba rural, 21.3.2000.
[56] Int. Mrs Mella Thombozi, Mwanafumu Baptist Church, Zomba rural, 21.3.2000.

| mbozi | | come a Baptist on her own after believing the Christian message. |
| h. Agnes Chikadula | Church of Christ | Because of distance. It is longer to go to the Church of Christ than to the Baptist Church[57] |

24. Mzuzu Baptist Church

Members	Former Church	Reasons
Mrs Elizabeth Njolomole	CCAP	Followed her husband[58]
Mr Njolomole Phiri	CCAP	Biblical films. Became a Christians through this and followed the missionary (Baptist preacher)[59]

25. Mandawala Baptist Church (1964)[60]

Members	Former Church	Reasons
Mrs Andisambula	Asimisi Church[61]	Heard of American starting a new church were to meet Baptist members, and became Baptist
Rev Gowelo	Church of Christ	The whole congregation left to join Baptist
Mrs Gowelo	Church of Christ	Followed husband[62]

26. Mwambo Baptist Church

Members	Former church	Reasons
a. Mrs Solomoni	Church of Christ	Divorced and the church did not like that because her husband was a key member of the church[63]

---

[57] Int. Mrs Agnes Chikadula, Mwanafumu Baptist Church, Zomba rural, 21.3.2000.

[58] Her husband became converted to Baptist faith earlier.

[59] Around 1964, the political environment was such that white people were suspected bringing confusion in the one party system under Ngwazi, as such they took with them police for an escort. Njolomole Phiri became the escort. Int. Elizabeth Njolomole, Mzuzu Baptist Church, 5.5.2000.

[60] Asimisi Church is a group of Churches of Christ led by Rev Smith. Int. Rev Gowelo, Mandawala Baptist Church, 9.3.2000.

[61] Ibid. The husband did not follow her.

[62] Ibid. Apart from Mrs Gowelo, most of the women in this Mandawala Church of Christ moved out of the church following their husbands. They were told to follow their husbands, because culturally that was right.

b. Rev Solomoni   Church of Christ   Took somebody's wife in the church. This was unbecoming in the eyes of the church.[64]

27. Mambala Baptist Church

Member	Former Church	Reasons
Mr and Mrs Walasi	Seventh Day Baptist	Converted to Baptist when Lichapa a Baptist Pastor challenged them about the keeping of the law[65]

28. Mulanje Baptist Churches in 1967

Members	Former church	Reasons
a. Nasela Baptist Church	??	Mainly through *phwando* meetings and developmental skills Mrs Wester taught to the women.
b. Thamanda Baptist Church	??	
c. Bongwe Baptist Church	??	

29. Khanda Baptist Church in 1978 *(cooking and Sewing Skills)*[66]

30. Chilumba Zone Baptist

Members	Before	Reasons
Mrs Rev Lutepo	CCAP	Followed husband at his command[67]
Mayi Nyauhango	??	Believed in the Baptist message and was converted to it in 1975[68]
Mrs Mlenga	??	Believed the Baptist message and was converted[69]

---

[63] Actually her husband married her while she was still considered to be married to this leader of the church. Both left church of church and joined Baptist church where they have risen even up to pastoral position. Int. Mrs Solomoni, Mwambo Baptist Church, 9.3.2000.

[64] Ibid.

[65] Int. Davidson Lichapa, Makolije Baptist Church, Zomba rural, 8.3.2000.

[66] Int. Rev Davidson Lichapa, Makolije Baptist Church, 8.3.2000.

[67] Int. Mrs Lutepo, Chilumba Zone Baptist Church, 17.3.2000.

[68] She was converted to the Baptist faith the first time she heard the Baptist message. Int. Nyauhango, Chilumba Zone Baptist Church, (north), 17.3.2000. The prefix Nya- in Tumbuka means Nee, so this lady is nee Uhango. The father was Mr Uhango.

[69] Int. Mr Mkwala, Chilumba Zone Baptist Church, 14.3.2001.

31. Makolije Baptist Church

Member	Before	Reason
Mrs Kanichi	Jehovah's Witness	In 1978 J.W. were banned and she left with children because of torture.[70]

32. Chirima Baptist Church

Members	Before	Reasons
Mrs Gunda[71]	?	Followed husband in 1996[72]

33. Bongwe Baptist Church

Members	Before	Reasons
Member x	CCAP Evangelical Baptist	Left CCAP for Evangelical Baptist because had a child out of wedlock. Left Evangelical Baptist because her uncle was a leader in Evangelical Baptist and because of disputes with him, she left in 1994.[73]

34. Mtokotha Baptist Church (Thyolo)

Members	Before	Reasons
Mr Kwalira	CCAP	Followed his wife[74]

35. Tambala Baptist Church

Member	Before	Reasons
Tambula	PIM	Because teachings in PIM were not for salvation. They preached that John Chilembwe was saviour as Jesus was.[75] He left and followed Baptist preachers (Abusa Lichapa and Chimenya) who

---

[70] Int. Makolije Baptist Church, Makolije Baptist, 22.3.2000. Her husband died in the persecution.

[71] She was second wife, because Mr Gunya's first wife died. However she was a leader of the woman at Chirima Baptist Church. Int. Mrs Gunya, Chirima Baptist Church, 3.5.2000.

[72] Ibid.

[73] Member x Bongwe Baptist Church, in chief Bongwe, Jali, Rural Zomba 3.5.2000.

[74] Int. Mrs Kwalira, Ntokota Baptist Church, Thyolo, 9.7.2000.

[75] John Chilembwe's uprising against the colonial government was seen as his shedding of blood to save the people. Int. Tambala Mwanakhu, Mpinda Baptist Church, 26.7.2000.

preached about salvation in Jesus.[76]

36. Namwera Baptist Church

Members	Before	Reasons
Mr Subayi and Mr Malemba	Church of Christ	Liked the teachings of Baptist Church[77]
Rila Baptist Church (Zomba rural)	Jehovah's Witness	??

37. Swang'oma Baptist Church

Member X	??	Tract "Ndichite chiyani kuti ndipulumuke" after reading this tract the Baptist man who had the track explained to him about the Baptist Church and he became Baptist.[78]

39. Govala Baptist Church

Member	Previous Church	Reason
Mrs Bakiri	Roman Catholic	Moved out of Catholic because of the teachings especially the teaching on Baptism. Baptists baptize a person who knows what she is doing. She was converted to this teaching in 1987.[79]

40. Mina Baptist Church

Member	Previous Church	Reasons
Mrs Jackson	CCAP[80]	Became Baptist in 1979 together with husband because they could not afford a church wedding which was demanded of them in CCAP.[81]

---

[76] Ibid.
[77] Int. Tambula Mwanakhu, Mpinda Baptist Church. 13.7.2000.
[78] Ibid.
[79] Int. Mrs Bakiri, Govala Baptist Church, 15.7.2000. Zomba rural.
[80] She was however not consistent but was born in CCAP. Int. Mrs Jackson, Mina Baptist Church, Zomba rural, 14.7.2000.
[81] Ibid. When they were told to wed, they told the church that they were not ready and the church disciplined them. So they went to join the Baptists in 1977.

41. Namachele Baptist Church

Member	Previous Church	Reasons
Mrs Modesta Nthambi	Roman Catholic	Followed her husband[82]

42. Lingadzi Baptist Church

Member	Previous Church	Reasons
Mrs Veronica Matiki	African International Church	Left to follow her husband who was a Baptist[83]

43. Naveya Baptist Church

Member	Previous Church	Reasons
Mrs Effelo Benson	Baptist	Born a Baptist[84]

44. Phazi Baptist Church

Member	Previous Church	Reasons
Mrs Anne Robertson	Church of Christ	Was told to follow husband[85]

45.

Member	Previous Church	Reasons
Mrs Bonongwe	Church of Christ	Became Baptist in 1987, after she heard a Baptist preacher preaching at her uncle's funeral.[86]

46.

Member	Previous Church	Reasons
James Mbewe	Baptist	Was born Baptist[87]

---

[82] She was a dedicated Christian in the Catholic Church. Int. Mrs Modesta Nthambi, Namachele Baptist Church, Zomba rural, 14.7.2000.
[83] Int. Veronica Matiki, Lungazi Baptist Church, Zomba rural, 14.7.2000.
[84] Int. Effelo Benson, Naveya Baptist Church, Zomba rural, 14.7.2000.
[85] Int. Annie Robertson, Phazi Baptist Church, Zomba rural. 14.7.2000.
[86] Her uncle was sick and admitted in Zomba General Hospital. He was a Baptist. When he died, there was a Baptist who preached at this funeral. Mrs Bonongwe was convicted by the message and became a Baptist. Int. Mrs Bonongwe, Chinangwa Baptist Church, 14.7.2000.
[87] Int. Mrs Mankhokwe (Mother to James Mbewe), Chinangwa Baptist Church, 14.7.2000.

47.

Member	Previous Church	Reasons
Mrs Mankhokwe and Mr Ma-nkhokwe	ATR	Was converted to Baptist church in 1976 when she and her husband heard the preaching of a Baptist, they became Baptist[88]

48. Thabwani Baptist Church

Member	Previous Church	Reasons
Member x	Roman Catholic	When her child was sick her church did not visit her, so she moved to Baptist[89]

Section B: Reverse conversion stories

The second key question that was asked was: "Why did you leave Baptist church". This question was asked only when it was reported that someone has left the Baptist church. The responses to this question were as follows:

1. SE Region members	Follow husband[90] and lack of able leadership[91]
2 Mwanafumu Baptist Church	Some pioneering women and men left to join a new church; for example Mrs Kala left the church around 1988 to Evangelical Baptist Church[92]
	-Because of polygamy. For example Mr Chikatola left in 1999 because he married a second wife[93]
	-Mr Nicholas Mlenga left because he become polygamous and joined APOSTLE[94]

---

[89] Int. Thabwani Baptist member, Ntokota Baptist Church, 19.3.2000.
[90] The key reason in this area is that women leave Baptist Church to follow their husbands.
[91] Int. Regional committee meeting, Zomba Baptist Church, 2.2000.
[92] Int. Makolije Baptist Church focus group (women), 22.3.2000.
[93] Ibid.
[94] Ibid.

3. Mwanafumu Baptist Church

Member	Church	Reasons
Mellen Thom-bozi (43) years	Baptist	Went to the mosque to follow her Muslim husband.[95]

4. Chaone Church at Mikolongwe Baptist (1972)

Missionaries started it in the 1970s but it now belongs to Ufumu wa Yehova ndi Amikaeli led by Mr Eliot Howa.[96]

5. Chilambe Baptist Church

Member	Church	Reasons
Member X	Baptist	Left on her own because of sexual promiscuity[97]

6. Namwera Baptist urch   Death of a key member[98]

7. Thabwani Baptist Church (Zomba rural).

Member	Church	Reasons
Member X	Baptist	Was removed from church because of divorce, the woman was at fault.[99]
Member y	Baptist	Brewed *kachasu* and was drinking beer.[100]

[95] Ibid.
[96] Int. Williot Howa, Mikolongwe, Thyolo, 28.3.2000. The Baptist church died because of lack of supervision from Blantyre leadership. The other reason is that they did not get iron sheets for their church.
[97] Int. Mr Chilambe, Chilambe Baptist Church, Thyolo, 8.7.2000.
[98] Ibid.
[99] Int. member, Thabwani Baptist Church, Ntokota Baptist Church, 19.3.2000. She was formerly a Catholic but left the church because she was divorced.
[100] Ibid.

Appendix no. 2

A Woman's Cry

Sister,
If you happen to meet him
Tell him that in matrimony
Hands are for caressing the wife's body
And fondling her breasts
Not a sjambok
For whipping her body
or slapping her face.

Sister, sister
If you see the man
forget not to remind him
That a man's chest in bed
is the woman's pillow
where she can pour her tears
In times of sorrow as well as joy
Not hardboard for manifesting his temper.

Sister, sister, please
If by chance you meet your brother-in-law
Whisper in his ears that in marriage
Lips are for kissing
And producing sweet non-sense
Thereby giving pleasure to each other

Not for kissing a calabash of beer

producing words fit for the bin thereafter.

Sister, sister, please, sister,
If you encounter the man I married
Remember to say to him that his eyes
Are there to admire his wife
The shape of her body
The beauty of her face
And the art of her hands
Not to lust after teenage girls.

Sister, sister, please, sister, Abiti Moya,
If you meet CHEJAFARI, my husband,
deliver to him this message:
Money in the home should be there
To maintain wife and young ones
Not to purchase risky pleasures
which he can have free and safe
from me, his wife, Abiti Daniel

Cecilia Hasha

Appendix no. 3

Box 431
Blantyre. Malawi
7 September, 1977

Mr. E. B. Muluzi
Secretary General and Administrative Secretary
Malawi Congress Party
P.O. Box 5250
Limbe, Malawi

Dear Mr. Muluzi

Thank you so much for all the assistance you gave me in the planning of the Baptist Women's Union of Africa Continental Congress Meeting in Blantyre during 25-29 July, 1977.

I appreciate the time you gave during your busy schedule to secure permission from Dr Banda, the Life President of Malawi, for this meeting to be held in Malawi and then for the leaders of the Baptist Women's Union of Africa and the Women's Department of the Baptist World Alliance to have an Audience with His Excellency, Dr Banda.

During the BWUA meeting we were especially pleased that you could attend the Banquet and bring greetings on behalf of Dr Banda and the Government of Malawi. We were also happy that you could lead us as we had the Audience with Dr Banda at State Lodge in Zomba.

The leaders and the women were thrilled that Dr Banda could meet the leaders, that you came to the Banquet, that services and food at the Mount Soche Hotel were first Class, and that they could be in an African country where peace and friendliness are so evident among the people.

Thanks again for all your help to me and this meeting.

Sincerely,

(Miss) Mary Ann Chandler

BIBLIOGRAPHY

Oral Sources

Anganeje, Chayima Baptist Church, Zomba, 20.3.2000.

Bakili, Mrs, Govala Baptist Church, 15.7.2000.

Banda, Mirriam, Nachiswe Baptist Church, 3.8.2000.

Banda, Mrs Roy, Lumbadzi Baptist Church, Lilongwe, 13.6.2000.

Banda, Rev Kalayitoni, Namachete Baptist Church, 3.8.2000.

Benson, Effelo, Naveya Baptist Church, Zomba rural, 14.7.2000.

Bonongwe, Mrs, Chinangwa Baptist Church, 14.7.2000.

Botoman, Efraim, Chisomo Baptist Church, Blantyre. 28.3.2000.

Botoman, Roseby, Chisomo Baptist Church, Chilomoni, Blantyre, 28.3.2000.

Chafunya, Mrs, Ntcheu Baptist Church, Ntcheu, 4.5.2000.

Chauluka, Linly, Mauluka Baptist Church, 24.3.2000.

Chidzambuyo, Mrs, Balaka Baptist Church, May 2000.

Chikadula, Agnes, Mwanafumu Baptist Church, Zomba rural 21.3.2000.

Chilembe, Mr, Chilambe Baptist Church, Thyolo 8.7.2000.

Chimkwita, Rev Emmanuel, Lilongwe Baptist Seminary, 12.3.2001.

Chinangwa, Maria, Chikwawa, 26.7.2000.

Chinangwa, Marina, Ndirande Baptist Church, 27.7.2000.

Chingota, Rev Dr Felix, Department of Theology and Religious Studies, University of Malawi, 20.1.2001.

Chipojola, Mrs, Ntcheu Baptist Church, Ntcheu, 4.5.2000.

Chirima Baptist Church, Focus group, 28.1.2001.

Chirwa, Akim, Blantyre Baptist Church, General Secretary, Baptist Convention of Malawi, 6.1998, 14.12.2000.

Chirwa, Martha, Zomba Theological College 14.12.2000, 9.1.2001, 12.1.2001, 15.3.2001.

Chisi, Mrs, Ufulu Baptist Church, Lilongwe, 23.6.2000.

Chisi, Rev A.C., Ufulu Baptist Church, 23.6.2000, 12.3.2001, 14.10.2001.

Chitsukwa, Mr V.W, Chisomo Baptist Church, 28.3.2000.

Emmanuel, Mrs Elias, Mauluka Baptist Church, Mphyuphyu, 13.7.2000.

Executive committee members of South East region, Focus group, 3.3.2000.

Galatiya, Mary, Likudzi Estate, Chipiliro Baptist Church, Balaka, 15.5.2000.

Galatiya, Stephen, Chipiliro Baptist Church, Likudzi Estate, Balaka, 15.5.2000.

Gawaza, Mr, Bangwe Baptist Church, Blantyre 30.4.2000.

Girls (23) at Youth South East regional conference, Zomba Baptist Church, 23.12.2000.

Goba, Olive, St Patrick Lwangwa Parish, Zomba, 22.12.2000.

Gowelo, Mrs, Mandawala Baptist Church, 9.3.2000, 25.11.2000.

Gowelo, Rev, Mandawala Baptist Church, 9.3.2000.

Gunya, Mrs, Chirima Baptist Church, 3.5.2000.

Gunya, Rev, Soche Baptist Church, Blantyre, 25.5.1999.

Howa, Williot, Mikolongwe, Thyolo, 28.3.2000.

Jackson, Mary, Mina Baptist Church, 26.11.2000.

Jali, Focus group, 21.3.2000.

Jonga, William, South Lunzu Baptist Church, 26.5.1999, 12.11.1999.

Joseph, Bertha and members, Ndirande Baptist Church, 27.7.2000.

Joseph, Bertha, Chikwawa, 26.7.2000.

Kachere, Bonwell, Chikwawa, 26.7.2000.

Kachere, Mrs Bonwell Marina Chinangwa, Ndirande Baptist Church, 27.7.2000.

Kalako, Liddah, Ufulu Baptist Church, Lilongwe, 13.12.2000.

Kalavina, Mrs, Nchalo Baptist Church, Chikwawa, 27.7.2000.

Kalavina, Rev, Nchalo Baptist Church, 26.7.2000.

Kalayitoni, Rev, Nachiswe Baptist Church, 3.8.2000.

Kalenga, Christina, Nsomo Baptist Church, Chikwawa, 5.5.2000, 28.7.2000.

Kalenga, Rev Jim, Nsomo Baptist Church, Ngabu, Chikwawa, 28.7.2000, 28.9.2000.

Kalenga, Rev Wilfred, Nsomo Baptist Church, 28.9.2000.

Kambalame, Agnes, Ntokota Baptist, Thyolo, 26.7.2000.

Kambalame, Filemon, Ntokota Baptist, Thyolo, 26.7.2000.

Kample, Mrs, treasurer for *Umodzi*, Chilambe Baptist Church, Thyolo, 8.7.2000.

Kamwendo, Rev Macfarry, Mtengo wa Moyo Baptist Church, 13.8.2000.

Kantunda, Mrs, Mpando Baptist Church, Thyolo, 26.7.2000.

Kantunda, Rev K.A.G.J., Mpando Baptist Church; Thyolo, 7.8.2000.

Kathumba, Rev Medson, Chirima Baptist Church, Mphyuphyu, Zomba rural, 31.7.2000.

Kawamba, Anne, Soche Baptist Church, Blantyre, May 2000.

Kawamba, Raynor, Baptist Convention Offices, Blantyre, 26.5.1999, 17.11.1999.

Kayipa, Mrs, Ntcheu Baptist Church, Ntcheu, 4.5.2000.

Kholomana, Martha, Mpando Baptist Church, Thyolo, 26.7.2000.

Khuzu, Mrs, pastor's wife, Tambala Baptist Church, 10.3.2000.

Kwalira, Mrs, Ntokota Baptist Church, Thyolo 9.7.2000.

Kwelakwela, Fanny (nee Malabwanya), Bangwe Baptist Church, Blantyre, 30.4.2000.

Leaders of South East Region, Zomba Baptist Church, 3.3.2000.

Lichapa, Elizabeth, pastor's wife, Makolije Baptist Church, Jali, Zomba, 8.3.2000.

Lichapa, Rev Davidson, Makolije Baptist Church, Jali, Zomba 8.3.2000, 20.3.2000.

Longwe, Molly, Lecturer, Baptist Theological Seminary, Lilongwe, 12.2000).

Longwe, Rev Hany, Principal, Baptist Theological Seminary, Lilongwe, 6.1.2001, 14.3.2000.

Lufani, Agnes, Zomba Baptist Church, 3.3.2000.
Lutepo, Mrs, Chilumba Zone Baptist Church, 17.3.2000.
Mafuule, Mary, Mpando Baptist Church, Thyolo 26.7.2000.
Magoli, Mrs, Balaka Baptist Church, May 2000.
Magombo, Mrs, Balaka Baptist Church, Balaka, May 2000.
Mahere, Anganeje, Chayima Baptist Church, 10.3.2000, 20.3.2000.
Maida, Rev, Chayima Baptist Church, Jali, 10.3.2000, 20.03.2000.
Makhaya, Mrs, Ntcheu Baptist Church, Ntcheu, 4.5.2000.
Makina, Mellia, Mwanafumu Baptist Church, 21.3.2000.
Makolije Baptist Church, Focus group (women), 22.3.2000.
Makondesa, Patrick, Kachere Research Centre, Chancellor College, 21.1.2001.
Malikebu, Rev David, Thundu Baptist Church, Jali, 28.11.1999, 28.10.1999,
    19.5.2000.
Mallungo, Hilda, Mtendere Baptist Church, Lilongwe, 14.3.2000, 14.12.2000.
Mankhokwe, Mrs, Chimangwa Baptist Church, 14.7.2000.
Marriage seminar, South East region, Zomba Baptist Church, 2000.
Matiki, Veronica, Lungazi Baptist Church, Zomba rural, 14.7.2000.
Mauluka, Mrs, Mauluka Baptist Church, 24.3.2000.
Mauluka, Rev, Mauluka Baptist Church, 24.3.2000.
Maya, Agnes, Zomba Baptist Church, 28.10.2000.
Member x Bongwe Baptist Church, in chief Bongwe's area, 3.5.2000.
Member, Thabwani Baptist Church, Ntokota Baptist Church, 19.3.2000.
Mkandawire, Annie, Capital City Baptist Church, Lilongwe 24.6.2000.
Mkandawire, Francis, Capital City Baptist Church, Lilongwe 24.6.2000.
Mkwala, Mr, Chilumba Zone Baptist Church, 14.3.2001.
Moses, Rev John, Chipimbi Baptist Church, Mozambique Border, 19.5.2000.
Moyo, Fulata, Chancellor College, Zomba. 2000.
Mpando Baptist Church, Focus group, 26.7.2000.
Mrs Makina, Mwanafumu Baptist Church, 21.3.2000.
Mtuwe, Rev, Chipinimbi Baptist Church, 19.5.2000.
Mtuwe, Rev, Malirano Baptist Church, Mozambique border, 19.5.2000.
Mussa, Regina, Ufulu Baptist Church, Area 23 Lilongwe rural, 14.6.2000.
Mwanafumu Baptist Church, Jali, Zomba rural, Focus group, 21.3.2000.
Mwanakhu, Mrs, Mpinda Baptist Church, 2.9.2000, 3.7.2000, 26.12.2000.
Mwanakhu, Rev Tambula, Mpinda Baptist Church, Mikuyu Association, Zomba rural,
    3.7.2000, 13.7.2000, 27.7.2000.
Nankwenya, Mrs, Mpinda Baptist Church, 2.9.2000.
Nanthambwe, Mrs, deacon, Mpinda Baptist Church, 22.9.00.
Nanthambwe, Nellie, Mauluka Baptist Church, 24.3.2000.
Nasimango, Sellina, Zomba Baptist Church, 28.10.2000.
Ng'oma, Rev, Mayera Baptist Church, Blantyre, 15.5.1999, 20.5.2000, 25.5.1999,
    31.3.2000.
Ngozo, Mrs, Balaka Baptist Church, Balaka, May 2000.

Njolomole, Elizabeth, Mzuzu Baptist Church, 5.5.2000.
Nkolola, Mrs, Balaka Baptist Church, May 2000.
Nsomo Baptist Church, Focus group, 27.7.2000.
Nthambi, Modesta, Namachele Baptist Church, Zomba rural, 14.7.2000.
Ntokota Baptist Church members, Jali, Zomba, Focus group, 19.3.2000.
Ntuwe, Rev, Chipinimbi Baptist Church, Zomba, 19.5.2000.
Ntuwe, Rev, pastor's meeting, Zomba Baptist Church, 19.5.2000.
Nyauhango, Chilumba Zone Baptist Church, (north), 17.3.2000.
Nyika, Margaret, Blantyre Baptist Church, 26.5.1999, 17.11.1999, 17.11.1999.
Oklahoma volunteer, Lilongwe Baptist Seminary, Lilongwe, 2000.
Oklahoma volunteers, Women, Lilongwe Baptist Seminary, 2000.
Oklahoma volunteers, Zomba, 25.9.2000.
Ott, Martin, Lecturer, Department of Theology and Religious Studies, Zomba,
     14.6.2000.
Paas, Rev Dr Steven, lecturer, Zomba Theological College, Zomba, 2000.
Pastor, Churches of Christ, Zomba Theological College, 23.3.2001.
Pastor's wife, Misesa Baptist Church, 13.3.2000.
Pastors' wives, Lilongwe Baptist Seminary, Focus group, 13.3.2001.
Phiri, Amos, Pastor, Living Stone's Baptist Church, Blantyre, 26.5.2000.
Phiri, Violet, Living Stone's Baptist Church, 26.5.1999.
Regional committee meeting, Zomba Baptist Church, 2.2000.
Regional women's meeting, Zomba, Focus group, 3.3.2000.
Robertson, Annie, Phazi Baptist Church, Zomba rural, 14.7.2000.
Sabola, Rev Paulo, Mwaleko Baptist Church, Mozambique border, 19.5.2000.
Salifu, Mrs Malesi, Mwanafumu Baptist Church, Zomba rural 21.3.2000.
Solomoni, Mrs, Mwambo Baptist Church, 9.3.2000.
South East Executive, Zomba Baptist Church, 2.2000.
South East Region women delegates to sewing and evangelism training school,
     Zomba Baptist Church, 3.5.2000, 13.10.2000.
South East region women's meeting, Zomba, Focus group, 3.3.2000.
South East regional conference, Zomba Baptist Church, Focus group, 3.3.2000.
Sumayili, Mrs, Mwanafumu Baptist Church, Zomba rural, 21.3.2000.
Taibu, Mary, Mwanafumu Baptist Church, Zomba rural, 21.3.2000.
Tambula, Rev, Mpinda Baptist Church, 3.7.2000.
Tanganyika, Mrs, Songani Baptist Church, Zomba 1999.
Tepula, Margaret, Makolije Baptist Church, Jali, 8.3.2000.
Thabwani Baptist member, Ntokota Baptist Church, 19.3.2000.
Thombozi, Mella, Mwanafumu Baptist Church, Zomba rural 21.3.2000.
Upton, Marylyn, Area 36 Baptist Church, Lilongwe, 5.1.2001.
Upton, Rev Dr Sam, Southern Baptist Missionary, Lilongwe Baptist Seminary, August
     1999.
Zomba Baptist Church, Focus group, 3.3.2000.

Unpublished Sources

Banda, Rachel, A Comprehensive Study of Christian Women's Organization in Southern Malawi, Module 3, MA, Department of Theology and Religious Studies, University of Malawi, 1999.

Banda, Rachel, Baptist Women of the Book and Culture, Paper presented at Postgraduate Colloquium, Department of Theology and Religious Studies, University of Malawi, 2000.

Banda, Rachel, The Writing of Post Independence History in Malawi, Module 2, MA, Department of Theology and Religious Studies, University of Malawi, 1999.

Banda, Rachel, *Umodzi* Uniform and its Implications, Forum Paper, Postgraduate Colloquium, Department of Theology and Religious Studies, University of Malawi, 1999.

Bible Way Records in the Baptist Publications Unit in Lilongwe, 13.3.2001.

Breugel, J.W.M. van, Traditional Chewa Religious Belief and Practices: a Study in the Explanation of Evil and Suffering and Ways of Dealing with them, PhD, London 1976.

Chaponda, Orison, *Gule Wamkulu* in the Catholic Church, Lilongwe Rural. A Cultural Phenomenon and a Pastoral Problem. MA Module, Department of Theology and Religious Studies, University of Malawi, 1998.

Day, Rendell, Conversion in the Baptist Convention in Malawi, University of Malawi, Unpublished First PhD Draft, 2000.

Day, Rendell, Emau Baptist Church, PhD module, Department of Department of Theology and Religious Studies, University of Malawi, 1995.

Day, Rendell, From Gowa Industrial Mission to Landmark Baptist . One Hundred Years of Baptist Churches in Malawi 1894-1994, PhD Module, Department of Theology and Religious Studies, University of Malawi, 1994.

Gazamiyala, D.J., Journal.

Koevering, Helen van, Dancing their Dreams. The Lakeshore Nyanja Women of the Anglican Diocese of Niassa, MPhil, University of Bristol, 1999.

Longwe, Hany, Identity by Dissociation: The First Group to Secede from Chilembwe's Church: A History of Peter Kalemba and the Achewa Providence Industrial Mission (APIM), MA, University of Malawi, 2000.

Longwe, Hany, The History of the Baptist Convention in Malawi, Research Notes, University of Malawi, 2001.

Matemba, Yonah, The History of Seventh-day Adventist Matandani Mission, Neno, Malawi 1908-1989, MA, Department of Theology and Religious Studies, University of Malawi, 2000.

Mwenembako, Sebastian, Funeral Customs, BA, Department of Theology and Religious Studies, University of Malawi, 2001.

Nsomo Baptist Church, Zolengeza.

Saunders, D.L, A History of Baptists in East and Central Africa, PhD, Southern Baptist Seminary, 1973.

Shelburne, G.B, History of the Church of Christ in Malawi, 4 pp. nd. (Copy in the library, Baptist Theological Seminary, Lilongwe).

Topesa, Mrs, deacon, Report to *Umodzi* weekly meeting, Zomba Baptist Church, 1999.

Published Sources

Baker, Robert, The Southern Baptist Convention and its People, Nashville: Broadman, 1974.

Barrett, David B, *World Christian Encyclopedia. A Comparative Survey of Churches and Religions in the Modern World. AD 1900-2000*. Nairobi: Oxford University Press, 1982.

Beaver, R. Pierce, *American Protestant Women in World Mission: A History of the First Feminist Movement in North America,* Grand Rapids: Eerdmans, 1980.

Bevans, Stephen B., *Models of Contextual Theology,* Maryknoll: Orbis, 1992, p. 31-46; p. 97-110.

Bilima, Ken, Press release, "Seventh-day Adventist Church," Daily Times, 17.5.2000, p. 17.

Breugel, J.W.M. van, *Chewa Traditional Religion,* Blantyre: CLAIM-Kachere, 2001.

Buku la Alangizi. Baptist Convention of Malawi, Lilongwe: Baptist Publications, nd.

Chakanza, J.C., *Wisdom of the People: 2000 Chinyanja Proverbs and Figurative Sayings,* Blantyre: CLAIM-Kachere, 2001.

Church, Henry, *Theological Education that Makes a Difference,* Blantyre: CLAIM-Kachere, 2001.

Fiedler, "Gender Equality in the New Testament. The Case of St. Paul," *Malawian Journal of Biblical Studies,* Vol. 1, 2003.

Fiedler, Klaus, "Christianity and African Culture, Conservative German Protestant Missionaries in Tanzania, 1900-1940", Blantyre: CLAIM-Kachere, 1999.

Fiedler, Klaus, "Even in Church the Exercise of Power is Accountable to God", in: Kenneth R. Ross (ed), *God, People and Power in Malawi,* CLAIM-Kachere: Blantyre, 1996, pp. 187-224.

Fiedler, Klaus, "For the Sake of Christian Marriage, Abolish Church Weddings", *Religion in Malawi,* no 5 November 1995, p. 22-28.

Fiedler, Klaus, "Bishop Lucas: Christianization of Traditional Rites, the Kikuyu Female Circumcision Controversy and the Cultural Approach of Conservative German Missionaries in Tanzania," in Robin Lamburn, *From a Missionary's Notebook. The Yao of Tunduru and other Essays,* Saarbrücken, 1991.

Fiedler, Klaus, *The Story of Faith Missions. From Hudson Taylor to Present Day Africa,* Oxford: Regnum 1994.

Fitts, Leroy, *A History of Black Baptists,* Nashville: Broadman, 1985.

Garner, Judy, *History of the Baptist Mission in Malawi. A Rambling Remembrance of some People and Events in the History of the Baptist Mission in Malawi.* Lilongwe: Baptist Publications, 1998.

Gramack, Robert, *New Testament Survey,* Grand Rapids, 1995.

Hammack, Mary L.H., *A Dictionary of Women in Church History,* Chicago: Moody Press 1984.

Kholowa, Janet and Klaus Fiedler, *In the Beginning God Created them Equal*, Blantyre: CLAIM-Mvunguti, 2000.

Kholowa, Janet and Klaus Fiedler, *Mtumwi Paulo ndi Udindo wa Amayi Mumpingo*, Blantyre: CLAIM-Mvunguti, 2001.

Kholowa, Janet and Klaus Fiedler, *Pa Chiyambi Anawalenga Chimodzimodzi*, Blantyre: CLAIM-Mvunguti, 1999.

Lusweti, B.M., *The Hyena and the Rock*, London: MacMillan 1984.

Makondesa, Patrick, *Moyo ndi Utumiki wa Mbusa ndi Mayi Muocha wa Providence Industrial Mission*, Blantyre: CLAIM-Mvunguti, 2001.

Mbiri ya aBaptist, Lilongwe: Baptist Publications, 1988.

McBeth, H. Leon, *The Heritage. Four Centuries of Baptist Witness*, Nashville: Broadman, 1987.

McCracken, John, Politics and Christianity in Malawi 1875-1940. The Impact of the Livingstonia Mission in the Northern Province, Blantyre: CLAIM-Kachere ²2000.

Mkamanga, Emily, *Suffering in Silence*, Edinburgh: Dudu Nsomba, 2000.

Mocorn, Dee, *"What do we Stand for as Baptists and Evangelicals?" Towards a Holistic, Afro-Centric and Participatory Understanding of the Gospel of Jesus Christ*, Johannesburg: Baptist Convention of South Africa, 1995.

Mthantauzira Mawu wa Chinyanja, Blantyre: Dzuka, 2000.

Neur, Werner, *Man and Woman in Christian Perspective*, London: Hodder and Stoughton, 1990.

Niklaus, Robert, John S. Sawin, Samuel J. Stoez, *All For Jesus. God at Work in the Christian Missionary Alliance over One Hundred Years*, Camp Hill: Christian Publications, 1986.

Phiri, Isabel Apawo, "Christianity: Liberative or Oppressive to African Women" in Kenneth R. Ross (ed.), *Faith at the Frontiers of Knowledge*, Blantyre: CLAIM-Kachere, 1998, pp. 198-217.

Phiri, Isabel Apawo, *Women, Presbyterianism and Patriarchy. Religious Experience of Chewa Women in Central Malawi*, Blantyre: CLAIM-Kachere 1997, ²2000.

Ross, Kenneth R. (ed), *God People and Power in Malawi: Democratization in Theological Perspective*, Blantyre: CLAIM-Kachere, 1996.

Schoffeleers, Matthew, "An Outline History of Territorial Mediumships between Traditional Rulers and the Spirit World among the Amang'anja", in: Matthew Schoffeleers, *Religion and Dramatization of Life*, Blantyre: CLAIM-Kachere 1996.

Schoffeleers, Matthew, *Religion and Dramatization of Life. Spirit Beliefs and Rituals in Southern and Central Malawi*, Blantyre: CLAIM-Kachere, 1997.

Selfridge, J.C., *Jack of All Trades Mastered by One*, Fearn: Christian Focus, 1989.

Sturley, D.M., *The Study of History*, Guildford: The Royal Grammar School, 1969.

Umodzi wa Amayi a Baptist a ku Malawi, Lilongwe: BCM 1961.

Virkler, A. Henry, *Hermeneutics, Principles and Processes of Biblical Interpretation*, Grand Rapids, 1985.

Walsh, Robert, *An Introduction to Philosophy of History*, London: Hutchison, 1970.

WMU Manual, Zimbabwe Baptist Church, 1979; Umodzi wa Amayi m'Malawi (WMU) Manual (Cyclostyled, nd, [1998]).

Index

Biblical References

www.ingramcontent.com/pod-product-compliance
Lightning Source LLC
Chambersburg PA
CBHW021900020426
42334CB00013B/415